Devotions
for the
God Girl

Devotions
for the
God Girl

A 365-Day Journey

Hayley DiMarco

Revell

a division of Baker Publishing Group
Grand Rapids, Michigan

Published by Revell
a division of Baker Publishing Group
P.O. Box 6287, Grand Rapids, MI 49516-6287
www.revellbooks.com

Printed in the United States of America

Library of Congress Cataloging-in-Publication Data
DiMarco, Hayley.
    Devotions for the God Girl: a 365-day journey / Hayley DiMarco.
        p.   cm.
    Includes bibliographical references.
    ISBN 978-0-8007-1950-0 (cloth)
    1. Teenage girls—Prayers and devotioins. 2. Christian teenagers—Religious
life. 3. Devotional calendars. I. Title.
    BV4860.D56 2010
    242'.633—dc22   2010021025

Scripture is taken from GOD'S WORD®, a copyrighted work of God's Word to the
Nations. Quotations are used by permission. Copyright 1995 by God's Word to the
Nations. All rights reserved.

Published in association with Yates & Yates, LLP, Literary Agents, Orange,
California.

Creative direction by Hungry Planet
Interior design by Michael J. Williams

16 17 18 19 20   15 14

Introduction

The God Girl wants what every other girl wants: to love and to be loved. She wants acceptance and laughter. She wants hope and peace. But her life, like everyone else's, isn't perfect. It's messy and lonely, it's stressful and hard, but one thing sets her apart, one thing makes her life amazingly different from others, and that's her heart. Her heart is set on something above, something greater than her that gives her strength and hope. She has found the truth, and the truth is that God lives. He lives above and he lives within. She calls him Father, she calls him God, and she calls him her salvation.

Because of that **the God Girl wants more than anything else to hear from him.** She wants his words to ring in her ears. This makes her crave him. It makes her look for him, listen for him, and wait for him. When other people are sleeping, the God Girl is waking up to wait and watch for him. She knows that a day that starts off in his presence is better than a day when he is forgotten or pushed aside for other more pressing things. Sure she has a lot to do, sure she is tired, but when a girl is in love, she must spend time with the object of that love.

If your life isn't what you would like and you wish you had more of God in your life, then you're on the right path. A desire for more is the first step. **Your willingness to be uncomfortable, to be put out, to be tired all mean spiritual success.** Each day you are given a finite amount of time, and often it doesn't seem like enough time to do all the things you have to get done. That can mean that God, in his graciousness and kindness, gets pushed to the bottom of the list. All that does is ensure that you will do life today on your own strength and not on his, and that leads to exhaustion and stress. But when you start your day off waiting for your orders from him and watching to see what he wants you to do next, life becomes almost effortless. Time seems to become more abundant.

In his book *The School of Obedience*, Andrew Murray calls this time spent with God **the "morning watch."** He challenges students all over the world to be faithful enough to devote a significant amount of time to the one they love the most, and to give their most important time at that. Take a look at his call to begin living a life fully devoted to the one you love the most by practicing the morning watch:

> You tell me there are many Christians who are content with ten minutes or a quarter of an hour. There are, but you will certainly not as a rule find them strong Christians. And the Students' Movement is pleading with God, above everything, that He would meet to train a race of devoted, whole-hearted young men and women. Christ asked great sacrifices of His disciples; He has perhaps asked little of you as yet. But now He allows, He invites, He longs for

you to make some. Sacrifices make strong men. Sacrifices help wonderfully to wrench us away from earth and self-pleasing, and lift us heavenward. Do not try to pare down the time limit of the morning watch to less than the half-hour. There can be no question about the possibility of finding the time. Ten minutes from sleep, ten from company or amusement, ten from lessons. How easy where the heart is right, hungering to know God and His will perfectly!

If you think you are too busy to spend a half hour with God, make a list of everyone you spend more time with in conversation during the day and list God below them. Yikes, right? My hope is that with the help of *Devotions for the God Girl* and maybe even the book *God Girl* and the *God Girl Bible*, you will find the passion and desire to devote more of your time to the pursuit of God and watching for him each day. But if you are ready right now, then by all means go for it. **Give your time to him and watch how it impacts your day and even your life.** As you do you will notice that your emotions soften, your fear diminishes, and your stress lessens. The more time you spend with God, the more things you can actually get done. If you want to spend your day in devotion to God, in obedience, and as far away from sin as possible, then you have to get close to him, talk with him, and listen to him.

I pray that God will give you the desire for more of him and the urgency to wake before the sun. Pay attention to your sleep pattern—if you find yourself awake in the early morning, then consider it his calling you to his side. Crawl out of bed and dive in. If

you aren't sure what to do, consider reading your daily devotion and then praising him and adoring him for who he is. Confess your sins and offer your repentance, then dive into his Word. Read. Study. If you need help knowing what to read, pick up the *God Girl Bible* and use the guides in the back. Get yourself some good worship music; it can really help you to get into the worship mood and draw you closer to him.

There is not one right way to devote your time to God. If this doesn't work for you, then try something else. If you have the *God Girl Bible*, you'll find a lot of ideas for study in the front of it, so check that out. Just don't delay. If you want more of him, then now is your time and this is your call. Devote yourself to more than a superficial reading of these devos—read, pray, study, and listen. When you do, you'll find your faith growing deeper and your love growing stronger.

I am praying for you, God Girl. **I pray that God will be your everything** and that you will discover his true worth. If you'd like, come by GodGirl.com and hang out. Tell me how your morning watch time is going. Share your ideas for study and get more ideas yourself. All for one and one for all! Let us lean on one another as we make this walk of faith. I look forward to hearing from you. Enjoy your God Girl journey.

Hayley

Obedience and Grace

I don't reject God's kindness. If we receive God's approval by obeying laws, then Christ's death was pointless.

Galatians 2:21

When it comes to God's Word, there are two popular lines of thought. One is that your salvation depends on doing all that it says. This is called legalism, and it's wrong. Salvation doesn't come from anything other than the death and resurrection of Jesus Christ. When you turn your life over to him and make him your Lord, then you are saved. Period. The end.

The other line of thinking when it comes to God's Word is that because of his grace, or great kindness, we are free to break the rules because his grace is relentless and he'll forgive us for it all, so why worry about it? This kind of thinking goes like this: "I really want to do this sinful thing, and since it's too hard to say no, I'm just gonna do it and then ask for forgiveness later." This way of thinking is just as bad as legalism, and it becomes a way of life that is contradictory to God's Word. God's grace isn't cheap, and it's not meant to be abused or used as a loophole to sin.

The truth about God's grace and your salvation is that you don't need to keep any rules to be saved or to keep yourself saved, but you love him because of what he's done for you. And out of that love flows your obedience to his Word. Only God himself gives you the power to keep his law. People who try to keep it on their own are gonna fail; it's just too hard. But through the help of the Holy Spirit, you can be faithful.

The law is powerless to save you and powerless to change you, but as you fall more and more in love with God, you will find yourself changing more and more into the image of Christ. That's because of his Holy Spirit in you. As you become more like Christ, you will naturally be pulled into a love affair with God's Word. You will want more and more of its life-giving message. You will want to know more about the one you love so that he may be the only one you serve, and you will find following his law becoming your delight and not a chore.

As you read God's Word, remind yourself of the gospel message. Speak it to yourself. Remember the life of Christ, his death, his burial, and his resurrection. And know that only this unmatched sacrifice can save you. Your life is a miracle. Your mind being opened to the life of Christ in you is a miracle. Your God has reached down and touched you, and because of that you are different. If you don't feel different or believe you are different, then take some time to read God's Word. Get to know him and his unfathomable kindness in that while you were dead because of your failure, he made you alive together with Christ (see Eph. 2:5).

Nothing can keep you from this salvation but your own decision not to accept it. It is there for you today: accept it and your life will be forever changed. What you could not do before, you will do today. What you were ruled by yesterday, you will be free from now. God promises to save you—all you have to do is believe it.

If the light hasn't come on for you yet and you aren't sure if you are saved or not, stop by www.godgirl.com and do some digging. You can start to answer the question of your salvation. Don't put it off. Start today to realize the amazing kindness of God and how freely he offers it to you.

The man and his wife . . . hid from the LORD God among the trees in the garden. The LORD God called to the man and asked him, "Where are you?" He answered, "I heard you in the garden. I was afraid because I was naked, so I hid."

Genesis 3:8–10

*T*he world might tell you that you are a victim. You were hurt, abused, rejected, and abandoned, and that's why you have issues, addictions, and drama in your life. But **when you believe that your messed-up life is because of something beyond your control, you give away the power over your own life that you so desperately want. As long as you are busy blaming someone else for your life, you'll never be free.** You'll never have control, and you'll never take responsibility for yourself.

Part of becoming a God Girl is choosing to stop running away from the stuff that will make you more holy and happy, and that is being honest about your role in your own messed-up life, no matter who started it. It's called confession, and confession is good stuff. It purifies the soul because it gets to the bottom of what's going on in yourself without worrying about what someone else did or didn't do.

Confession agrees with God and his Word about sin and says to him, "You are holy and I want to be holy too." It says, "No matter what others do or have done, I'm siding with God and living a life that pleases him because I know that's his will." And when you do that, you'll have all the protection and hope you need. Don't accept the pattern of avoiding honest confession like the first people did or like the world around you does. Confession might hurt, and it will probably feel totally uncomfortable and even dangerous, but the truth is, it's the safest and healthiest thing you could do. Confessing is good for the soul, and it proves that you don't belong to yourself but to God.

The man answered, "That woman, the one you gave me, gave me some fruit from the tree, and I ate it." Then the LORD God asked the woman, "What have you done?" "The snake deceived me, and I ate," the woman answered.

Genesis 3:12–13

When someone makes you mad, who is more to blame, them or you? After all, if they hadn't done what they did, then you wouldn't have to get all mad. Or if someone tempts you to do something you know you're not supposed to do and you do it, whose fault is it? Where does the blame lie? The truth is that at the first sign of trouble, the human mind tends to look for someone to blame. The mind is like a super detective: always getting to the bottom of things, always searching to figure out who started it and who is responsible for the mess we're in.

So it's not surprising that blame was the first response to the first spiritual mess people got into. Adam and Eve both blamed someone else instead of taking responsibility. Was it the snake's fault? Would they have taken a bite without him? It's hard to say. But either way, the result of pointing a finger at the "real" problem wasn't quite what they had hoped.

When you blame others for your mess-ups or misery, you miss out on the one thing that can help you, and that's taking responsibility. Taking responsibility for the things you say, do, and think is the first step in the life of faith. When you confess your sin and accept Christ, you are taking responsibility, and suddenly something amazing happens: he takes responsibility for you as well. And voila! You have found all you wanted by doing the very thing you didn't want to do—accepting responsibility for your own life. If Adam and Eve hadn't tried to shift the focus off themselves, would life have been different for them? We'll never know, but what we do know is that blaming others doesn't please God.

Enoch walked with God; then he was gone because God took him.

Genesis 5:24

*T*he test of your faith is not in the amazing moments but in the boring and mundane ones. Your true faith shows through when you can be happy when you aren't in the spotlight and when no one of any importance is looking on. That's when your true character is revealed. When you are with someone who can't do anything for you, who you really are comes through. When you aren't trying to impress someone you think is important, then the real you comes out.

So who are you when no one is looking? And who are you when the people you are with can't do anything for you? Do you notice a different character than the one that shows itself when the spotlights are on or the popular people are around? Only you can judge, since you are in both situations, but take a look at your home life versus your friend life. Are you less holy, kind, and compassionate at home with the people who know you and can't improve your standing? Or are you just the same? Why is it easier to be cranky with your family than your friends? Usually it's because you know they can't do much for you as far as your social life goes. You aren't trying to impress them like you are your friends and even acquaintances. But who you are in your most unimpressive moments is who you truly are.

The God Girl is the same no matter who she is with, and if she sees some differences, she's willing to get to the bottom of it. She doesn't blame her failures on the people around her but on her own moral mistakes, and so she does something about it. When it's all about you and not them, you have the power to change. So take an inventory of your life and see if there are two you's, and if so, decide which you is better and ditch the other one. Your life will be better, and so will the lives of the people around you.

The LORD said to Noah, "Go into the ship with your whole family because I have seen that you alone are righteous among the people of today."

Genesis 7:1

God's commands don't always make sense. They sound unrealistic, unsafe, and crazy at times. Build an ark in the middle of town? Spend your money on the poor? Turn the other cheek when bad people hurt you? Pray for people who persecute you? **Sometimes the things God asks you to do are going to hurt, and they might even make you look crazy.** But you have to decide now, before that time comes, if you're gonna do what he says no matter how it looks or how crazy it seems or if you're gonna run everything through your "common sense" filter.

You get it all backwards when you use common sense or the world's ideas of right and wrong as the final say on what you're going to do or think. Relying on your own smarts is rejecting the mind of God and saying your own mind deserves more respect and worship. As a God Girl your final filter should always be God's Word, not the world's ideas. You have to ask yourself, "Is what I'm being asked to do consistent with God's Word? Is it crazy-sounding but biblical?" If so, then the question is, "Am I willing to do it anyway?"

It couldn't have made any sense to Noah and his family to build an ark where there was no body of water, but it was all part of God's plan. Faith can mean you have to do some things the world thinks are crazy. Take the pack of gum back to the clerk who forgot to charge you for it. Tell the truth when everyone else is telling lies. Pray when others panic. Faith doesn't always make sense, but what does make sense is God's dependability. No matter what he wants you to do, you can be sure that it is for the best.

Then Abram believed the LORD, and the LORD regarded that faith to be his approval of Abram.

Genesis 15:6

*T*he only way to become right with God is to believe in him. It was faith that made Abram righteous in God's sight. It was his faith that made him do what God told him to do. And it's faith that will give you the power of God on your side.

People who don't believe don't get the gifts of God. **Belief—not doubt, not suspicion, not fear, but belief—is your permission to allow God to work in your life.** Because you have free will, you can choose not to believe and not to take the gifts of God into your life. You can choose not to hear from him, not to serve him, and not to love him. That's your prerogative. But you can also choose to believe, like Abram did, and get more of what you need from the God who knows everything you need. Abram could have doubted God's promises—after all, they were preposterous—but he chose to believe them anyway. And thousands of years later Abraham is known for his faith.

During the time Jesus walked on this earth, he healed everyone who came to him with faith that he could heal them and save them from their sins. If they hadn't believed him, they wouldn't have found what they were looking for. As a God Girl your faith defines you and sets your limits. You'll be blessed to the exact degree of your faith. Want more faith? Then you have to know God more so that you are able to believe him, trust him, and wait upon him for the things he promises. You have to believe that God's Word is true, relevant, and practical for your daily life before you can grow in your faith. So think about what you believe: is it consistent with what God says? Don't let the world tell you a lie that sounds godly but is really just sin dressed up as righteousness. Go after the truth as if your life depends on it, and you'll be rewarded for your faith.

Abraham remained standing in front of the LORD. Abraham came closer and asked, "Are you really going to sweep away the innocent with the guilty?"

Genesis 18:22–23

*P*rayer is direct contact with God. It isn't meditation or contemplation but a conversation, a back-and-forth with the God who has the power to do all you could ask. Our prayers can get repetitive and boring. But the prayers you see in the Bible are totally different. When these men and women of God pray, they are relentless, not passive. They beg, plead, and ask over and over again. Abraham wouldn't give up asking for God to save the town of Sodom from destruction (see Gen. 18:20–33). Moses pleaded with God (see Exod. 32:11). Hannah "poured out her heart to the Lord" so much that people thought she was drunk (see 1 Sam. 1:15). King Hezekiah and the prophet Isaiah called to heaven (see 2 Chron. 32:20). Paul fell to his knees in God's presence (see Eph. 3:14).

Prayer is where you plead with the one who can do anything to do what he wills. Prayer is free

access to the Creator of the world, available to all who make Jesus the Lord of their lives. And the Word of God says you can be sure that he hears your prayers and he will answer according to his will (see 1 John 5:14–15). He listens to your pleadings. In fact, he expects them. When Jesus told the parable of the widow and the judge, he said we should "cry out to him for help day and night" (see Luke 18:2–8).

So make your prayer active. Be fearless about asking for what you need, knowing that God answers prayers and no matter what answer you get, you can be sure it's the best thing for you. Just don't neglect to pray. That's where the power lies. Be persistent. Be vocal. Talk to God as the only one who can. And you'll find that he is truly the one who will.

Take your son, your only son Isaac, whom you love, and go to Moriah. Sacrifice him there as a burnt offering on one of the mountains that I will show you.

Genesis 22:2

*A*braham was told to sacrifice his son Isaac—not for just any old reason but to reveal the truth that only through death can your life be truly devoted to God. But it wasn't the death of Isaac that was really the point here but the death of Abraham. It would be worse than death to have to kill the one you love, but that's what God wanted Abraham to do in order to prove his faith, die to himself, and die to his feelings that fought against him with every bit of their energy, telling him not to do what he was being commanded to do.

Dying to your urge to do what makes sense even when it's directly opposed to God's commands is at the foundation of faith. Dying to self is refusing to let you be your boss any more and deciding that no matter what God asks, you'll do it. No matter how crazy it sounds, you're in. You're in because you know that God can be trusted and that you want his best. That makes it easy to do the hard things; they are no-brainers when you know that of course God is good and can be trusted, so you can do whatever he asks without any worry about the outcome.

Abraham was asked to do an unimaginable thing, but he never hesitated because he knew God and he knew that if God asked him to do it, it must be for the best. The world might consider that insanity, but the believer considers it necessity. When doing what God commands seems impossible, remember Abraham, and remember who God is. Either he is perfect or he is imperfect. What you decide to do after he commands you to do something proves which one you think he is.

Now I know that you fear God, because you did not refuse to give me your son, your only son.

Genesis 22:12

*G*od is the giver of every good and perfect thing, but what happens when that thing he's given you is so good that you start to think it's more important than anything else, even him? We humans have a tendency to give the gift the same kind of worship and honor meant for the giver.

Abraham never expected to have a kid. So when God gave him Isaac, it would have been easy for Abraham to fall deeply and even obsessively in love with his kid. And when God demanded that Abraham kill the one he adored, how easy it would have been to say, "No way, José!" But Abraham proved his faith in God when he refused to give in to his desire to protect the boy he loved so much and instead did what God asked him to do. Not many have felt this kind of agony of obedience as much as Abraham. But in the end that obedience would bring more glory than any agony could ever steal.

Obedience isn't always comfortable; in fact, true obedience demands something of the obedient. It demands complete reliance on the wisdom, power, and love of the one who knows what is best, and it demands a ruthless determination to do whatever has to be done to prove that following is much better than rebelling.

If God isn't demanding something of you, then you're not listening, God Girl. What could you do right now out of obedience that would lead you closer to the God you love and deeper into the life of faith? To listen, turn the pages of his Word. Study his law and make his kindness part of your very essence. Love the unlovable, give to the needy, obey authority, offer forgiveness, turn the other cheek, humble yourself, and he will lift you up. Obey him today and find a reward far greater than you ever imagined could be yours. Nothing gives more to the life of a God Girl than obeying her Lord.

Then Jacob prayed, "God of my grandfather Abraham and God of my father Isaac! . . . Please save me from my brother Esau, because I'm afraid of him."

Genesis 32:9, 11

*I*f you want more faith, then you're going to need more prayer. As you pray you learn to trust the God who answers prayer. It is like exercise. The more weight you lift, the stronger your body gets, and the more you pray, the stronger your faith gets. Neglecting God's call to prayer leads to spiritual weakness and failure. If you want more trust, if you want more hope, more faith, and more strength, then you need more prayer. You can't let prayer take a backseat in your life. It has to be the most important part of your day. It sets the tone for your life. Without it your faith is useless and weak.

When you love someone, you want to spend time with them and talk with them, and when you need something from someone, you have to communicate to ask them for what you need. Prayer is your communication with God. It's the way you connect, the way you come into his presence and learn his character. It's the way your life comes to really mean something, because through praying for others you can change their lives. And as those lives change, your trust in God deepens and their lives improve. It's a win-win.

Prayer is a powerful thing in the hands of a God Girl. **Don't ever underestimate its strength and its ability to change not only your life but the lives of the people you pray for.** Jacob's willingness to go to God for his needs brought divine help for his entire family. And your prayers may just serve to help not only you but the people around you as well.

While Joseph was in prison, the LORD was with him. The LORD reached out to him with his unchanging love and gave him protection.

Genesis 39:20–21

f you feel depression coming on, you can stop it before it digs in and takes over, and all it takes is a decision: decide not to think about it. Impossible, you say? No, no, no. It can be done.

As soon as you feel depressing thoughts coming on, think about something else. When you pray, don't agonize over your misery; just say to God, "Your will be done," and then get on with something else. Sometimes prayer can just be an excuse to wallow in your pain and agony, and that's not right. Don't pretend to be praying when what you're really doing is worrying. Let your prayer remind you who God is, not what your problems are. What seems bigger, the thing closest to you or the thing off in the distance? The closer the bigger, so bring God closer by adoring and praising him, and put your worries in the distance by refusing to stare at them, even in prayer. Know that God knows your situation, and then ask him to show himself to you so that you can find truth instead of the lie of depression.

The depressed mind is not trusting God to be who he says he is or to do what he says he'll do. You can kick the most common depressions of life, but you have to know and trust the one who is truth. God's Word confirms that faith should override feelings. Hebrews 11:1 says that faith is being certain of "things we cannot see"—in other words, not being controlled by what we feel. It might feel like all is lost, but the truth is that nothing—not angels or rulers, not devils or evil men, not trials or suffering—can take us away from him (see Rom. 8:38–39). Nothing will be our destruction, but it can all be used for good if you, like Joseph, are just willing to trust that God wouldn't let it happen if he wasn't going to make something amazing out of it. **There certainly can be chemical causes for your depression, but the beginning of all efforts to lift your thought life up out of darkness should be to place your mind on God.**

Pharaoh said to Joseph, "Because God has let you know all this, there is no one as wise and intelligent as you. You will be in charge of my palace, and all my people will do what you say."

Genesis 41:39–40

*O*ne of the hardest things you'll ever do is stay hooked up to God in the good times. Bad times always drive you to your knees. You need so much help and protection when times get tough that you run full speed to him. But look out for the good times: they can soften your faith and drive you off into a different direction.

Whenever you have a win, you have to consciously remind yourself to bring everything back to him to give him the credit and the thanks and then to move on. You can't concentrate on your wins any more than you should concentrate on your failures. But spend your energy on him and you'll find your faith on the increase. And when the bad times come, just think about them as a blessing in disguise, because the bad times are a reminder to your heart of the one who works everything out for the good of those who love him. They remind you that you can do nothing in this world without him. So be thankful and happy in the bad times, knowing always that this too shall pass as you rest under the graceful hand of the Savior.

Joseph said to his brothers . . . , "I am Joseph, the brother you sold into slavery in Egypt! . . . God sent me ahead of you to make sure that you would have descendants on the earth and to save your lives in an amazing way. It wasn't you who sent me here, but God."

Genesis 45:4, 7–8

When people try to destroy you, God Girl, don't worry. You can't look at life from the world's perspective anymore; you have to look at it from God's perspective. Why would he let something bad happen if it wasn't for your good? Just look at the life of Joseph, whose brothers hated him and sold him into slavery, who was sent to jail unfairly, but who never stopped trusting God. God's plans aren't always like ours. They might seem totally off track from ours and even dangerous, but they're always the best. No one should go looking for their own destruction, but when it looks like the world is bent on yours, don't freak out. Trust him and go to him for comfort. Have faith and know that he works all things together for the good of those who love him.

When life throws you a curve ball, don't worry, God's got your back. You've got to know that like Joseph, you can rise above mean people and overcome through faith in the one who sets the moon and the stars in place. You, child of the living God, are protected no matter how tragic your situation. No matter what they do to you, you will continue to go in the right direction if you trust that God works it all out in the end. When the world attacks, remember Joseph. All those things had to happen to him— even slavery and imprisonment—in order for him to get to the position of power where he needed to be to save his family and many other people. Suffering isn't something to worry about but can be something to take hold of when your will is only that God's will be done.

Joseph said to them, "Don't be afraid! I can't take God's place. Even though you planned evil against me, God planned good to come out of it."

Genesis 50:19–20

ood can come out of the evil others plan. Don't limit your life by thinking that when bad things happen, your life is ruined or things are out of control. Bad things don't always mean your end. People might plan to hurt you, but no one can hurt you unless you decide to let them. How you think about who is ultimately in control of life and what trials are for will decide how much they hurt you. You can be attacked on all sides, trapped, and wounded, but if you trust that God is who he says he is and decide that nothing matters except pleasing him, then you won't be destroyed, only made stronger.

Suffering builds the life of the God Girl; it doesn't tear it down. She knows that suffering can lead to pure joy because it builds her perseverance and character. She knows that it is through suffering that her faith is proven and her strength increased. Resistance, not ease, makes you stronger. So consider adversity to be only a part of your training. When you look at life from this perspective, no one can control you or hurt you. When you are a slave to God and God alone, no one else will tell you what to do, how to act, or how to feel.

This trial is only meant to make you better. So rise above your human nature that whines and complains and pushes back against trials, and stand on his nature that knows all, sees all, and ultimately controls all. As you stand on the solid rock of your salvation, you will overcome anything the world might throw at you. And whatever they plan for evil, he'll use for good.

In the course of time Moses grew up. Then he went to see his own people and watched them suffering under forced labor.

Exodus 2:11

Moses saw his people suffering and was sure that he was the one who would save them, but when he tried, he failed miserably. But forty years later he was the one who set them free. So why the big-time gap between his dream and reality? What took him so long?

When Moses decided to set the Hebrews free, he did it on his own and got to work with his own power. He wasn't relying on God but on his own sheer brute strength. It turned out that his vision wasn't wrong; the time just wasn't right. Be careful that you don't jump the gun when it comes to your *dreams.* They might be meant to come true someday, but not today. God may want you to do something, but he doesn't want you to do it in your own strength; he wants you to do it in his. So wait for his prompting, his lead, and his power. When you do, that thing you want to get done will succeed, but if you jump ahead and take matters into your own hands, then you can't be sure of the outcome.

You want to be happy, you want true love, and God might want that for you too—but don't take matters into your own hands and try to manipulate the situation. Don't jump into things and try to control them. Let them be what they will be while you trust God all the way. If you know that a vision is from him, then you can trust him to fulfill it; you don't have to take charge. So rest in the truth and prepare yourself not only to hear God's voice but also to act as soon as he says to act.

Moses said to the Lord, "Please, Lord, I'm not a good speaker. . . . I speak slowly, and I become tongue-tied easily." The Lord asked him, "Who gave humans their mouths? Who makes humans unable to talk or hear? . . . Now go, and I will help you speak and will teach you what to say."

Exodus 4:10–12

Shyness is never an excuse for sin. Just because you don't *feel* capable of reaching out to love and serve others doesn't mean you can disobey God's call. Nothing should keep you from reaching out to the world around you—not your tendency to fear rejection or to assume they all hate you, and not your fear of social situations—nothing is bigger than the God who commands you to go.

This should be good news to the shy girl, not something that freaks you out. It means that contrary to popular belief, you don't have to be controlled by your shyness. You don't have to panic or be afraid of people, because God promises to help you do the things he tells you to do. God's people are called to have compassion and empathy, to treat others as we would want to be treated, to teach, to preach, and to share truth with others—yes, even with strangers. That means that if shyness is getting in the way of these commands on your life, then it is leading you to sin, and so it must not be obeyed. You're a God Girl—you serve the one true God and not the god of fear. There is your freedom!

The cure for your fear is the love of the Father. When God's will is your will, nothing anyone says or does can hurt you, and that's the source of your confidence. You are truly free when you label yourself a God Girl instead of a shy girl and when you choose his will over your own!

Then the LORD said to Moses, "Go to Pharaoh. I have made him and his officials stubborn so that I can do these miraculous signs among them. . . . This is how you will all know that I am the LORD."

Exodus 10:1–2

When you are faced with impossible odds, just think of it as a chance for God to show up.** Nothing that happens in the life of the God Girl is failure; everything is an opportunity. Adversity is a good thing when you use it to help you turn to the only God who can save you.

Don't let terrible situations or stubborn or angry people keep you from believing that God can and will do as he pleases on this earth. After all, he is all-powerful and always present, remember? His will ultimately wins. Even though times might look tough, you can be sure that he is still God and still in control.

So don't fear what others fear. Just look at a trial as an opportunity for God to do what God does best: perform miracles. When you look at the world from that perspective, nothing can get you down, nothing can scare you, because you are sure of one thing, and that is God's presence and power. Relax and let others who don't know him do all the worrying. You are a God Girl and you are a child of the King. His hand is always on you to protect you and to guide you. Just look to him, trust him, and be sure that nothing happens without his ultimate permission. Because of that you can be sure that you are able to overcome any tough situation.

On the tenth day of this month each man must take a lamb or a young goat for his family—one animal per household. . . . Your animal must be a one-year-old male that has no defects.

Exodus 12:3, 5

Since the cross, sacrifice no longer has to be made for our sins (see Heb. 10:18–19). Today, sacrifice for a God Girl is associated with giving up something that matters to you, and it is a part of how you worship God. When the Israelites were told to sacrifice a lamb for the Passover (see Exodus 12), they were told to select one that was special, with no defects, aka perfect. This perfect little lamb was to be cared for by the family for four days and then to be slaughtered. So why didn't God tell them any old animal would do? Why didn't he just say kill a pigeon or a rat? Because the sacrifice was not only about killing the animal but also about the people who needed and maybe even loved the animal giving up what they needed and loved. Sacrifice isn't about giving up things that are easy to give up; it's about giving up what is hard to give up.

A lot of times we say we're giving up stuff or making sacrifices for God when we're really not, like saying we won't date anymore even though we haven't had a date in a year. In that case, saying that not dating is your sacrifice to God is not technically true since you weren't dating anyway. But giving up any daydreaming or thinking about dating would be a great sacrifice if that would be almost impossible for you without God's help. So whatever you want to give up for God, make sure that it's yours before you give it. In other words, if giving it up hurts and you'll notice its absence, then that's a valid sacrifice.

When you give up something for God, you also have to make sure that it's not a sin you are giving up. Choosing not to sin is not sacrifice. Remember the lamb: it was to be without defect, a symbol of sinlessness. Not dirty and unclean, a symbol of sin. Sacrifice has to do with giving up what is good, not what is evil. Giving up what is evil or sinful is repentance, not sacrifice, and is a daily requirement.

In the desert the whole community complained about Moses and Aaron. The Israelites said to them, "If only the LORD had let us die in Egypt! There we sat by our pots of meat and ate all the food we wanted! You brought us out into this desert to let us all starve to death!"

Exodus 16:2–3

*A*re there times when you hate your life? That was the case for the Israelites in the desert. "We're sick of this food," they complained. "We need meat." Really? God has just brought you out of slavery, and you're going to complain? Sheesh! What's up with that? From where we stand it all seems so crazy, doesn't it—complaining after what God had just done?

But have things really changed? After all, isn't complaining about your lot in life, like having a big nose or not being popular, like accusing the God who gives you all that you have of not giving you enough? Did you know that everything that happens to you has to come through God to get to you? Does that make him a tyrant in your eyes? It might if you don't know the big picture.

The truth is that God has a purpose for everything in your life. And he promises to work all things together for good. All your aches, pains, and emptiness—he'll use it all for good if you'll do just one thing: trust him. Can you trust that the place where you are in life right now is exactly where you should be? **Everything that he gives or takes away is for your benefit.** Even if it feels like the exact opposite, don't believe your feelings but trust him. When you do you will find a life filled with hope and direction. You won't be wandering in the dark, dry desert, but you'll find your promised land, the place where you can be content no matter what happens.

Are you tired of being unhappy? Do you want victory? Then choose it. Choose to trust God and believe that your life is under his control no matter how lost you feel. You must believe God's Word when it says, "all things work together for the good of those who love God" (Rom. 8:28).

If you carefully obey me and are faithful to the terms of my promise, then out of all the nations you will be my own special possession, even though the whole world is mine.

Exodus 19:5

*Y*ou've read your Bible a million times and still nothing. *What does it all mean? Where is God when I need him? Why do I feel so empty? Am I missing something?* Then suddenly you obey him in some way and *poof!* That same verse you've read a hundred times means something. Why didn't you get it before?

Well, it's simple: it's a matter of action. When you read God's Word and then do what it says to do, something funny happens: he shows you more truth. He blesses you, as his Word says he will. If you just aren't finding God and want something more, then consider just doing it—whatever God commands. Do what he is asking you to do and you'll find more of him than you've ever found before. *Obedience*, the art of just doing it, brings you face-to-face with *God*.

You won't ever have that connection you want to have until you do what he says. Once you take that first step and do what he's telling you to do, this obedience stuff will get easier and easier. He's not a tyrant that tells you to do something only to punish you and wreck your life. No, he tells you to do stuff so that your life will be better. **Don't expect the worst from obedience; believe in the best.** His Word promises it. Don't wait another minute; do what God is asking you to do today, and you'll see more of God than you are seeing right now.

Honor your father and your mother, so that you may live for a long time in the land the LORD your God is giving you.

Exodus 20:12

Sometimes the hardest people to love are the ones closest to you. It's easier to love people you see only from a distance, but the ones you see up close can be unimpressive, even unkind. But the truth is that we're all like that up close. No one is perfect, and the closer you get the more you see those imperfections. And that's why parents can be so much trouble. Not only do you see all their blemishes and smell all their stinks, but you have to deal with all their emotional, spiritual, and mental weaknesses. When they tell you what to do it can be hard to respect them, hard to not roll your eyes or to laugh, but then God knew that, didn't he? "Honor your father and your mother" (Exod. 20:12). It was such an important command that it made the Top 10 list.

Your parents were given to you to make you stronger. And though they might sometimes do that by godly example and insight, sometimes they do it by accident. **No matter what your parents do, the most spiritual response to them is honor and respect, if only for their position as parents.** Knowing this can help you to stop taking everything that comes from them as insanity or old age setting in and start thinking about it like direction from God. Each time you give up what you want to do to do whatever your parents want, you build your spiritual strength and show God and the world that his desires are more important to you than your own. Doing what God wants you to do means doing what your parents want you to do, plain and simple. So unless they are asking you to sin, the God Girl has got to obey, and out of that will come holiness.

In the tent of meeting outside the canopy where the words of my promise are, Aaron and his descendants must keep the lamps lit in the LORD's presence from evening until morning.

Exodus 27:21

Light is a symbol of God and godliness. Before God created the seas teeming with creatures, the land growing with plants, and the first people, he turned on the light. "Then God said, 'Let there be light!' So there was light" (Gen. 1:3). Light is always associated with goodness. God is said to be dressed in a robe of light (see Ps. 104:2), and 1 John 1:5 says he is light. His Word is a light that helps us to see where to walk (see Ps. 119:105). And the gospel itself is considered light to a dying world (see 2 Cor. 4:4).

God wants his people to live in the light. He wants the light to keep burning continually. There was a time when we lived in darkness, but when we met Jesus the lights were turned on and everything that was hidden was seen. As a God Girl **you can't let yourself go back into darkness.** Darkness is the opposite of light. In darkness evil lurks, sneaks, and pounces. **Sin hides in the dark, but when we shine the light on our lives, it can no longer hide.** And that is why the light should always be on.

God Girl, you too are a light to the world, revealing truth to those who are lost and shining light on what people do in secret (see Matt. 5:14). But if you put your light out, hide it, or are ashamed of it, then you give in to the darkness. You have to trust that truth is what this earth needs, and that truth is found in the light.

No more hiding, God Girl. No more "lights out" moments where you do what you would never do if the lights were on. Encourage the light by praying, studying, and looking for opportunities to bring your own sins into the light.

Build an altar out of acacia wood for burning incense. Make it 18 inches square and 36 inches high. The horns and altar must be made out of one piece of wood.

Exodus 30:1–2

*Y*ou can find God even in the boring stuff, like the dimensions of the altar and taking a census. But don't expect to find him there before you do the work. God calls you to get up and get going, and sometimes it's not until after you get a move on that he shines his light on what you've done. When you have a dull or boring job to do, you have to look at it as a character builder, because when you are willing to do the boring things in life with a good attitude, you will be changed, and so will the job you do.

You can't look at anything as beneath you, because that would be putting yourself even above Jesus himself.

When he washed the feet of the disciples, he did the most "beneath him" job there was.

It takes inspiration to go through the boring stuff. Don't think for a minute that the amazing saints of history had exciting and glorious jobs to do every day. It's the exact opposite: those boring, difficult, and dull tasks that they committed to every day were what made them shine and made them go down in history forever. When you let God do something through you, he always changes it into something beautiful. So don't avoid the dull and boring things you've got to do. Be like Christ and dive in to the hard stuff knowing that God has called you to do his work and because of that, he will do an amazing work in you.

Choose something of your own to give as a special contribution to the LORD. Let everyone who is willing bring this kind of contribution to the LORD: gold, silver, and bronze.

Exodus 35:5

Is there something you can't part with? If someone asked you to give it up, could you do it? The thing you say you can't give up is the very thing you have to give up. **When something you own becomes the most important thing in your life, it teeters on idolatry.** An idol is anything that you obsess about, that you need, that you can't live without. The only thing that you truly can't live without, other than food and water, is the presence of God in your life. And when things overshadow that need or even try to fill it, danger is in the air.

God asked the Israelites to give something of their own to him (see Exod. 35:4–9). Do you think he meant "your least favorite thing" or "the one thing you don't really like, use, or want"? Or do you think he was looking for something important that they really loved or thought they "needed"? Look at the things listed in Exodus 35:5: gold, silver, bronze. Do you think they were important to the people? Worth something? Yep, they were. In fact, all the things on that list would have been very valuable in their time and hard to part with. Why do you think God asked for this contribution? Why would he want his followers to give up what they love and even need?

Maybe it is because those things seem so important that they can easily start to replace God in our lives. Think about what you really need. What things are essential? Air, water, food, shelter. Everything else is an opportunity for misplaced worship.

Look at the things in your life and see what you worship. What can you not live without or give up? Think about what that thing means to you and how it could be meeting some of the needs in your life that God wants to meet—for comfort, physical needs, hope, or joy. In what way do you worship things rather than God, and how will you change that in order to save your soul?

The burnt offering will be accepted to make peace with the LORD.

Leviticus 1:4

Imagine giving up something you need or love to God every morning and every evening. This was the system the Israelites lived under (see Leviticus 1–2). Each morning and evening the community sacrificed things like food, grains, and animals (see Num. 28:1–8).

The guilt or sin offering was made to clear people of all the sins they had committed prior to the sacrifice. There was also the burnt offering, where they would burn up entire animals into ashes. This offering represented their total dedication to God, giving him their all. A third offering was the fellowship offering. This was basically a family meal where everyone had fellowship with one another and with God.

Let's look a little closer at those three things: You have the forgiveness of sin, complete dedication to him who forgave the sin, and then fellowship. And that pattern still exists today. The sacrifice of Jesus is your guilt offering, but it only had to happen once—forgiveness in full, once and for all. All that is required for forgiveness is for you to confess, repent, and accept Christ's blood as all you need. Then comes your complete dedication, and then fellowship with God.

If you were completely holy as God is, then there would be no separation between you to bridge. But since that isn't the case, something had to happen to get the two of you together, and that was the sacrifice of Jesus. He is your one and only sacrifice. He is all that you need to be made holy in the eyes of God. No longer do you need to bring your choicest items to the altar in order to come near to God, but you now have full access to him because of your position in Christ. As you read the book of Leviticus, consider how much God requires of those who worship him.

I am the LORD your God. You must live holy lives. Be holy because I am holy.

Leviticus 11:44

*G*od isn't your buddy. He isn't a genie in a magic lamp sent to grant your wishes. He is holy, he is perfect, and he requires honor and reverence. But because he is also forgiving, kind, and loving beyond compare, it can be easy to get so relaxed around him that you verge on being disrespectful. The Bible does talk about being a friend of God and how when you make him the Lord of your life he adopts you as his own child, but that doesn't give you permission to lose your awe and reverence for him. As a God Girl you can't forget your place. Don't get so relaxed around God that you treat him with disrespect. Don't get so casual with him that you forget the reverence he deserves.

Reverence isn't something that weakens you to make him strong. You are actually made strong by admitting how powerful God truly is. When you get relaxed around God and think of him as more of a buddy than a deity, you run the risk of not giving God the faith he needs in order to be able to act in your life. Reverence reminds you not only who he is but who you are, so that in everything you do you will act in godliness and awe and not in childishness and disrespect. As a God Girl you must live a holy life because the one you worship is holy. Wanting anything less is disobedience and disrespect.

I am the LORD. I brought you out of Egypt to be your God. Be holy because I am holy.

Leviticus 11:45

Seven times in the book of Leviticus God commands us to be holy because he is holy (see Lev. 11:44, 45; 19:2; 20:7, 26; 21:8; 22:32). Holiness isn't something to be watched from a distance. It isn't an unreachable goal or one that you're allowed to avoid because of the abundance of kindness poured out on you. **God's kindness isn't something that excuses you from holiness but something that helps you get holiness.** Kindness, or grace, shouldn't be reserved for the occasional offense, but it should be accepted as the very hand of God on your life, giving you the ability to do what is holy instead of being a slave to sin. The kindness of God brings mercy and forgiveness, but just as importantly, it brings his help. You can't live a holy life without the Holy Spirit on your side. And it is through the help of that Spirit that you have the ability to do what God commands to be holy. If holiness feels like a totally unattainable goal, it's because you've tried to get there in your own power. Holiness can't be attained by the flesh. No act of strength can muster it. But you can willingly reach out and accept the gift of God's kindness and his Holy Spirit, and through that gift you then can get the strength and ability to be holy.

The God Girl can't dismiss the idea of holiness as an unattainable goal, one that is better ignored than pursued because of her inability to be perfect. Holiness is yours for the taking, God Girl, and you can start taking it today if you are willing to trust that God will be your strength and that it's not through your own power but through his Holy Spirit that you can become holy.

You used to live in Egypt. Don't live the way the Egyptians do. I am bringing you to Canaan. Don't live the way the Canaanites do. Never live by their standards. Follow my rules, and live by my standards.

Leviticus 18:3–4

The world or God—which will it be? How easy it is to listen to the ideas of the world and to fall in line with them. But the world has always had a different standard than God. What's morally encouraged in one society is punishable by death in the next. Even the standards of purity for drinking water in your city may be more strict or lax than in the neighboring town. But God's Word says don't live by the standards set when you lived in Egypt, Canaan, or California, but remember you are a citizen of the kingdom of heaven. Live by those standards. You can't allow the standards of the world to creep into the truth of Scripture.

Don't just assume that just because you've heard something all your life, it's gotta be true. That's just plain lazy. You've got to learn the standards of God and test everything against God's Word. **Find out what makes him happy and what he has to say about the decisions in your life.** His Word makes the standard of conduct for a God Girl clear, and though much of the Old Testament law was fulfilled by the life of Christ and so no longer applies to your life, there is still a lot in its pages to look at in the light of the cross.

Understand God's demands on the life of a believer and his requirements for faith. See what Christ has saved you from and how much you owe him for that. Appreciate the history of our faith and the gift of God's kindness. Read the Old Testament through the lens of the New Testament, considering how life this side of the cross is different from life before Jesus. And take into account the entirety of God's Word as you decide what it means to be a God Girl. The truth of the Old Testament has not been rejected but has been fulfilled in the life of Christ. Learn what that means by reading your Bible. Study God's Word and make it your way of life, and you will be blessed.

Those who treat their God with contempt will be punished for their sin. But those who curse the LORD's name must be put to death.

Leviticus 24:15–16

*M*any laws found in the Old Testament are no longer required. A lot of commandments are no longer commanded. A lot of the Old Testament law is ancient history this side of the cross, but some commandments will never, ever be removed. Some sins will always be sinful, and this is one: to curse the Lord's name.

Though death is no longer the punishment for sin in the life of the believer, using the name of the Lord as a curse word is still sinful. When you use his name in anger, frustration, pain, or even excitement, it's a sinful and ugly thing. In the time before Christ it was so ugly that unlike a lot of other sins mentioned, it had no sacrifice. The punishment was death. This shows you what an ugly and unacceptable sin it is in the eyes of God.

God's name must be honored and respected, not used as a curse. As a God Girl you should make your faith obvious to all, and cursing his name proves your disobedience. Don't let God's name be used in vain. Get rid of all that kind of talk, and honor God by honoring his name. Give God the respect he deserves.

Give the silver to Aaron and his sons. It will buy back those Israelites.

Numbers 3:48

*S*inning is as easy as falling off of a bike. You don't have to sin, but it **is your tendency;** in fact, we all have that tendency. That's why God says that no one has God's approval, not one person is righteous, and everyone has turned away and fallen short of the glory of God (see Rom. 3:10–12). And so a price has to be paid to get your life back, just like a ransom to a kidnapper. Sin kidnaps you and puts you into slavery and bondage to itself. Sin calls out your name and says, "Come on, I will make you happy." But as soon as you turn to it, it grabs you and chains you down, making it almost impossible to get free.

But there's a way out of those chains, and it is called redemption, the ransom for your soul. When you accept Jesus as your Lord, your ransom is paid and you are set free. That means you're not only free from the penalty of sin but free from its bondage as well. Sin doesn't have power over you anymore (see Rom. 6:14). So you don't have to keep saying yes to it, giving in to it, or being weak because of it. God set you free. He doesn't save you just to give you a one-way ticket to heaven but to set you free. The only reason you continue to struggle with the same sin you fought before your redemption is because you choose to go back to it, like an abused wife goes back to her abusive husband. It's not right or good. It makes no sense; you've been set free, so why do you return to the place of torment? You don't have to! Turn to God and be free.

If this is how you're going to treat me, why don't you just kill me? I can't face this trouble anymore.

Numbers 11:15

The normal human reaction to failure is despair. That feeling that there's no way to fix the mess you've found yourself in is what makes you sound like Moses and say, "It's all over. I might as well give up now." But you can't let that despair beat you. You have to realize that there's nothing special about your particular drama. Missing an opportunity to do something right is a really ordinary thing that happens to all of us. If you ignore that and think something tremendously unique has happened to you, you're probably going to sink into the pit of despair and not know how to get out, or even be willing to. The solution is in Jesus' words to his disciples, who were just as depressed about their lot in life. He said, "Get up! Let's go!" (Matt. 26:46). He didn't let them wallow in their mistake. He told them essentially to get over it and to get going on to the next thing.

So what's the next thing in your life? What is Jesus calling you to get over and to get on with? If you wallow in your past and refuse to move on, you recommit your failure all over again. Only when you obey and get moving do you lessen the sting and the power of your past failure. In fact, it remains a present failure until you get up and get over it.

If you don't know what the next thing for you is, then let it be this and this alone: to trust Jesus completely and to pray continually. Then ultimately know that he works all things together for good—even your failures (see Rom. 8:28). By doing these things you let this failure move you forward instead of backward into hopeless despair.

He never lets the guilty go unpunished, punishing children . . . for their parents' sins to the third and fourth generation.

Numbers 14:18

God promises to punish those who do evil. That's a relief when you're the victim of evil, but what about when you're a victim of the punishment? God's law says that when parents sin, those sins will be punished for generations to come. And so if one parent serves the idol of drunkenness, you see that pattern repeated for generations. Sin seems to be passed on in the DNA, but that doesn't have to be the case for you.

As a God Girl you are no longer a slave to sin. You're no longer controlled by its power. **While some children may continue on in the sinful ways of their parents, forever condemned to a life of bondage, you, God Girl, are now set free.** Jesus came to set the captives free, and that means even you who used to be captive to the sins of your family. You might not have realized you're free, and you might have been living under the deception that your parents' sins will be your own, but that is rubbish. The price for those sins in your DNA has been paid. You are no longer living under the curse, because "Christ paid the price to free us from the curse that God's laws bring by becoming cursed instead of us" (Gal. 3:13).

When you read the Old Testament, you also have to take into consideration the New Testament. Yes, God curses the kids of sinners, but he also offers freedom from the curse to all those who are willing to repent and to make Jesus the Lord of their lives. If there's a familial sin in your family, confess that sin as if it were your own, and then promise God you will turn from it and never do it. You can be sure that when you do, you will be set free from the curse and given a new life in the area where your family has previously been in bondage.

How long must I put up with this wicked community that keeps complaining about me? I've heard the complaints the Israelites are making about me. So tell them, "As I live, declares the LORD, I solemnly swear I will do everything to you that you said I would do."

Numbers 14:27–28

Complaint is disbelief—disbelief that God is who he says he is and is alive and well in your life. When you complain, you criticize the things God has given you. It's shortsighted and naive to act like God has in some way swindled you out of something you should have gotten, but it is not unusual. The Israelites had been freed from slavery and set free to enter a promised land, but when life got dry and the desert got hot, they complained. They started to doubt God's faithfulness and love, and they took matters into their own hands. But when God heard them whining, he was not happy. In fact, he decided that he would give them exactly what they were afraid of, and so it was a self-fulfilling prophecy of sorts. The same is true today: **believe the negative things this world pours on you,** and **you'll find yourself in possession of those same things, but believe the power and truth in the Word of God, and you will find everything it promises in your hot little hands.**

It's easy to be lied to by what you see and easy to believe that the way things look is the way things are, but how sad it is to believe what you can see more than you believe the God you can't see. When God gives you a vision of things to come, when he shows you a path you've got to take, don't be surprised when you're tested along that journey. And don't run in the opposite direction when the testing comes, but stand still in your faith and hold on to the title of God Girl. Even though everything in the world says he's wrong or absent, your heart and your mind have to hold fast to the truth that he is always right and always present.

The people complained to Moses and said, "If only we had died when the other Israelites died in the LORD's presence! Did you bring the LORD's assembly into this desert just to have us and our animals die here?"

Numbers 20:3–4

*G*od never does anything stupid. What he does might seem crazy, like taking you out of a perfectly good job as a slave and moving you into the middle of the desert with nothing to eat but manna, but it's not stupid. God has a plan. And when you complain about your circumstances, you're not trusting God's wisdom, kindness, and love.

The Israelites were saved from bondage to the Egyptians, and still they wondered if God had saved them just to kill them. Even after seeing so many miracles (the parting of the Red Sea alone should have been proof of God's hand in their lives), they still weren't sure God could protect them and save them.

When your life seems hopeless and your world is a barren desert, remember the Israelites. Remember that they could only see today, not tomorrow or the next day. They didn't know what God had in store. And they weren't considering that God's best is far better than anything the world could have offered.

Even if you have to live in the desert for a time, trust him. After all, how weak is your faith if you trust him only in the garden or on the high mountain top? No, trust is valuable only when it is practiced in the face of adversity. Each trial you live through is your chance to grow in faith and trust. Use it—don't lose it by complaining about where you are or what you are being told to do, like the Israelites did. Maybe if they had learned to trust sooner, that first generation would have made it to the Promised Land. Instead they wandered around for the rest of their lives, only to leave the land of promise to their children (see Num. 14:22). Don't make that same mistake. Learn to trust today.

Bring a burnt offering as a soothing aroma to the LORD.

Numbers 28:27

Scent is an amazing thing. It can affect your mood, your emotions, and your thoughts. Smelling is so powerful that it can make you feel just like you felt the last time you smelled the same thing. Good smells have a way of calming us, and some say certain scents even help us to concentrate, but smells can also be disgusting. A lot of scents leave you running in the opposite direction. They can hit you like a slap in the face and make you wanna cover your nose and mouth in self-protection.

In the spiritual realm, think of obedience to God as a good smell that God loves to inhale. Love, kindness, selflessness, giving, and serving all are soothing aromas to God. And they are what he looks for in the lives of his children. But sin is a stench that makes him turn his head and disregard even the prayers of the stinky (see Prov. 28:9). What is the aroma of your life? Does it drift up to the Lord in heaven with a lovely scent, or is it a disgusting stench?

If you aren't sure, then check your thoughts and your actions. Do they match God's Word, or are they in conflict? A life in conflict is an unpleasant aroma. But a life set on pleasing him and finding out what he likes and dislikes is a soothing aroma. May you find out what pleases God and do it. May he be charmed by the fragrance of your actions rather than repulsed by them.

(It takes 11 days to go from Mount Horeb to Kadesh Barnea by way of Mount Seir.) On the first day of the eleventh month in the fortieth year after they had left Egypt, Moses told the Israelites everything the LORD had commanded him to tell them.

Deuteronomy 1:2–3

The Israelites took forty years to make a trip that should have taken eleven days. Forty years! Can you imagine? It seems impossible, doesn't it? But what about you—how long does it take you to learn what God wants to teach you? **Have you been tested in the same thing over and over again?** Do you see the same trials coming to you on a regular basis? If you say to yourself, "This keeps happening to me!" then it might be time to consider that you may be wandering in the desert because of your disobedience, and you aren't going to get out until you get it—until you pass the test.

So look at your life. If there's something you can't get past, get over, or get away from, then it might just be time to take a fresh look at it from the perspective of God's Word. Find out how you could act more like someone who agrees with Scripture and less like someone who agrees with their sinful side. Talk to God. Ask him what lesson you need to learn so that you can get out of your desert wanderings. As soon as you are willing to try things God's way instead of insisting on your own way, you'll be brought into your own promised land. So stop asking "Why me?" and start asking "What about me needs to be changed?" Let God's Word be your guide, and choose to stop letting your emotions, your desires, or your dreams lead the way.

*But if you look for the L*ORD *your God when you are among those nations, you will find him whenever you search for him with all your heart and with all your soul.*

Deuteronomy 4:29

*D*o you find it hard to connect with God? Hard to hear his voice? Don't worry, this is to be expected. **God wants to see how much energy you're gonna put into finding him** and getting to know him. He's interested in the chase. So don't give up just because you've given quiet time a shot and gotten nothing from it. You've got to prove to God that you are devoted to knowing him, and that takes time and persistence.

God promises you that you will find him, but he makes the point that it will take energy—in fact, all the energy your heart has to give. Have you run after God with all your heart? Or is part of your heart somewhere else? It takes time to get your heart to concentrate, so don't give up when it doesn't focus immediately. You have to keep taking its hand and bringing it back to him.

A lot of people just go to God for direction: "Which way is best for me?" But God is more concerned with you knowing him than he is with getting you what you want and where you want to go. So if you're having trouble hearing him, don't give up. Just trust that if you are persistent in wanting to know him, you will find him.

But remember the Lord your God is the one who makes you wealthy. He's confirming the promise which he swore to your ancestors. It's still in effect today.

Deuteronomy 8:18

*M*oney—who doesn't want it? And who doesn't need more of it? It's how you get food, clothes, and shelter. But is that all money is good for? The most important thing about money isn't having as much as you want in order to get all the things you want but having enough to give to others in need. **God doesn't give his children money in order to make them happy but in order for them to distribute it to the people around them who are in need.**

When you give to others, don't expect to get anything at all back from them, but know that your reward will be from God alone. In fact, you have a choice: are you gonna choose to seek your reward from people or from God? Whenever you give to others without looking for a reward, you really are giving back to yourself, because someday you'll see what God has in store for the God Girl who gives not to please herself but to please him.

What you have isn't your own. It all came from God so that it could go out to those who are in more need than you are. When you are blessed with something, ask God who you can now bless. Find out how to spread the wealth, how to share the gifts, and how to change the world through giving to others as God gives to you.

Today I'm giving you the choice of a blessing or a curse.

Deuteronomy 11:26

*L*ove and fear are archenemies in the life of the God Girl. They are a blessing and a curse, complete opposites. As the children of Israel grouped up near the land of Shechem, they were shown the mountain of blessings (Mount Gerizim) and the mountain of curses (Mount Ebal), and God gave them a choice between the two. The choice before them was obedience or disobedience. If they obeyed God, then blessings would be theirs, and if they chose the opposite, then they would receive the curse (see Deut. 11:26–32).

Today you have the same kind of choice: you can choose between disobedience (fear) or obedience (love), and one comes with a curse while the other comes with blessing. Most of the time fear promises protection and pretends to come from wisdom, but the truth is that it's a thief. It steals your peace and your hope, and it weakens your will. But love provides you all the hope, peace, and happiness you could ever handle. Fear leads to slavery; love leads to freedom. The enemy tells you that love is dangerous and leaves you vulnerable. And when you buy that lie, choosing love seems like a dangerous choice. But the God Girl doesn't need to protect herself from what God says to do. His call to love is to be obeyed no matter the cost. When you make decisions out of fear or self-protection, you push God off of the throne and stand on it with your hands on your hips in total defiance.

Fear should never be a barometer for action, telling you when the weather's right for you to do this or that—not the fear of losing something you love or of loving someone you don't even like. If you trust God and his Word, fear will never be your master, but God's Word will be. Learn the truth about loving God's way in 1 Corinthians 13. This kind of love isn't dysfunctional. It doesn't love for what you get out of it. Study God's Word, look for truth, and make it a part of who you are, and you will be set free from the bondage of fear.

The LORD your God is testing you to find out if you really love him with all your heart and with all your soul.

Deuteronomy 13:3

When temptations come at you like gunfire in a battle, don't be surprised. There are gonna be times when your life will be free from temptation, and those are sweet times. But those times when the going gets tough will be used to teach you to trust Jesus completely. Don't give up or condemn yourself for being so easily tempted to sin; after all, you are just a beginner in this life of holiness. You aren't expected to be immune to temptation. But what you need to do is trust these words: "If you live by what I say, you are truly my disciples. You will know the truth, and the truth will set you free" (John 8:31–32). According to Jesus, all you need for peace is obedience. No matter what comes at you, obey. No matter how absurd obedience might seem, obey. Obey, obey, obey, and he promises you that you'll know truth, and miraculously that truth will set you free.

Is there something you want to be free from? If something plagues you and is making your life miserable, then you've just found the answer. Obey God and you will be set free.

*You may be wondering, "How can we recognize that the L*ORD *didn't speak this message?"*

Deuteronomy 18:21

*H*ave you ever been sure that you were doing just what God wanted and then been shut down by a door slammed in your face? Would God tell you to do something that he knew wouldn't happen? Or was that not the voice of God but your own hopes? What is more possible, that you heard him wrong or that he lied? How do you know when it's God's voice and when it's just your own wishful thinking?

Maybe it just takes time. **If what you think you are hearing agrees with Scripture, if** you see the **doors open** to you as you move forward, and if **other people actually agree** with what you are hearing, then it might just be the voice of God. But what if it's just mass hysteria or high hopes? How can you really know you are tapped into God? The only answer seems to be to look at his Word. What does his Word command? What does it say for you to do, God Girl? Stick to that and you will be sure to do the will of God. And if for some reason a door that you've been knocking on doesn't open, don't blame it on the voice of God or the sinfulness of whoever stopped you, but blame it on your inability to always hear the Word of God over your own desires. Don't beat yourself up over your mistake. Just take note of the sound of your flesh versus the voice of God so that next time you'll more quickly recognize the difference.

Carefully obey the LORD your God, and faithfully follow all his commands that I'm giving you today. If you do, . . . these are all the blessings that will come to you.

Deuteronomy 28:1–2

Obeying God's Word can seem not only impossible but downright painful. Saying no to the things you really want is a royal pain, which is why not many people actually do it. After all, why can't you have what you want when you want it? But can God's wants and your wants survive together?

Deuteronomy 28 should be your inspiration. God promises a lot to people who obey him instead of their own wants. Sure, this side of Jesus we have God's kindness that gives us a pardon from all our sins, but the question is this: which is better, pardon from what you've done wrong, or the list of blessings in Deuteronomy 28?

Obeying God's Word clearly offers a lot, lot more than doing whatever you want and then just asking forgiveness ever could. That's called cheap grace, and all it does is prove how little you truly love the giver of that grace. After all, what shows your love more, your choice to do what he says, or your stubborn insistence on doing whatever you want whenever you want because "he's so forgiving"? Obedience is clearly the most rewarding choice between those two. If you aren't sure, spend some time considering the blessings of obedience—not the difficulty but the reward. Rather than being bondage, obedience is freedom. Do one simple act of obedience and haul in the reward. Obedience should be your friend, not an enemy that you fear and avoid. Do what God says to do and you'll find out that what he says is true.

On the seventh day they got up at dawn. They marched around the city seven times. . . . When they went around the seventh time, the priests blew their rams' horns. Joshua said to the troops, "Shout, because the LORD has given you the city!"

Joshua 6:15–16

*A*re you facing a battle that you have to fight? Do you have a big trial in front of you that you aren't sure how you're gonna overcome? Then take a look at God's Word for help. Look at the life of the people of Israel. In almost every case all Israel did was go through the motions of the battle while God himself did all the actual fighting. When you get up, get going, and go through the motions of something that you've got to do, then God will do what he does: win the battle.

When you see something that has to be done, you can't sit on your couch waiting for God to do his thing. You are called to participate, like the Israelites walking around Jericho. You have to move and trust that when you get moving, God does miracles. Why would God repeatedly ask the Israelites to step out in faith and do things that ultimately he himself would do for them? It was a test of their faith. Moving, acting, doing what God calls the God Girl to do proves that you trust and believe in him. You have to know that God does the work through you, but he works through you when you start to work. So even if the job ahead of you seems ridiculous or scary, get up and get going so that you can see the hand of God at work.

The LORD said to Joshua, "Don't be terrified or afraid. Take all the troops with you, and march against Ai. I am about to hand the king of Ai, his people, city, and land over to you."

Joshua 8:1

/ f God promised to help you do something that sounded impossible in the same way he promised to help the Israelites capture first Jericho and then Ai, would you step out in trust and do what he said, or would you doubt his ability to deliver on his promise? Doing the things God asks can seem totally impossible. Walk around the city and the walls are gonna crumble? Just walk onto the land and I will take it from them and give it to you? The Israelites must have had a hard time believing that everything God told them to do could actually be done, but history proves that he came through. Never once did God not fulfill his promise or work things out for the people who did what he commanded. **God would never command you to do something that couldn't be done.** Knowing that, you can be sure that he's gonna help you do whatever it is he asks so you will have success. So if there is something in your life that seems impossible or something you know you should do but you just can't seem to do, know that you're not alone. God promises to help you. You just need to call on him and trust him to answer. Then move out in trust. Take the first step, walk, enter the door—don't just wait but get moving. Your life can change for the better today. You can walk away from whatever is plaguing you or bringing you down. Freedom can be yours, but you've got to get moving. Walk out the door; it's unlocked. Take off the shackles; he's released you. Today, take back your life by giving it over to God. And remember, you can do everything through Christ who strengthens you (see Phil. 4:13).

Joshua waged war with all these kings for a long time.

Joshua 11:18

When your enemies are relentless and just won't back down, don't be so quick to freak out. Obviously it's no fun to be attacked and made fun of. It's no pleasure cruise to have enemies, but when you've looked for peace, when you've loved them and nothing has changed, when you've humbled yourself and done things God's way rather than your way and they still are after you, you might want to consider that **their aggression might be part of God's plan.** God doesn't want to hurt you, but he does want to teach you.

We always have something to learn in the trials of life, and this situation is no exception. **What will you take from this relentless enemy of yours?** How are you going to grow in faith instead of in anger and bitterness? Find out what reaction to your trials pleases God instead of pleasing your flesh. When you believe that God lets mean people in your life for a reason, you take away their power to hurt you and instead allow God to shape you. So don't be afraid of your enemy, but trust God to show you the path of righteousness in how you react to them.

In this life you're gonna have enemies. You're gonna run into people who hate you and people whose goal it is to punish you for whatever bothers them, but take heart: God is still God and no one, not even a mean person, can take away his power in your life.

Joshua asked the Israelites, "How long are you going to waste time conquering the land which the LORD God of your ancestors has given you?"

Joshua 18:3

How long are you going to keep on worrying about something the Lord has already given you? How long are you going to stress about your salvation or believe you are "too bad" to be forgiven? Holding on to discipline or punishment in order to "serve your time" like some common criminal is unbelief. Rejecting the promises of God because you believe you are "not worthy" to receive them is not trusting him. God wants your faith and your trust, but unless you let go of your fears and doubts, you will never be set free.

God had given the land to the Israelites, but seven tribes had failed to move into it. They just wasted their time trying to get the land God had already given them. Hello! From where we sit that's insanity, but at the time it made total sense to them. And the things you believe about yourself and your God might make sense to you, but don't let your feelings fool you—if they disagree with God's Word, then they are wrong. You can't get anywhere **playing God, and that's what you're doing when you insist that God's promises don't apply to you because of your past or even your present.** His promises always stand true, and if you want to get in on them, all you have to do is to believe them. The land is yours and all that goes with it—freedom, safety, and hope—but not until you reach out and take it. Your salvation requires something of you, but it's a simple thing: let go of any judgment you've brought down on yourself and accept the forgiveness of God. It can feel like a tough challenge, but it's one you certainly can handle.

But Joshua answered the people, "Since the LORD is a holy God, you can't possibly serve him. He is a God who does not tolerate rivals. He will not forgive your rebellious acts and sins."

Joshua 24:19

*D*o you count on anything or anyone other than God? A rival to God is anyone or anything that you let do the things God has said he would do in your life. As long as you have a fallback, something that's there just in case God doesn't come through, then you have a rival in your midst. It seems preposterous that a believer would believe that something else was as powerful as her God, but the truth is, all of us are prone to thinking like this without even realizing we're doing it.

So look over your life and see where you have put your hope. What kinds of things or people do you count on when the chips are down? What do you do to make it through? Go shopping? Cut yourself? Gossip? Eat? Anything that you rely on to save you is a rival, or an idol, taking the place of God. Don't let it go on any longer but chuck the idea that anything else can save you other than God. When you do, you'll find out that salvation was right there the whole time, just waiting for you to notice.

So the LORD became angry with the people of Israel. He handed them over to people who robbed them. He also used their enemies around them to defeat them.

Judges 2:14

The wake-up call: something that happens in your life to get your attention. Sometimes hard times come from the world, sometimes they come from your sinful choices, and sometimes they come from God. Whatever their source, their cure is always God's presence. Trials and suffering should never be a time for you to freak out or give up but should be a time to take a spiritual inventory and to look at God and his Word to find out what direction to go next.

All through the history of Israel you can see a people bouncing back and forth from faith to disbelief. They struggled with focus, and a lot of times they would get off track by looking only at what they could see instead of at the invisible hand of God. But the beauty of history is that you get to see God's hand at work in the lives of other people and to learn about his nature and his love for his children from what you see thousands of years later. Though God never saved his people from the consequences of their actions, he was always willing to send help their way.

When your life takes a detour and you find yourself somewhere you never thought you'd be, don't give up hope: he is near and ready to take you back. You might not know today how to change your life and get closer to the God you love, but as you read his Word you'll find that you're not alone. Though your life might seem like a joke, it can change. You just have to be willing to cry out to him, confess your sins to him, and then wait for him to do what only God can do: save you from your sin and the mess it's gotten you into.

Gideon said to God, "You said that you would rescue Israel through me. I'll place some wool on the threshing floor. If there is dew on the wool while all the ground is dry, then I'll know that you will rescue Israel through me, as you said."

Judges 6:36–37

*A*re you waiting for a sign from God? Do you believe you are supposed to do something but are still waiting for proof? Beware of putting God to some kind of test, making him jump through hoops to prove himself to you. The only sign you need is the sign of his Word. What he says in it is true and doesn't need more proof. If God is asking you, through his Word, to do something, then you have to do it at the moment he asks you. **To demand some kind of a sign first cheapens the Word of God.**

In Judges 6 God comes to Gideon several times and tells him what he wants him to do. But Gideon asks God for a sign, a reassurance that what God said to do is really what God wants him to do. God's words to him weren't enough; he, like a lot of us, needed a miracle. Because of his fear or doubt Gideon needed more, and though God in his kindness did give Gideon a sign, Gideon did nothing but delay doing what he was commanded to do.

Most demands for signs come out of fear—the fear of being wrong or the fear of doing whatever God has asked. Fear doesn't come from God; it comes from the enemy. The most powerful thing Satan can do to destroy the life of a believer is to convince him or her that God's Word has to be proven, backed up, and supported with signs that it's really the right direction to take. But as a God Girl, you should have no question that following the Word of God is the right direction for your life. So don't stall any longer, and don't operate in the same fear that Gideon lived in. If you've been called by the very Word of God to do something, then get to doing it.

Wherever you go, I will go, and wherever you stay, I will stay. Your people will be my people, and your God will be my God.

Ruth 1:16

*W*hen life looks like it's over, when the one you love is gone and you have nowhere to go, what do you do? Curl up and die? Or get up and get going? For Ruth the answer was obvious: she would get up and get going. Her destiny was tied to her husband's mother, and no matter how hard it would be, she would not walk away. So instead of staying home to be with her family, where things were familiar and safe, she decided to leave Moab with Naomi. This trip would have been scary. How would they survive? What would they do? But Ruth accepted Naomi and her God as her own and didn't look back. This confidence in a God she barely knew and willingness to do whatever her mother-in-law asked her to do gave Ruth a brand-new life.

When all looks lost, when your dreams have been destroyed and you wonder what to do next, your eyes are probably going to be on what you've lost, but the only way to move forward is to trust in the God who will never let you down. You are going to face times in your life when doing the right thing seems like a waste of time and following God rather than following your feelings seems impossible, but you have to **find the strength to reject your feelings and move on in faith,** even if that faith feels far less convincing than your emotions. Ruth is a good example of a girl who fearlessly did what she had to do even though she didn't know what would happen next. Now her name is written for all to remember as being an ancestor of Jesse and a part of the root of David, which is the lineage of Christ himself (see Ruth 4:13–22; Matt. 1:5). You never know what your pain will give way to, but you can know that something good is coming around the bend when you put your faith in the God who never fails.

Praise the LORD, who has remembered today to give you someone who will take care of you. The child's name will be famous in Israel.

Ruth 4:14

*N*o matter how bad things get, you can be sure that what God wants to happen will happen. A lot of times **God gets his people to do what they need to do by letting them suffer.** Naomi had to move to Moab because her family suffered from a famine, and famine was also the reason Jacob and his sons went to Egypt. Every time that things seemed to be the worst they could be, it turned out to be all part of God's plan.

In the midst of trials you never know what good's gonna come, but if you only concentrate on the bad parts of life, then bad is all you're gonna see. When you can see your trials and suffering as just a crucial step to where you were meant to go, then nothing can get in your way. You can be depression-free, worry-free, lonely-free, and fear-free. In fact, when you aren't free from those things but are ruled by them, you are believing a lie about God—the lie that he isn't in control and he can't work all things out for the good of those who love him. But as we see time and again in Scripture, God is not a distant observer but an active participant. He has plans for the lives of his kids, and all you need to do is trust him enough to find out what his plans are.

Ruth was not from the family of faith. She didn't know Naomi's God, but she chose to trust him and to commit to following Naomi to her homeland. Even though Ruth didn't know what would happen to her, she was not going to give up her devotion to her mother-in-law, her people, and her God. Through the fearless faithfulness of Ruth, God would bring the lineage of David and then Jesus himself.

Though fear and doubt surround you and all seems to be lost, take heart, God Girl—he is in control and he won't let you suffer for long. Just cling to the truth and refuse the sins of worry and fear, and you will be set free to soar.

The LORD causes poverty and grants wealth. He humbles people; he also promotes them.

1 Samuel 2:7

laming all the hard times in your life on Satan can be easy; after all, he's out to get you and all of God's kids. But remember, it wasn't Satan who sent Jesus to the cross. It wasn't his idea to torture and kill Jesus—it was God's. So when something totally painful happens to you, don't blame it on the enemy, because that's making it about him. Just focus on the one who will give you hope and peace; trust God and make it about him. Each attack and each abuse you experience should be a stepping-stone to lead you closer to God and not closer to the enemy.

As you watch the world fall apart around you, remember that God is in control and that out of this misery can come something beautiful, just like salvation came from the bloody cross. That's just what Hannah was acknowledging in her prayer (see 1 Sam. 2:1–10). **Don't let the enemy take what can be a tool in the hand of God and make it a weapon to cripple you.** Rise above the pain into the realm of holiness and know that God lets suffering in your life to help make you holy, should you choose the path of perfection over misery and complaint. Don't allow your pain to be wasted or to be used against you, but harness it and take advantage of the perfecting power of it. Then and only then will you be set free from the power of the enemy.

The LORD told Samuel, "Don't look at his appearance or how tall he is, because I have rejected him. God does not see as humans see. Humans look at outward appearances, but the LORD looks into the heart."

1 Samuel 16:7

Think about all the ways that God has led you. Your life has been filled with times when God pulled you out of trouble, led you to safety, and kept you from harm. It's been filled with divine encounters that you didn't even recognize till a whole lot later. He was never far away, even when you felt like he was. He pulled you out of trouble and kept you from death.

It's easy to look at life as one freak accident after another and to see people as in control instead of God. But God isn't a distant observer who created you and then let you go. He keeps you from things that could hurt you and promises to get you away from things that try. He's always present and always powerful. He is forever standing beside you asking you to look his way and take his hand. As a God Girl you are never truly alone. **If there is a gulf between you and God, it's because of your refusal to accept his outstretched hand, not because he's disinterested in your life.** He is supremely interested in everything that happens to you. And he is forever ready to make something beautiful of your pain and suffering. He is the only one who can.

David was once just a humble shepherd boy, but everything in his life—even down to being a shepherd who learned to defend the sheep—was used by God to prepare David to be king (see 1 Sam. 16:1–13). The girl who has the watchful eye of God on her can't fail to make something amazing out of her life when she is willing to consider God's power, his love, and his hand in her life. Let go of your urge to blame your situation on outside influences, and instead search for God's influences on your life. He is, after all, the one ultimately in control. And that's a good thing, even if it doesn't look like it right now—in the end you're gonna see how he used it all for good.

But the LORD told Samuel, "Don't look at his appearance or how tall he is, because I have rejected him. God does not see as humans see. Humans look at outward appearances, but the LORD looks into the heart."

1 Samuel 16:7

Some of the hardest times in your life can be the best. Your trials and suffering prove who you are: a girl who will run either to God or away from him when the going gets tough. When you run to him you end up on your knees. And from the ground it's easier to look up to God and miraculously find the comfort you need. Through this process you discover not only who he is but who you are: a child of the living God.

David, whose story starts in 1 Samuel, is a good example of the stress and strain of suffering making one kid into a strong and powerful man of faith. His time on the run from Saul didn't destroy him; it made him into a man who understood the hand of God in his life. The same can be true for the God Girl: **she grows in faith when she doesn't look for the easy way out and doesn't spend all her time daydreaming about the good life or whining about her miserable life.** The God Girl looks at all the things that come to her as an opportunity to get stronger. It takes a lot of exercise reps for your muscles to get bigger, and it takes a lot of reps of faith for your trust to get bigger.

When you're young, life comes at you guns blazing, but it's only temporary. Who you are today is not who you are going to be tomorrow. The tests and trials you are going through right now are going to shape you into either a victim or a victor. So what's it gonna be?

If you want to avoid being the victim, then don't run in fear the next time suffering knocks on the door. Just look it dead in the eyes and know that its arrival means a chance for you to get your spiritual exercise. The greatest people in history had to be tested and proved faithful before they could do the things they did in the name of God. So don't let your pain go unused.

Then David said to Nathan, "I have sinned against the LORD."

2 Samuel 12:13

*D*avid was called a man after God's own heart (see 1 Sam. 13:14), but he sinned in a big way with Bathsheba. How could a man after God's own heart do something like that? And how could a righteous God keep on blessing him and not just slap him upside the head?

The answer starts with David's confession. When the prophet Nathan confronted King David on his evil choices, David was quick to confess the whole thing (see 2 Sam. 12:13). And what's most important is that he recognized that ultimately his sin was against God more than any person. David didn't argue for himself; he got right to the confession and agreed with God that he was a total sinner. And that one confession proved that even though he had sinned in such an awful way, he still loved God and wanted what God wanted.

Immediately after David's confession, the prophet Nathan told him that the Lord took away all his sins, but that didn't mean that God would also take away the slap upside the head (see 2 Sam. 12:13–14). Sin has consequences regardless of how sorry you are for what you did. Once you confess your sins to God, you can know that you are forgiven and set free from the punishment that usually comes along with them in the spiritual world, but that doesn't mean you are free from the consequences they carry in the physical world. Sin is never the best choice, not ever. Even though it promises all kinds of payoffs and perks, in the end its payoff is just death and destruction.

Look closely at the life of David. See how his choices affected not only his life but his kids' lives. And think about how your sin can bring others down with it. As a God Girl you can't let the temptations you face draw you into the cycle of sin. You can have a heart after God's own heart if you want to do what God wants, and you can find out what that is in his Word. Study the lives of those who have gone before and learn about the life of faith and its effect on those around you.

But since you have shown total contempt for the LORD by this affair, the son that is born to you must die.

2 Samuel 12:14

*A*ll sin is against God. Sure, others might be involved in or around it, but even if people get hurt and lives get messed up, sin is still an act of violence against God, and that's the real tragedy. A lot of times when you sin you ignore the fact that your rebellion was a rebellion against God's law and because of that against him. You get caught up in the feelings of guilt associated with the people you have hurt or what you have done, and you ignore the main one you have turned against. But you can find great freedom from guilt in standing up courageously and honestly to say what David said, and that is the simple statement, "I have sinned against the LORD" (2 Sam. 12:13). In that moment David came back to his senses and called sin what sin was, and his sins were forgiven. And because of that he was set free from their stranglehold but not from their consequences.

See, a just God doesn't let his children go without discipline. So even though freedom comes to you when you confess, a price still has to be paid in the natural world. But don't confuse that price with your guilt. Once a sin is confessed, even if the pain of it still stings and the consequences still belong to you, you are guilt free (see 1 John 1:9). You have passed from enemy of God to forgiven. It's when you hold on to that guilt and nurture it like you were in charge of your own discipline that you remain chained up. Forgiveness is instantaneous, not long and laborious. You might have a long road of consequences in front of you, but it is good for the soul to know that your guilt is no more.

*I won't offer the L*ORD *my God burnt sacrifices that cost me nothing.*

2 Samuel 24:24

King David said, "I won't offer the LORD my God burnt sacrifices that cost me nothing" (2 Sam. 24:24). Why? Because **in order for something to be a sacrifice, it has to cost you something.** It's no sacrifice if it doesn't hurt you somehow. **Giving up something that's easy to give up isn't what makes you holy,** but giving up the very thing you don't want to, that is what makes you holy. Look at the things you won't let go of in your life, and then think about whether they should be sacrificed to the Lord.

For the God Girl the act of sacrifice is an act of cleansing. It cleanses your heart and brings it back in line with God's will. When you don't allow your natural desires to rule your choices, you are free to obey God's Word and to worship him. But when you reserve those things you love only for yourself and never give them up to God, then you've gotten off track.

As a God Girl you've got to learn to identify what God is asking you to sacrifice and how he wants you to obey him. Your sacrifice has to be offered with a happy heart, not in resentment, or it is useless. Think about your sacrifice as your expression of joy and love for your Father.

King Solomon loved many foreign women . . . from the nations about which the L*ORD* *had said to the people of Israel, "Never intermarry with them. They will surely tempt you to follow their gods." But Solomon was obsessed with their love. . . . In his old age, his wives tempted him to follow other gods.*

1 Kings 11:1–2, 4

*A*s a God Girl you can never let chasing boys get to be more important than chasing God. When anything in your life becomes more important to your heart than God, it's called an idol. **Idolatry rips God from the throne of your life by making someone or something else the main focus of your day.** Boys should never be so important that getting one is your number one thought. Chasing love can quickly distract you from what's really important, especially if the one you're chasing doesn't love God the same way you do, or even at all. Any love that you find at the cost of devotion to God isn't healthy spiritually or emotionally.

Loving people is a good thing, but real love is about serving God and not yourself or your hormones. When loving is more about getting than giving, it isn't love at all; it's selfishness. As a God Girl you have to make sure that the love you chase is a love that serves God and not just you. All of your worth and your hope should be in the hands of God and not in the dream of a boy. Guys are almost always going to disappoint you in some way or another, but God isn't. When you put all your faith in the one who never fails, you are preparing yourself to love the way the Father created you to—not out of your need but out of your faith in the one who is love (see 1 John 4:8).

[Elijah] sat down under a broom plant and wanted to die. "I've had enough now, LORD," he said. "Take my life! I'm no better than my ancestors." Then he lay down and slept under the broom plant. An angel touched him and said, "Get up and eat."

1 Kings 19:4–5

f you never felt depressed, then you wouldn't be human. It's the nature of a rock to never get depressed, but you're not a rock; you're a human and humans have emotions. The lows of life are what give you the ability to feel the highs. This world includes some bad things that are depressing. Don't get mad at yourself when those things show up in your life and sometimes get the best of you.

Elijah was depressed in this story. The world seemed to be out to get him, and he wanted nothing to do with it any longer. But look how God intervened. He didn't give Elijah some big revelation; he commanded him to do something simple but powerful: "Get up and eat" (1 Kings 19:5). Elijah didn't have a vision. He didn't see God in all his glory at that moment. He just did what he was told.

Depression doesn't have to win. If you're willing to do what God asks you

to do the minute he asks you, you can kick depression before it becomes too much for you to overcome. If God helps you to intuitively know that you have to do something like get out of bed and eat, then you've got to do it. When you get up and do something, you'll see the depression start to lift. You have to make the effort to decide today who you will follow—the voice of depression or the voice of God.

After the earthquake there was a fire. But the LORD wasn't in the fire. And after the fire there was a quiet, whispering voice.

1 Kings 19:12

*T*he heart of a God Girl should always desire to hear others rather than yearn to be heard. In other words, you should speak so that you can listen and understand others, not so that you can use as many words as possible in a day. When you like to talk just in order to be heard and understood, you steal the silence that might have been meant for someone else to fill so that you could better understand and even help them.

Talking too much is taking away the chance for God to be God in the lives of others. When you talk incessantly, you don't leave a lot of opportunity for miracles or divine intervention because your words drown out the whisper of God. It isn't your job to justify, explain, or position yourself. And it isn't your job to manipulate, control, or handle the lives of the people around you. Your focus shouldn't be on your life here on earth but on the kingdom of heaven.

So the next time you want to talk, ask yourself this quick little question: "Will this benefit the kingdom by nurturing the soul of the one I'm talking to, or am I just looking to be heard or understood?" The more you learn to listen with that idea in mind, the more you'll find God in your conversations.

When he couldn't see Elijah anymore, he grabbed his own garment and tore it in two to show his grief.

2 Kings 2:12

When God gives you your own Elijah, someone to teach and disciple you, it's okay to lean on him or her. That person is there to teach you and to be your example, but once they are gone, you can't panic. You have to trust what you've learned from them and know that this road is your own to walk and not theirs. When you reach the place where you have to go it alone, know that this is how it should be. The solitude is for a purpose: **in the aloneness you'll learn that no one can take care of you but God.** It's good to have the support of people you can lean on, but when they are all gone, it's not the end but the beginning. As you walk on as you have been taught, you will get stronger, and pretty soon you will find yourself becoming someone else's Elijah.

So don't look at your loss right now as something you can't overcome. It's something you must overcome, and you are not alone. Everyone has to go through these moments when they realize it's up to them and the one they leaned on is no longer there. But the one who carries you is always there. God will never be far. He is always closer than you can imagine. If you've lost your Elijah, now you can rely fully on God and his presence. Know that you can do it with God alone and that your solitude won't last forever.

Elisha answered, "Don't be afraid. We have more forces on our side than they have on theirs." Then Elisha prayed, "LORD, please open his eyes so that he may see." The LORD opened the servant's eyes and let him see. The mountain around Elisha was full of fiery horses and chariots.

2 Kings 6:16–17

When life starts to get hard, it's not a bad thing to have God and no one else but God. When everyone has walked away, you can't find a friend, and no human arms are there to hold you, then you can know that God has cleared a path straight to his arms. Because when you have all kinds of people to comfort you and everything you need to be soothed, then you don't really need God, do you? You're looking across the table instead of up to heaven.

Jesus didn't come to save the healthy people who have everything they need but to save the sick, the frightened, and the worried. People who have it all don't need him. But people who want something deeper, people who are being tested, who have been left alone, and who are living on a steady diet of pain and insecurity—these kinds of people are the ones who know what it means to need him and to be kept alive by him and him alone.

Each time you feel the sting of your so-called life, thank him that he is pulling you closer to him instead of to some earthly comfort that would just distract you from his presence. Don't pray for more of what you want but for more of what you need. The truth is that what you need isn't always the same thing as what you want. God's desire for you equals your need. And what God wants is always the best. His love for you shows up in the tough times just as much as in the amazing ones—sometimes even more.

David's fame spread through all lands, and the LORD made all the nations fear him.

1 Chronicles 14:17

What's your legacy gonna be? When you're dead and gone, what are people going to remember about you and treasure that was yours? How will they be better because you existed? Generations from now, is your family tree going to be different because of who you are today and who you're gonna be tomorrow?

When you're young you can feel like you have no control over future generations, but then something starts to change in you, and you start to think about things like how your life is gonna make a difference. You see that every decision you've made affects not only you but also the people who love you and even the ones who will never even know you but will hear stories about your life generations from now. If your spiritual heritage is noble or pathetic it doesn't make much difference, because starting with you your family history is changing. It's either getting healthier or getting sicker. Even though historical books of the Bible can sometimes be boring, we need them so that we don't forget where we've come from so we know where we can go.

As a God Girl you can give hope to not only your family but your generation by being a shining light in the darkness, a girl of peace and hope. Think about how one guy, David, changed the world, and then think about how your life can make a difference to your generation and even ones to come. It's up to you: **are you gonna change today and start thinking of your devotion to the Savior as something that can empower you to make life matter,** or are you gonna stay lost in your own powerlessness and need? For the God Girl the answer is clear: change today and every day to move in the direction of faith. Know what you believe and why you believe it. Learn to live up to the name of God Girl, and the world won't soon forget you.

That night God appeared to Solomon. He said, "What can I give you?" Solomon responded to God, . . . "Give me wisdom and knowledge so that I may lead these people. After all, who can judge this great people of yours?"

2 Chronicles 1:7–8, 10

When God offered to make King Solomon's biggest wish come true, Solomon's request was kind of shocking. Of all the things in the world he could have asked for—more money, fame, a long life—he asked for wisdom. Amazing! What kind of person would think that if they could ask for anything at all, they should ask for wisdom? But that's exactly what this man asked for, and his request was so impressive that God decided to give him more wisdom than anyone before or since.

Why would wisdom be the first thing out of his mouth? Why would Solomon want that? Think about your life and how different it would be if you had the wisdom of God running through your veins. Wisdom changes everything. It changes how you think, how you feel, and how you act. Wisdom, especially for the spiritual girl, is of highest value. It's the secret to success and even to power—the power to get things right and so to avoid discipline, failure, punishment, and bad consequences.

How often do you work at growing your wisdom? How many times do you look into God's Word in order to make a wise decision about the trials in your life? Wisdom is just as important today as it was in the day of Solomon. If you lack wisdom you should ask for it.

Wisdom will change the way you think and act, and if you make it the most important thing in your life, then you will be set free from the pressures faced every day by girls who have no desire for wisdom. Make wisdom your goal, and your life will naturally improve.

The LORD has kept the promise he made. I've taken my father David's place, and I sit on the throne of Israel as the LORD promised. I've built the temple for the name of the LORD God of Israel.

2 Chronicles 6:10

*I*t isn't always true to say that success is a blessing from God. Sometimes real success can end in spiritual failure, and failure can become a spiritual blessing. When the land of Israel split into two nations, Judah and Israel, the covenant that God made with David went with Judah, the smaller nation. You'd probably think that God's hand would be behind the big guy, the most powerful people, but nope, he went with the little guy.

It's easy to compare your life with the lives of others and to say that because your life doesn't look as good or glamorous as theirs, you're not blessed. But that's looking at the world through the eyes of the lost. God's ways are not our ways. His choices don't always make sense and his gifts can be hard to spot when you are looking at blessing through the world's eyes.

Even though things look bad, even though failure seems imminent, you have to believe. Think about the land of Judah: when the heirs of David failed and they were led astray, still God was faithful. Even though the little nation sinned, did that mean that God wouldn't honor his covenant? Of course he would honor it, and he did. Don't let the way things look fool you. The promises of God can't be removed. And the promise to you is that he will love you and save you as long as you will trust him.

When your people turn, praise your name, pray, and plead with you in this temple, then hear them in heaven, forgive the sins of your people Israel, and bring them back to the land that you gave to them and their ancestors.

2 Chronicles 6:24–25

o understand how much God hates your sin, you only have to look as far as the cross. Everything in you that is selfish, envious, bitter, resentful, or angry—everything in you that is not part of the character of God—is what put Christ on that cross.

When you confess your sin every day, you agree with God that a lot of you is broken and at odds with godliness and so you honor the cross. But when you forget or skip over that very crucial part of each day, you start to take Christ's death for granted and so dishonor the cross. If you stop becoming aware of the ugliness of sin and start to ignore it, or worse yet, accept it, you start a steady downhill slide that will take you farther and farther from God. When you think you are forgiven just because God loves you and you forget the bloody cross of his Son, you are acting like that very cross was unnecessary. It's important to really understand that it isn't simply God's love for you but Christ's death and your acceptance of that sacrifice that saves you. Don't let yourself get so comfortable with your sin, which was his death sentence, that you can't see it anymore. Agree with God every day about your sinfulness. Confess everything that doesn't come from him and agree that it's what sent his Son to the cross. God promises that when his people turn away from sin and pray to him in repentance that he will listen. When you do that, you will also find that your relationship with God grows in depth and power and peace. Confession is good for the soul.

If my people, who are called by my name, will humble themselves, pray, search for me, and turn from their evil ways, then I will hear their prayer from heaven, forgive their sins, and heal their country.

2 Chronicles 7:14

Sin has a cure, and it's humility. Humility is the foundation of all righteousness. Without it you can't get away from your sin and you can't make Jesus the Lord of your life. Humility sounds weak, uncomfortable, and even dangerous, but **humility is just acknowledging your complete dependence on God and making a deliberate decision to make life not about you but about him.** When your life is centered on your wants and needs and you lose sight of who you live for, humility sneaks out the back door and danger sneaks in.

When the Israelites' military and financial victories puffed them up, they lost their humility, and then all of a sudden they stopped worshiping the true God. But God made a way out for them. He didn't write them off like you might think, but he kept his promise to David to bring success for generations to come. But even so, his hand of protection was off of David's heirs while they lived their prideful and evil lives.

It's easy to let pride and confidence in your own abilities color your vision of what you were meant to be or to do. All day long you live with thoughts about yourself, your feelings, your wants, your needs, and your experiences, and it's easy to get all self-occupied. But you've gotta be careful. When things start to look bad and you notice that the waves are getting rough, then it's time to stop all the navel-gazing and start looking up. You have to turn away from the sin of self-obsession and toward the strength of humility. When you walk humbly, without any regard for yourself or your wants but with an eye on your God and what he wants, your life will be blessed. You'll find that your prayers are more effective, forgiveness is yours, and your life is healed.

King Rehoboam sought advice from the older leaders who had served his father Solomon while he was still alive. . . . But he ignored the advice the older leaders gave him. He sought advice from the young men who had grown up with him and were serving him.

2 Chronicles 10:6, 8

*F*aith isn't just about communion with God; it's also about being part of God's people. When you have a big decision to make or when troubles hit you from all sides and you don't know what to do, God doesn't want you to play the fool. The fool is the one who won't ask godly advice but listens to the crowd. The fool goes to her friends, who may have little or no wisdom, and does whatever they say. But that's a stupid move.

True wisdom comes from people who are older and more mature and who can see things from a broader perspective. You might not like what you hear, and you might even say they are "out of touch" or "too conservative," but it's foolish to ignore them and just do what your friends say.

Friends are a good thing, but their wisdom isn't always quite ripe for the picking. Usually they give advice with self-protection in mind—they say what will make you happy, or they encourage you to sin because they are just as heated about things as you are. **You can't let a friend or anyone else tell you that sin is the way to deal with your problems,** even when you're dealing with the sins of others. Nope, you've gotta go to people who are more removed from the situation and have nothing to gain or lose by your ultimate decision. Then don't play the fool by returning to your friends and choosing their more immature and earthly response.

Friends are not always selfish, and they aren't completely clueless, but they just don't have the wisdom that comes with age. So think about where you get your advice, and look for godly counsel when you have a decision to make, especially one with spiritual ramifications.

The battle isn't yours. It's God's.

2 Chronicles 20:15

*D*o you ever feel the need for vindication—to defend or justify yourself to others? Sometimes people get you wrong. They misunderstand you or they lie about you. But what do you do next?

Vindication is your attempt to fight the battle yourself, to fix things and to prove yourself to everyone who has you wrong. But God never asked you to vindicate yourself. The obsession to prove to other people that they're wrong and you're right is never an act of faith. When you say to yourself, "I have to explain myself, and they have to listen," you don't sound like our Lord. Jesus never fought to prove himself to human beings. If they misunderstood him, he left it to God to do the correcting. When you see that someone is wrong or misunderstanding you, you've got to let them have their opinion. The God Girl has to trust God to intervene where he's gonna intervene, and then she has to refuse to criticize his creation by complaining about people. Her job at this point is prayer, not judgment. This means that you have to remain calm and let people misunderstand you. What they think doesn't define you, so don't get all up in arms. Your job is to stay obedient and just keep on walking like Jesus walked, in faith and trust, knowing the battle isn't yours—it's God's.

The LORD became angry with Amaziah. He sent him a prophet who asked him, "Why do you dedicate your life to serving the gods of those people? Those gods couldn't save their own people from you."

2 Chronicles 25:15

*H*as God ever sent you a prophet, a voice of reason sent to point out the sin in your life that you have chosen to ignore? When he does it can hurt something awful, and your first response can be the common one, and that is to argue with them and to totally reject their warnings. But don't be so quick to fight for your sinfulness. Don't be so quick to try to prove you're right when others say you're wrong. Just stop and listen, thank them for their insight, and take it home with you. Then don't let another day go by without asking God for his word on the subject.

In order to have this kind of response, you have to tear down the wall of self-protection that you have built around your life. This takes a large dose of humility, but ignoring your sinfulness was really not self-protection in the first place. The wise girl refuses to lie to herself anymore and really wants to figure out where she's getting it wrong. Getting it wrong, after all, is a cause for concern. Do you want to live your life in ignorant bliss, or would you rather turn the lights on and see into all the dark places of your life? The best way to destroy the arguments of the enemy in your life is by turning on the light and confronting the lies you have been accepting as truth.

Ignorant bliss is really no bliss at all; it's just a down payment on destruction. Sin's payoff isn't happiness; it's death. So don't trust your own deceitful heart anymore, but be willing to listen when others correct you. Even though it tears at your heart, listen. Even though it sounds absurd, listen. You'll have a teachable heart, and a teachable heart is a peaceful heart.

As they praised and gave thanks to the LORD, they sang antiphonally: "He is good; his mercy toward Israel endures forever." Then all the people shouted, "Praise the LORD," because the foundation for the house of the LORD had been laid.

Ezra 3:11

*N*othing happens that God can't use to get things done in the lives of his people. Through the most horrible and trying circumstances God cleanses, teaches, and delivers his people. Things might look lost and the end might seem to be near, but when God promises to rescue you, you can be sure he's gonna do it.

When the Israelites went into exile and were taken away from everything they knew, it seemed like the end for them. But God had a plan: "They will be taken to Babylon and stay there until I come for them, declares the LORD. I will take them from there and bring them back to this place" (Jer. 27:22). In the middle of a trial it might look like God has forgotten you. You might say something like "This always happens to me" or "I'm sure it's something I've done wrong." You might see only the bad in it, blame yourself, and think that God has left the building. But you might just want to look closer. God uses these times for your good. Look at the lives of the Israelites: they were sent into captivity, but it wasn't for nothing. While they were there they learned to look at their God in a new light. Instead of thinking of him as absent, they began to see him as involved. And so when they returned home from exile they were changed people, ready to serve God by rebuilding the temple that had been destroyed.

The book of Ezra stands as an example to all of us that God will restore us if we are willing to come back to him and obey him. He is ready to rebuild your relationship even after you have sinned in a big way. **He isn't a God who holds a grudge forever; he doesn't reject you and refuse to hear your cries.** Consider how faithful he is to his promises and how he works everything together for good.

I am ashamed, my God. I am embarrassed to look at you. Our sins have piled up over our heads, and our guilt is so overwhelming that it reaches heaven.

Ezra 9:6

When all the people around Ezra sinned, Ezra confessed their sins as "our sins" and said, "Our guilt is so overwhelming that it reaches heaven" (Ezra 9:6). He'd had nothing to do with their disobedience in mixing with pagans and turning their backs on God, but that didn't stop him from making himself a part of the confession. They were, after all, his people, and he was well aware of what their acts meant to a holy God. And so Ezra grieved as if he was the one who had walked away from God, and he prayed as though his very life depended on it (see Ezra 9:5–15).

How often have you shared the burden of the sins of the people you love and confessed them as your own? Probably never. It's not a normal thing to do, but think about what Ezra did and why he did it. Then think about how often you have judged the sins of others with disgust and revulsion. Which reaction is more holy? The next time you see the sins of the people you love, think about standing in spiritual grief with them, pleading with God to forgive "our" sins and to heal "us" of our unfaithfulness.

After the people saw Ezra crying in front of God's temple, they were so moved that they too started to "cry bitterly" and to confess their unfaithfulness to God (Ezra 10:1). Ezra didn't force them, but he influenced them by taking on their condition as his own and responding as a godly person would after having come face-to-face with sin in his own life. As a God Girl you play a role in the spiritual lives of those in your family, community, and nation. Don't stand by as an observer, but become active in prayer and confession.

*I am praying to you day and night about your servants the Israelites. . . .
Lord, please pay attention to my prayer and to the prayers of all your other
servants who want to worship your name.*

Nehemiah 1:6, 11

*W*here you are and who is around you right now isn't just by
chance. There's no such thing as chance in
the life of a believer; that would imply that God
isn't in control and that things happen without any reason whatsoever.
But God has a reason for everything he allows. That means that he can
bring you into relationships that make no sense, that drive you crazy,
and that you want to get out of, but if you look to him you might just
find something amazing. Think about the people around you and ask
yourself if God hasn't given them to you in order for you to intercede
for them, to come to him with requests on their behalf, to help
them and even save them.

Praying for sinful people in your life isn't an option; it's a
requirement for the God Girl. If they are in your life, then
they need your prayers, even the bad people—especially
the bad ones. Don't let what you feel dictate how obedient you are. Think about the fact that each person
in your life needs your prayers. This prayer of inter-
cession doesn't have to be hard; you don't have to
get involved in their drama, but bring them before
the throne of God and plead with him. Your pleas
to God can help them be saved.

Don't ever think things happen by chance and
that you weren't meant to be where you are. You
were meant to be just where you are, and your prayers
were meant to bring the freedom that others need.

I went out with a few men without telling anyone what my God had inspired me to do for Jerusalem.

Nehemiah 2:12

When God gives you a vision for your future or your purpose, you don't have to share it with everyone in order to make it more real. Sometimes your service to God will go unannounced and your devotion won't be seen or understood by anyone. You don't need to brag about the vision you've been given or explain why you are doing what you are doing. If it's really a vision from God, then it's gonna happen, and if not, then you won't have made a fool of yourself. As you spend more time in the presence of God, you will find yourself with all the encouragement you need to do what you are being asked. His approval is the only approval you need.

A lot of visions are meant to be shared, but only at the right time. Visions have to be tested. They aren't served to you on a silver platter, but most often they are going to take some effort on your part, and a lot of times that effort is its own reward. When you need another person to validate your vision, you are looking to people who don't have the same relationship with God that you do and who haven't seen the same vision you have seen. So act as you are called to act and say what you are called to say, but don't be too quick to explain that you are sure God has called you to do the things you do.

God made me strong.

Nehemiah 6:9

When you pray, does God give you strength? If not, then take a look at your prayers. All God's responses are good responses, including "no." **If God doesn't give you what you ask for, then he has a very good reason.** You have to trust him so much that when your prayers seem to go unanswered or the answer is a loud "no," you can look up, smile, and say, "Thanks for knowing what's best for me." After all, what do you know about the future? How can you predict the outcome of this or that desire of your heart? You can't.

But as a God Girl one thing you can do is be sure that God's will is the best possible will for your life, and if he sees fit to not give you something that you really, really want, then it's for a really, really good reason. So instead of worrying and freaking out about not getting what you want, think about why he might not want you to have it or, better yet, why he does want you to have exactly what he has given you and nothing more.

God will make you strong when you trust his strength. And he will answer every prayer you'll ever pray when you trust his Word. Find out about prayer. Do your homework and learn God's promises on the subject. Prayer is your lifeline, your hand reaching out to the Father who protects you, so why wouldn't you want to know everything about it that you could? And all you need to know is found in the pages of his Word. So go after the wisdom and truth in Scripture and become a God Girl who prays.

The fact is, even if you remain silent now, someone else will help and rescue the Jews, but you and your relatives will die. And who knows, you may have gained your royal position for a time like this.

Esther 4:14

A lot of stuff in the Bible can seem contradictory, but just because you can't conceive of something, that doesn't make that something impossible. God can allow two opposites to both exist without contradicting each other. Think about free will and God's hand in your life. Everybody has the free will to do whatever they want. We all make choices on our own, not as God's puppets but as sinful human beings who have the power to choose between obedience and defiance. But God also says that he controls our destiny (see Exod. 7:3; Rom. 9:10–13). So which is it? Free will or predetermination? It's both.

Esther and her cousin made decisions and took actions that affected an entire generation of Israelites, but you could also say that God had planned for them to do just that (see Esther 4:14). Whether you think what happens is a result of God's hand in your life or your own free will, live your life like one who is devoted to his commandments and committed to loving him in all you do. Do this and your life will unfold in the power and grace of God, but reject God's commands and you'll find yourself destined to live a life of regret.

God wants to use you to change a generation. He wants you to take risks, to be fearless in defending the defenseless, but your will has to agree with his. As a God Girl you have to know that his purpose for you is clear and **what matters most is your daily worship and pursuit of holiness, not your perceived destiny.** As you go after God every day, God's hand in your life will be obvious to everyone.

Faith knows that there is more to life than meets the eye. The human mind can't easily conceive of free will and predetermination coexisting, but with God anything is possible. Some things you have to have the faith to believe without fully understanding.

Job stood up, tore his robe in grief, and shaved his head. Then he fell to the ground and worshiped.

Job 1:20

God is found at the end of yourself. When you are beat down, worn out, bruised and battered, God becomes everything. The less you can rely on yourself or your past success, the clearer and more impressive his presence becomes. When the hard times hit you often feel powerless, and with that there is less of you, and with less of you there is more room for him.

Prayer really takes wings and changes lives when it's not about you, your problems, or your fears but instead it's about him, his will, and his ways. At that point everything you want and even need fades to the background. You don't need peace with where you are or how you feel. You don't need to feel comfortable with who you are or with who people think you are because you know who he is. **You'll find some rest for your soul when you don't care if you are distrusted, disputed, rejected, or shamed.** When you come to that point, you have found all you need in the one who knows what it is to be misunderstood, doubted, and horribly rejected. Remember that the lack or trial in your life is nothing more than what millions before you and to come have experienced and will experience, and hardship is the fuel of faith. Faith proves itself in the hard times, not in the good ones. Faith is born and grown through stress and turmoil, not through ease and comfort.

Whatever junk you're living through right now, just know that without this junk today, you might never find the need or passion for more of God. Don't let this stuff be wasted on your soul. Let it scrub you clean of any hint of self-obsession and sweeten you with a pure and humble God-obsession.

Naked I came from my mother,
and naked I will return.
The LORD has given,
and the LORD has taken away!
May the name of the LORD be praised.

Job 1:21

Nothing happens in your life that God didn't let happen. It's true that God only gives good and perfect gifts, but he also lets other things in your life like trials, persecution, and trouble happen for a reason. Job's life is a good example of this. God didn't inflict destruction on Job's life; Satan did, but not without first asking for God's approval.

When God lets bad things happen in your life you may wonder why he would allow you to be hurt, but the answer can be found in the lives of people who have come before you, like Job. Because of Job's suffering, you now have an example of how to live in the midst of your trials. You can see from Job's experience what the answers are when questions on suffering come. You can also see that God is never very far away, and all he wants is your faith in him and your obedience to his Word. As Job obeyed God he got out from under his suffering, and in the end he had more than he could have ever imagined. So even if you have to suffer for a while, think about the fact that much greater and more amazing things will come to you—if not in this life then most certainly in the next—if you are willing to trust him no matter what happens to you here on earth.

After all this, Job finally opened his mouth and cursed the day he was born.

Job 3:1

*Y*ou don't have to feel good to be godly. Everything in you might scream "Yuck!" Your emotions drag, your heart aches, and you feel like you can't go on, but you have to push through and trust. You have to act like you don't feel those things at all and just push on into action, doing what you've been called to do—love, serve, give, trust. In spite of how things look, your mind has to focus on what is true and honorable and commendable (see Phil. 4:8). **You can't use your sadness as an excuse to be ungodly.** Feelings lie and feelings manipulate, and if you let feelings be your guide, you're gonna spend more time off track than on the road to success. So listen to what your feelings have to say, but if they're bringing you down, like they did to Job when his trial first hit, then turn down the volume. You can acknowledge they are there, you can even mourn and grieve as Job did, but then say, "Even so, I'm moving on as if everything's okay, because feelings aren't my God." When you act as if you feel good even when you don't, something amazing happens: you start to feel good. It's weird, but it happens. When you **work at making what you know more important than how you feel,** eventually your mind will be able to control your feelings and stop letting them control you. Then you'll be free.

People who are controlled by their feelings are like waves on the ocean, blown by the wind and tossed around by the sea. Want stability? Then take your life back from your emotions.

I wish you would keep silent. For you, that would be wisdom.

Job 13:5

*C*an you trust the silence of God, or do you feel the need to keep the chatter going? When you fear silence, it's easy to start listening to the emotional noises that roll around inside of you and think of them as the voice of God. After all, how could he be silent—isn't he supposed to be talking, guiding, helping? The answer is yes, but he doesn't always do it with sound. Sometimes he lives in the silence.

Silence isn't really just the absence of sound; it's the absence of your stress over not being heard. The real question is, do you trust God to care for you without you having to tell him what you need? Does he know all or doesn't he? Is he aware of what's going on in every aspect of your life? The answer is yes, a thousand times yes. He knows it all and he isn't avoiding your need. He's fulfilling it in the way it needs to be fulfilled.

You have to trust the silence in order to find the comfort of God. When you can shut off the chatter of your emotional needs and just look at the amazing face of God—studying his Word, listening for his presence, and trusting that even if you never hear from him again, he is still right with you, never leaving you—then you can start to rest and lose the worry. In the silence you can hear better and learn to shut off your pesky emotions that want to yell and shout and pout over all that they feel they need.

Don't confuse what the monk and writer Thomas Merton calls "the echo of our own emotional noise" with the voice of God. We grow so accustomed to the sound of our thoughts that it becomes hard to shut them off and live in the silence of God. Can you trust him to know what you require without you speaking of it? Can you trust him to fight your battles and defend your name? Can you trust the silence of God?

God has worn me out.
You, God, have destroyed everyone who supports me.

Job 16:7

When Job's life was a miserable mess, his body was covered in painful sores, and he had lost everything, his friends were useless. They cut him down and blamed him for everything bad in his life. But Job claimed that God had turned his friends against him and destroyed everyone who should be supporting him. He looked at God as the all-powerful one who controls the wind and even the choices of man. When you have this point of view, you don't need to get all up in arms about mean people. And you have no reason to fear the old meanies because you are certain God has allowed all this for a reason. When you are sure that God never gives you anything that isn't designed to make your life better, you're impermeable—no mean can get into you. So why complain or worry?

Other people aren't ultimately responsible for your lot in life. So don't blame them for the things that happen to you, but look for God in everything. Where you are today isn't where you're gonna be once you can find your way to God. After all, he knows all and sees all, and he promises to never abandon you or leave you (see Deut. 31:8). Nothing can separate you from his love, not even mean people. So choose to believe God rather than fear mean.

As long as there is one breath left in me
and God's breath fills my nostrils . . .
I cling to my righteousness and won't let go.

Job 27:3, 6

When you first start out as a God Girl, you are passionate, hopeful, and excited, but as the storms start to hit your life and the winds get to blowin', you start to bend under the stress of it all. When that happens you have two choices: you can either reject your first love, God, or hold on tightly to him. You can either forget all that you know about him and run for cover, or you can just keep on keepin' on, trusting him like you did in the beginning.

In the life of faith trials are gonna come. Your faith has to be tested, purified. You have to prove your faith is real. So don't look at trials as something you've got to worry about but as a natural part of growing up. The strong tree isn't the one planted inside a warm, comfortable box in a climate-controlled building. Nope, the strong tree is the one planted outside in the elements, forced to live with extreme temperatures, drought, and snow. This hardy tree digs deep into the ground to keep itself alive, always reaching for more life-giving nutrients, always holding on, even against all hope. Your roots can grow strong too when you survive every season and keep on getting those life-giving elements from the Father. A small little sapling grows into an enormous oak when it holds tightly to the soil that surrounds it. You too will grow in strength when you hold tightly to the Word of God.

*If I have walked with lies
or my feet have run after deception,
then let God weigh me on honest scales,
and he will know I have integrity.*

Job 31:5–6

*B*ad habits are like weeds. They dig down deep and wrap them-selves around your heart, so removing them takes strength and wisdom. You could just yank 'em out by the roots, but if you've ever pulled weeds then you know how hard it can be to get those things out, especially if the roots have really dug down deep. But there's another way to kill the roots choking your spirit. Follow Job's example by asking yourself what sinful habits have crept into your life, and then begin to choke them out with something far better and more powerful—a good habit from God's Word. **A good habit is the best way to suffocate a bad habit.** When you make living God's Word out in your life the most important thing to you, then you fill your life with the good habit of integrity or right living.

So don't sit around feeling bad about your bad habits or sins, and especially don't think about the sins of other people—that's a total waste of time. You need to spend your strength looking for the good in people and your situations. When you find good things in people, try to imitate them. Watch how they overcome situations and feelings you aren't so good at overcoming. Refuse to be negative, always seeing the bad in things, and instead pay attention to the hand of God.

Bad habits can be totally wiped out when you stop treating them like they have more control over you than God. When you made him Lord of your life, you became his slave. You can't be a slave to two masters. That means you aren't in chains to your bad habits and sinful way of living anymore. You are set free; all that's left to do is to step out of those old chains and run in the direction of God. You are no longer a prisoner but have been set free—so go ahead and act like it!

After Job prayed for his friends, the LORD restored Job's prosperity and gave him twice as much as he had before.

Job 42:10

Are you suffering? **Your suffering will end when God is done using it.** Suffering isn't meant to destroy you, like you might think, but it's meant to make you into something more than you are right now. Unless your suffering is self-inflicted, it will set you free if you will look in thanks on the one who allows it. All suffering should lead you to worship and thankfulness, not to resentment and distrust. When the suffering God Girl trusts God instead of blaming him, her prayers are focused not on getting rid of the problem but on serving the Answer. The most effective prayers aren't the prayers begging for relief but the ones that look outside of yourself instead of inside.

The life of Job gives us a good example of powerful prayer. Job suffered a lot, but it wasn't until he prayed for his friends that his life was healed: "After Job prayed for his friends, the Lord restored Job's prosperity and gave him twice as much as he had before" (Job 42:10). The best and most powerful prayer is always the prayer for someone else. When you take your eyes off of your own suffering and instead put them on serving others, you will find yourself free from grief and moving on to more important things—things that make a difference eternally.

Blessed is the person who does not
follow the advice of wicked people,
take the path of sinners,
or join the company of mockers.
Rather, he delights in the teachings of the LORD
and reflects on his teachings day and night.

Psalm 1:1–2

*G*od is all about your life's process, not purpose. Purpose is a big deal, but not as big a deal as obedience—just doing what you are called to do right now. It's easy to start to freak out when you can't figure out your purpose in life, but God doesn't want you to focus on some great purpose off in the distance; he wants you to find him in the moment, right now. He wants you to rise above yourself, your needs, and your desires and to trust him right now, not someday in the future when you find your purpose. God's purpose for your life isn't for later; it's for now. His purpose for you is the process of continually doing what he asks you to do, no matter how much it hurts. If you can move through the turmoil, stress, and strain of life by obeying God's Word and looking to him for each step and each action, you will have found your purpose.

It's a human and even prideful thing to focus on looking for a "greater" purpose. **God doesn't need your grand accomplishments, but he wants your heart,** fully devoted and trusting in him. When you give your life to him with that in mind, you'll see that every day you have fulfilled your purpose of loving the one who gave you life. The more you live with this goal in mind, the better your days will be and the more of an impact your life will have.

So don't think like other people think. Don't focus on yourself but focus on your God. Don't ask "What's my purpose?" You know your purpose: to love and serve the one true God so that his will may be done on earth as it is in heaven. Line up your life with his, and your life will be a true success.

*I fall asleep in peace the moment I lie down
because you alone, O Lᴏʀᴅ, enable me to live securely.*

Psalm 4:8

Some things you don't have to pray about: your moods, for example. **Bad moods don't need to be prayed away—they need to be kicked out!** Your mood comes from your way of thinking about the stuff in your life. The more you listen to your flesh and feelings, the easier it is to miss the truth of Scripture. But the more you flat-out refuse to let the world around you decide your moods, the freer you become.

Growing into the God Girl you were meant to be means step-by-step, day-by-day grabbing your bad moods by the scruff of the neck and tossing them out the door. When you start to make the Holy Spirit's thoughts your own, when you study his Word and find out what pleases him, and when you want what he wants, then controlling your emotions gets easier and easier. You start to recognize your bad moods quicker, and sometimes you just refuse to let them live.

Your bad moods don't have to control you, but you can control them. Think about what your mood is railing about: is it your problem, your environment, or something someone said or did? Is it reacting to what God said? Does it care more about people or God? If it's caring more about the creation than the Creator, it's up to no good. Bad moods don't have to plague the God Girl because her mood is based not on her changing circumstances but on a God who never changes. Having a bad day? Think about how you can be happy in the trial God has set out for you. Having a hard time? Think how perseverance can change your life.

As you grow from a God Girl into a woman, you'll get better at refusing to listen to your moods and instead choosing to listen to God. Each time you do you'll build your strength, character, and faith.

The LORD is my inheritance and my cup.
You are the one who determines my destiny.

Psalm 16:5

Thinking that success is God's goal for your life is a total lie. When you pray, don't ask him to give you fame and fortune. Those things of this world mean nothing in the life of faith. God might give you success and fortune if you are faithful, but this success is never his goal or the goal of the God Girl.

God doesn't need you to be successful in order to save lives or to get done what he wants to get done. All the cattle on the hills are his (see Ps. 50:10). He created every living thing; they all belong to him (see Ps. 24:1). So it's wrong to believe that he needs your success or that you need success in order to serve him. God is concerned about your holiness, not your comfort. He wants you to be more like his Son, Jesus. His goal wasn't popularity, fame, or even success, but sacrifice. He's our living example. When your focus is success, your focus is yourself. But your focus should be God and his kingdom. Your first question should be, "Will this benefit the kingdom?" When your first thought is, "How will this benefit me?" you are proving you worship not God but yourself. What a sad state it is to be more concerned with your own life than with the life giver! Instead, be one of those the psalmist talks about as people who "lead holy lives on earth" (Ps. 16:3).

As you realign your goals with the Father's, every minute becomes a success—even in your failures. Failure in the eyes of the world isn't always failure in God's eyes. Throughout time he has used the failed actions of his people to achieve his desired end. Don't let your failure to succeed in this world get you off track from the true success of following Jesus no matter how crazy that might seem.

Let the verdict of my innocence come directly from you.
Let your eyes observe what is fair.
You have probed my heart.
You have confronted me at night. . . .
I have called on you because you answer me, O God.

Psalm 17:2–3, 6

*W*ho are you? Do you know? When others laugh at what you do, make fun of you, or hate you, do you immediately look inside yourself to see if those mockers are right? Have you ever done that and felt like you just don't know yourself? Some people call knowing who you are "self-awareness" and spend days, if not years, looking for it. Self-awareness isn't a sin, but constantly chasing after it means your heart is set on the wrong thing.

When things go wrong and when people cut you down, you don't need to find yourself but to find Jesus. Looking inward will only drag out the pain and dig you deeper into a pit, but if you look up to the source and goal of your faith (see Heb. 12:2), you're gonna find freedom. Who you are on the inside isn't as important as who you believe Jesus is. When you've messed up, your only hope is to run to Jesus and to depend totally on him. Learn his thoughts. Study his Word and run to his throne. Then you will be set free from your failure and your self-preoccupation, and you will be free to love the way Jesus loved.

Keep me from sinning.
Do not let anyone gain control over me.
Then I will be blameless,
and I will be free from any great offense.
May the words from my mouth and the thoughts from my heart
be acceptable to you, O Lord, my rock and my defender.

Psalm 19:13–14

*T*he God Girl doesn't give control of her life over to anyone but God. And that means she only lets those who are assigned authority by God have authority over her. Certain authorities here on earth, set up by God, will control your life in certain seasons, like your parents, teachers, the police, or judges. But giving control to anyone who God has not given control to is idolatry.

When you're young it can be easy to look for people to tell you what to do. You don't have the answers and you want help. You want to know how to dress and how to act. You want help, but help and advice can become control, and just as quickly your life can become less about pleasing God and more about pleasing people. When you make decisions and run your life based on what someone else wants you to do, you walk away from the will of God and into the will of his creation. No friend, no boyfriend, and no enemy should have control over your life. And when you do the things you do out of a fear of rejection or manipulation, you don't just make a mistake; you commit a sin.

Make it your prayer that no one should gain control over you but that you can learn to love others God's way. Work on humility instead of pride. Don't worry about what others might do or say; just always choose God's way and trust that he will truly work everything out for the good of those who love him.

My God, my God,
why have you abandoned me?
Why are you so far away from helping me,
so far away from the words of my groaning?

Psalm 22:1

*W*henever something turns out different than you expected, it's easy to blame God. The first question is always, "Why, God? Why me? Why this?" But those kinds of Qs can easily become a whine or a complaint. They can easily start to sound like an accusation: "I did what you asked—why didn't you hold up your end of the bargain?" Well, maybe he did. **God isn't really concerned about making you happy. He wants to make you *holy*.** And the process of making you holy, which is called sanctification, doesn't always involve the easiest and most comfortable way.

When a trial comes into your life, your first response should be to ask God, "How can I serve you in this?" Any other response means you are trying to serve two ends—your own and God's. And that can't be done (see Matt. 6:24; Rom. 6:16). You have to focus completely on the end that God has in mind for your life. Once you do, living a godly life will become more like second nature. That's because God promises that as soon as you obey him, he will give you peace. The apostle Paul puts it this way: "Make sure that you improve. Accept my encouragement. Share the same attitude and live in peace. The God of love and peace will be with you" (2 Cor. 13:11). And again: "Practice what you've learned and received from me, what you heard and saw me do. Then the God who gives this peace will be with you" (Phil. 4:9).

No matter what the results of your plans or dreams are, and even if it feels like God totally let you down, trust him, believe, and know that this too shall be used to make you a holy woman if you will just let it. Like the psalmist, get good at knowing that even if things seem miserable, God is always there and always in control.

I will sing and make music to praise the LORD.

Psalm 27:6

Worship music was meant to help us do one thing, and that is to worship God. When you worship you tell God how amazing he is and pour out your sense of awe, thanks, and reverence to him. It's like Christmas morning for God when you shower him with the gift of your praise. But what's amazing about worship is that it serves not only the God you sing to but also the one who sings. Worship was never meant to be a selfish act that you do so that you can feel better or feel inspired, but those feelings are a side effect. A lot of times the songs you sing to God express your human emotions of fear, worry, and stress—at least that's what they did for King David, who wrote many of the psalms.

Music isn't the only way you worship God. You worship him when you live in obedience to what he commands, when you thank him for all you've got, and when you talk with him about your life. Worship is more than just singing, but worship music can be a powerful way to connect your heart and soul to him. Check out the book of Psalms, and see how the godly men who wrote them were often scared, lonely, depressed, and suffering but at the same time always got back to hope and to a total belief that God would work it all out. Check out how the psalmist can spend most of his energy on complaining but wind up in worship when he finally remembers the truth. And remember that you are reading these psalms from this side of the empty tomb. Like all the books of the Old Testament, the book of Psalms should be read through the filter of the New Testament. And always consider what the life and death of Jesus mean to your emotional life and how you relate to the Father.

Psalms can be a great way to speak to God. Read them out loud and make them your conversation with God. Trust the wisdom they speak, and know that communication with God is the most important thing in the life of a God Girl.

I trust you, O Lord.
I said, "You are my God."

Psalm 31:14

he Lord never made a promise he's not gonna keep. It's impossible for him to promise something and not do it, because that would make him a liar. If God were a liar, then he would not be holy but sinful. And God cannot sin; therefore, God cannot lie. Make sense? Knowing that, now you can be sure that any promise he makes, he's gonna keep. You can trust that he will always protect, guard, and bless those who obey him, because he is holy and he promised it. He promises to never walk away from those who love him (see Heb. 13:5), and those who love him are the ones who do his will (see John 14:23; 1 John 2:5).

As a God Girl you have to be confident in God's Word and sure of his promises. Then when hard times come you can rely on the truth and live in the peace of knowing that he will truly work everything together for your good (see Rom. 8:28). In this life a lot of people are gonna disappoint you. They will reject you, walk out on you, and even hate you. But God's character can't be judged based on the sinful character of humanity. God can be trusted, even when things look completely bleak. When trials come and God seems silent, you can still be sure that he is present. If he wasn't, then he wouldn't be God. By his very nature he knows everything (he's omniscient) and he is everywhere (he's omnipresent). The God Girl knows her God, so she knows that no matter how things look or feel, everything is well. She trusts that when she looks for him, she will find him and that if she trusts him, he will bring her only what is good for her.

I made my sins known to you, and I did not cover up my guilt.
I decided to confess them to you, O LORD.
Then you forgave all my sins.

Psalm 32:5

Sin is an internal action that leads to an external result. You might think it's all external and say things like "The enemy is making me sin" or "I can't control myself." You want change but you feel powerless. When you blame your actions on being addicted to something or on having an illness that makes you what you are, you are saying that your actions are beyond your control. But that's a lie. After all, how could a just God condemn sin if sin was out of your control?

The truth is that your sin is within your control. God has defined sin in Scripture, and because of that we know what he is completely against. If God is against your sin and he wants you to be free from it, then why aren't you? It comes down to the way you think. In order to be free from sin, you have to change what you think about that sin. The beauty about calling a sin a sin is that it gives you power to overcome it. When you label things as they are, you take responsibility and therefore take control of your life. Since God never commands you to do the impossible, if he has commanded you not to do something (sin), then you can be sure that not doing it is totally doable. Sin does not have power over you (see Rom. 6:14). As long as you are willing to call sin what it is, God Girl, you can overcome everything that offends God by the power of his Spirit.

O LORD, your mercy reaches to the heavens,
your faithfulness to the skies.
Your righteousness is like the mountains of God,
your judgments like the deep ocean.
You save people and animals, O LORD.

Psalm 36:5–6

When you love a boy it's easy to say why. "I love the way he talks with me and the way he can fix things. I love how he cares for people." When you love him, you love who he is and not just how he looks. If your answer to why you love a guy was "Because he's so cute!" then most people would probably say that's just puppy love, because true love is about more than feelings and looks. When you are truly in love, you can go on and on about the guy with all kinds of deeper reasons why you love him.

So what do you love about God? The fact that he is love? The fact that he can and will use everything for the good of the people who love him? The way he keeps his promises? The way he gave his only Son so you could be saved? When you know God, you can't help but love him, and when you love him, your reasons go on and on.

If you don't have a long list of reasons why you love God, then it's time to make one. And the place to start is in his Word. Look at who he is, what he does, and how he does it and be thankful for all those things. Then tell people about him. When a girl loves a boy she can't shut up about how amazing he is, so why would it be any different when she loves God? And tell God too, because when you do you are giving him praise and thanks for all he is. And that not only brings him glory but also lifts your mind out of the darkness that can so easily engulf it. It reminds your soul who you belong to and gives your emotions the freedom to rest in his faithfulness and let go of things like worry, fear, and pain. So decide why you love him—there's a lot of reasons you should.

Do not be preoccupied with evildoers.
Do not envy those who do wicked things. . . .
Be happy with the LORD,
and he will give you the desires of your heart.

Psalm 37:1, 4

What are you most preoccupied with lately? What's the main thing you think about, worry about, and work so hard at? Have you asked God about it? Pleaded with him for help? Bugged him to death and gotten no reply? Do you want to know what might be the disconnect? Your focus. When your main issue is anything but the kingdom of God, then that's called worry, and worry separates you from God and messes up your relationship with him.

Think about all the time you spend bugging God with your questions. Now think about what would happen if you could be totally free to concentrate just on him. Think about the lilies of the field. They don't worry about their lives, but they are so beautiful, just living where they were planted and not worrying about how nice the field across the street is. Don't you know that you are more important to God than the flowers? And don't you know that means that he will take care of you, no matter what (see Matt. 6:28–32)? Where's your faith? It's not faith till it's been tested by adversity and stuck with you. Don't fail the test by putting the worries of this world ahead of the plans of God. No matter what comes your way, God Girl, you can be sure that God is in control and no amount of complaining or whining will change that. So be satisfied with his omnipotence and forget your troubles, and God will work it all out.

God is our refuge and strength,
    an ever-present help in times of trouble.
That is why we are not afraid
    even when the earth quakes
        or the mountains topple into the depths of the sea.

Psalm 46:1–2

You get closest to Jesus in the tough times, not the good times. That's when you learn who he is and what he can do to save you.

For a weak swimmer who doesn't understand the currents and the crashing waves, the surf is a scary thing to go into—deadly, even. But to the surfer who knows the waves and really loves riding them, they are nothing to fear. Just like a surfer riding a wave that might destroy an ordinary person, **you have to learn to look at the waves of your life,** the tough times and hard relationships, **as something to go through and not to fear.** You are overwhelmingly victorious because of who he is (see Rom. 8:37), and not just in the easy things, but in all things. In the hard things of life you can find not only his hand but the strength of your faith. Don't panic when the waves come; just see them as something you've got to ride on and go through in order to find the good part of life.

Nothing can separate you from the love of God, except when you yourself let it. So hold on tight, keep your eyes on the Father, and enjoy the water.

I admit that I am rebellious.
My sin is always in front of me.
I have sinned against you. . . .
Create a clean heart in me, O God,
and renew a faithful spirit within me.

Psalm 51:3–4, 10

When you first come to Christ you agree with him that what you used to believe was a lie. That's called repentance, and it's what you have to do in order to be forgiven and saved. The things the world told you, the pain you inflicted on yourself, the loneliness, the guilt, the emptiness—everything that a life without Christ gave you was a lie, and you finally agree with that.

But repentance doesn't stop as soon as you accept Christ. It goes on every day. Every day, guaranteed, you do something sinful, something that proves you've bought the lies again. So every day you have to consciously repent of that stuff. Every day you have to clear the slate by calling a lie a lie and agreeing with God that you missed the mark. This doesn't mean that you have to feel unending guilt, but you do have to admit that you were a fool for being stupid enough to forget the truth yet again. It happens to everyone everywhere, and that's why God has made a way out: repentance.

God doesn't just put up with your junk. He isn't your best friend who overlooks your sins; he is God, and he requires holiness (see Matt. 5:48). Don't let your idea of a loving God cloud your need to recognize that he is a holy God and to agree with him about your sin. Choose to confess your sin and repent, and then bask in the joy of his unending love.

My soul waits calmly for God alone.
My salvation comes from him.

Psalm 62:1

When God is silent, don't freak out. Just because you feel like he's not there and not talking doesn't make it the truth. Just look at the silence as your chance to chase after him. It's a gift, really, because once you feel like you have him, it's easy to get lazy and stop chasing after him. But when you need more of him, that's your chance to run full bore in his direction. You just have to know that he is right there, even in the silence of the desert. And you have to know that he's offering to quench your thirst; you just have to be thirsty for him.

Silence isn't your enemy. It can be your friend, so don't run away from it but keep listening for God's voice. Don't try to cover up the silence with more words and emotions; just know that **it won't kill you and it doesn't mean God has walked away.** Just keep looking at his Word and consider that his voice captured on paper. Hear all he has to say as you read. Then once you start to quench your thirst for him, don't be satisfied and start to walk away again. Keep on drinking from his Word and listening for his voice. If you will do that because you want to hear from him and not just impress others, then you will be satisfied—if not today then someday very soon. Just don't give up believing. Your life and his life in you are too important to give up.

You have been my confidence ever since I was young.
I depended on you before I was born.

Psalm 71:5–6

*A*re you where God wants you? If not, get out of there. But if you are, stop complaining about it, because you are where you are so that God can work out his purpose in you and you can become the very image and likeness of his Son.

Unless you have moved yourself, by sinning, into a situation or condition that God wants you out of to protect your soul, you are where God wants you. You can be sure that things are as they should be even if you are surrounded by strife, disease, pain, or suffering. When you let experiences make you bitter, resentful, or sad, you can be sure that you have turned against the very God who ordained your life and who you depended on even before you were born (see Ps. 71:6).

The freedom of being a God Girl is in knowing that everything in your life has a divine purpose. It's in knowing that you are never where you are by accident and in finding hope and opportunity, instead of despair, in your trials. Hope is what will distinguish you from the lost. You should never give up and surrender to emotional anguish. You have nothing to fear and nothing to complain about when you are where God wants you to be. He is to be your rock and your fortress (see Ps. 71:3). You can depend on him.

So don't complain about your circumstances or try to get out of them by doing something sinful, and you'll soon find a ton of spiritual growth and hope. Resist the temptation to complain to others about your sad state, to dwell on it, or to worry about it. That's not fit for a God Girl. Sin never produces a healthier or happier life. It only pulls you farther away from the giver of life and threatens your perseverance and character. But thanking God for never leaving you and trusting that he's got everything worked out will do more for your healthy state of mind and emotions than any complaint ever could.

They ate more than enough.
He gave them what they wanted,
but they still wanted more.

Psalm 78:29–30

A re you ever satisfied? Do you ever have enough? Or is there always something more you want or think you need? It's easy to see all the world has to offer and to have a continual wish list. "I want this, and this, and that . . ." and the list goes on and on. But what does all this wanting say about you? And what does it sound like to the ears of God?

In the desert, the Israelites complained because they were tired of just eating manna all day every day, so God dropped all kinds of birds out of heaven for them to eat. But then they were bored with just birds and bread and wanted something different, and God got mad.

Discontentment is disgusting. How awful it must feel to give and give and continually hear "That's just not enough." Seems like if that happened to you, eventually you'd just want to give up trying—after all, the person is never going to be satisfied.

But when you love God and you know the lengths he went to in order to save you, you start to realize that you really don't deserve anything, but he has given you everything. Discontentment only becomes a problem when you get your head stuck in the world and lose your focus because you see pretty things and you want them. But when you can get your focus back on the big picture and the things that really matter, all that fades away into the background.

If you want to be free of the wanting and not getting, quit looking in front of you and start looking up. Forget what your eyes, ears, and mouth want and go after what your soul needs. When you do, God will be right there ready to give it to you.

Mighty LORD, even your faithfulness surrounds you.
You rule the raging sea.
When its waves rise, you quiet them.

Psalm 89:8–9

*A*re you suffering from a big strain on your life? Have you lost your sense of peace? Do you feel like your life is blown and tossed about by the wind and God has let go and left you adrift? Then take your eyes off the waves and look at his face. Every sailor knows that when a boat rises and falls on the ocean's waves, you can steady your stomach by looking at the steady horizon, not the side of the boat. When you look at something that is immovable, your stomach gets some peace. In the storms of life, your horizon is the face of God. He's the only one who can quiet the crashing waves. And if you keep your eyes on him, you won't get sick. If you look to his Word and not stare at the rough waters, you can find peace.

If you aren't right with God, you can never get your mind off of yourself, and looking at yourself gets in the way of seeing his face. Are you looking to the horizon, to Jesus, right now in the problems in your life, or are you looking at the rough waters of life? If you look up to him, you can be sure you will find peace. The peace that only he can give is dependent not on circumstances or other people but only on your relationship with him. When you take your eyes off him and worry, you get freaked out and depressed because you don't think about him, just yourself. When you take time to talk things over with him, to know him, and to worship him, your worries dry up and your only thought is how to stay near to him. Jesus is never stressed or freaked. So get close to him in your difficulties and let him say, "I'm giving you my peace" (John 14:27).

Whoever lives under the shelter of the Most High
will remain in the shadow of the Almighty. . . .
He will cover you with his feathers,
and under his wings you will find refuge.
His truth is your shield and armor.

Psalm 91:1, 4

There are a lot of places you can look for protection and rescue. A lot of people, things, and actions promise to save you from your life, your misery, and your pain, but the truth is that there's only one salvation, one rescuer, one protector, and that is God.

When life overwhelms you and when storms come, there is a safe harbor. God's hand is reaching out to protect you, but you have to lift your arm and reach back. You can't sit with your arms crossed and eyes down just wondering when the rescue is gonna get here. He's already here, and he's just waiting for you to take his hand. **The only condition to this rescue is your love.** When you love God, he stands strong and tall by your side. He becomes your strong tower, your rock, your sure foundation. He is everything you need to build on and to grow. He is your source of strength and protection.

So when the storms come, when the attacks fall, don't look around for help but look up to the helper. Trust his Word to be true; it will never steer you wrong. As soon as you are willing to accept his protection, you immediately have it. His Word is your lifeline, his Son your salvation. Don't be so blind that you don't see the very hand of God reaching out to save you. Reach out in faith and grab hold of it. When you do you will find all the protection you need, and your life will be saved from the pit of despair.

Shout happily to the LORD, all the earth.
Serve the LORD cheerfully.
Come into his presence with a joyful song.

Psalm 100:1–2

appiness and joy aren't the goal of faith but are the symptoms. When your love of God is real, the natural result of that love in your life is happiness. His presence is like candy to a kid and a smile to a stranger. For the God Girl, coming into his presence after being in a war-torn world can be pure exhilaration, and that's where the shouts of joy come from. "Shout happily to the LORD, all the earth" (Ps. 100:1). Have you ever shouted for joy? The most expressive and passionate sounds to come out of the mouth of the God Girl are most often directed to her God. His goodness fills her heart to overflowing, his power draws out her sense of awe and admiration, and she has to shout. And when she serves him it's with pure joy, because to serve the one you love is to truly live.

As a God Girl you are called to come into his presence with a joyful song (see Ps. 100:2). Is your song joyful? Or is it robotic? Do you mean it when you sing it? If not, then close your mouth. Don't lie to God as you worship him. Be honest as you sing; be loving as you praise. Believe what comes out of your mouth, or don't say it.

The fear of the Lord leads to a joy that must be expressed back to him. Experience more of God by learning more about him. As you learn how he thinks and what he has said and as you do what pleases him, you yourself will also be pleased.

Teach me, O Lord, how to live by your laws,
and I will obey them to the end. . . .
Direct my heart toward your written instructions.

Psalm 119:33, 36

*D*o your feelings control you? Are they your master? Your experiences and how you feel about them should never be your only guide in life. Moods, emotions, and feelings can be misleading. All they talk about is "me this" and "me that." They aren't focused on God. As a believer you should never let your feelings get the better of your faith. Worry, fear, and loss of self-control can all be signs of a life that worships feelings instead of the Father. How can you make decisions and take action based on faith in God instead of feelings? You have to learn to see past what you're experiencing right now and look to the Word of God. Just as a blind person feels for walls to guide them and obstacles to avoid as they walk, you have to steer clear of the obstacles in your path and instead reach out for what you know to be true and solid. Take your eyes off of the things that weaken your emotional state and draw you away from truth. You were meant to be a slave not to feelings but to the one true God. Trust God's written instructions to you—they aren't for show or just for reassurance but are for guidance and direction. When your feelings falter, his Word will not.

It was good that I had to suffer
in order to learn your laws.

Psalm 119:71

uffering is not your enemy but an essential part of life,
because it was suffering that saved you. The suffering of
Jesus rescued you from certain death. But there's more: that
suffering also produces obedience. "Although Jesus was the Son of
God, he learned to be obedient through his sufferings" (Heb. 5:8).
Knowing that what God commands is gonna be hard, knowing that
it might even hurt, but doing it anyway gives you more strength
and spiritual insight than a perfect day ever could. In fact, you are
called to be happy when you suffer because suffering produces
endurance, character, and confidence (see Rom. 5:3–4). So if you
lack any of those things and refuse to run away from the
suffering that comes your way, you will be sure to get
them to overflowing.

When you suffer at the hands of somebody else
or when everything seems to be against you, don't
ask "Why me?" and don't run for dear life, but
stand and decide that this suffering isn't going
to scare you and you are going to let it do its
work. If you're a girl with strong emotions and
a tendency to fear and worry, this can be a tall order, but you're
no ordinary girl. You were made for a time just like this, and your
story will inspire others to overcome when you prove that it can
be done. So take this chance to fearlessly suffer without complaining or worrying, and trust that what God says about your trials is
true and good. Don't fear, just stand in faith, and you'll be greatly
rewarded, I promise.

Make my steps secure through your promise.

Psalm 119:133

*S*ome people say that if things are going great in your life, look out, because something bad is coming. Sounds logical, right? No one has a perfect life without any problems, so it makes sense that when it's been good for a while, something bad must have to happen to keep up the law of averages. And besides, God promises that we're gonna have trials in this life, so we know bad stuff is going to happen. But does that mean that you always have to be on alert for the next bad thing that's about to happen? No way! **Expecting the worst is not trusting the God who promises to care for and protect you.** He promises to never abandon you or leave you and to use everything in your life for your good if you are only willing to let him do that. That means that even when bad things happen, they're actually good because of what he's gonna do with them.

So if your life is going great today, don't worry about tomorrow (see Matt. 6:25–27). **Fear and worry are sinful, not holy.** Don't let anyone scare you into thinking that if life is good, you'd better prepare for the worst. That cheapens the gifts of God. Instead you have to learn to be content with whatever you have, enjoying what he gives you and what he takes away. Fearfulness is never an acceptable character trait for a believer unless it's the fear of the Lord, which means that nothing scares you except walking away from him.

I was glad when they said to me,
"Let's go to the house of the LORD."

Psalm 122:1

*A*re you glad when you get to go to the house of the Lord? Or is it something you have to do but aren't really excited about? Going to church shouldn't be something a believer does begrudgingly. Church is the place where you get to worship God like you will worship him in heaven, with a chorus of voices. Church is a place where you get to learn what pleases him, talk about how great he is, hear about the amazing things he's done, and read what he has to say. Church is the place where you get to be with others who think the same way as you do about him and where you can be free to praise him and give him thanks. So why is it so hard to get up in the morning and get out the door? Why do you feel so bummed about taking a day to do church?

The most common answer is "I'm just not getting anything out of it." But that answer sounds like church is all about what you get out of it and not what he gets. Change your way of thinking about church and maybe you'll change the way you feel about it. **Instead of thinking of church as being for your benefit, think of it as being for God's benefit.** Go there to give him your heart, your voice, your presence. Go there to serve him by loving other members of the faith. Go there to be taught how to obey God and how to minister to the lost. Go there to be trained to serve. Go to church for the one whose church it is, and church will no longer be a pain but a blast. When you make it all about him, it can't help but be all good.

Do not be afraid of sudden terror
or of the destruction of wicked people when it comes.
The LORD will be your confidence.
He will keep your foot from getting caught.

Proverbs 3:25–26

*Y*ou don't have to be afraid of what other people are afraid of. Nothing can destroy you when you are a God Girl. Not going broke, not war, not crime, not natural disaster—nothing can destroy you unless God allows it in order to serve his purpose, and his purposes are always good. When people around you panic, when they are afraid of the future and are unsure where they can stand, show them the life of Christ in you and stand faithfully without panicking. God has promised to keep your foot from getting caught. He has promised to not let you be left behind or left unprotected. He provides for his people—you can count on that.

What makes you different from the rest of the world is your faith, and because of that faith you believe that everything is gonna work out like it should work out. When you think like that, there's no worry, no fear that can get you down. When you let God be who he is and you take him at his word, you are set free.

You can handle anything the future brings in his strength. No danger can overwhelm you when you are hidden in him. You will not go without anything you need as long as you don't start thinking like the world and getting all paranoid and panicky. Trust God. If you are a worrier, then read God's Word to learn more about the God you can't yet fully believe in. Find out the truth so that it will set you free from worry and fear.

Guard your heart more than anything else,
because the source of your life flows from it.

Proverbs 4:23

our heart can make some bad choices if left to its own devices, mainly because your feelings demand immediate attention and want what they want when they want it. But just because your heart feels something, that doesn't make it true. A lot of times your heart lies. That's because feelings are often based on your experience of the world around you, not necessarily on God's truth. The beauty of knowing and obeying God's law is that it's unchanging and sure; it doesn't go back and forth based on the actions or feelings of humanity. It doesn't tease you by saying one thing only to change to something else when the winds pick up. No, God's law is constant, and its stability gives you a chance to rise above the trials of this life. It's an outstretched hand in the storm, and it helps you find your way safely through the fog of emotion.

When God's Word says to guard your heart, it doesn't mean the beating organ in your chest but your mind, your thoughts, and your emotions—all that is you. You have to guard your thoughts and feelings because out of those come your love for God and his commands, and out of that comes your ability to serve, to find joy, and to trust God. **If you let your heart be led astray, then your faith gets derailed.** A lot of girls let emotions alone guide all or most of their decisions. They say, "I feel it, so it has to be real," but that isn't always true. Faith isn't about feeling; it's about knowing. We don't say, "I feel like I believe in Jesus." We either believe and follow him or we don't. And before, during, and after we believe, feelings go with that. But feelings can be fickle. They rise and fall like the wind and are prone to rebellion, but you can overcome them if you refuse to think things based solely on how you feel, and instead you judge everything based on God's Word. So guard your heart and let truth be your guide instead of random experience.

The fear of the LORD is the beginning of wisdom.
The knowledge of the Holy One is understanding.

Proverbs 9:10

f you need wisdom, fear God. If you want more understanding about the things in your life, then understand God. The fear of God is the beginning of all righteousness. If you don't fear his power and his hatred of sin, then you never find salvation. This kind of fear isn't a kind that makes you run the other way, but it makes you fall to your knees in grief and want only to set things right. The fear of God isn't a horrible thing; it's a blessed thing. It leads you to righteousness and wisdom. The more you know who God is, the more you are gonna fear him. Just be careful of making God a "friend" only and forgetting his power, his wrath, and his jealousy. He is not a person to be trifled with but a power beyond compare. He is also a love beyond compare—such a wonderful combination. To have such an amazing power love you so much? Nothing compares.

You got wisdom the first time you feared God, and it keeps on growing as you keep on fearing him and wanting to please him. Just don't confuse this fear with the fear of evil or of man; it's not the same thing. That kind of fear puts you under fear's control, but the fear of God puts you under the loving hand of God. You need to **understand the God you fear so that your fear will be a fear of reverence and not a fear of punishment,** because as a God Girl saved by the blood of Christ you can be sure that your punishment has been taken by Jesus himself (see 1 John 4:18). What you need to fear is rejecting God, turning your back on him, and failing to honor him in everything you do. That kind of fear will give you strength, hope, and more wisdom than you ever dreamed possible.

Whoever loves discipline loves to learn,
but whoever hates correction is a dumb animal.

Proverbs 12:1

*L*ove hurts, especially when it comes to discipline. Out of his love for you God lets pain come into your life so that you can grow and learn. It's called discipline, and it is done not out of anger or rage but in love and kindness. It's designed to correct you so that you won't fall into disaster again. Discipline is the teacher of the righteous; it teaches you where you have gone astray and reminds you how to get back on track. When you only want what's best for your life and your faith, then you won't hate discipline, but you'll look at it as a chance for improvement.

Correction is like the holy reset button. It lets you stop and see where you're off track and how to get back on track. The longer you fear or hate correction, the longer you'll be trapped in the turmoil of your sin. When you're ready for wisdom and a peace that goes beyond anything you can imagine (see Phil. 4:7), accept correction as a wise disciple, and don't run from it like a dumb animal.

When a stubborn fool is irritated, he shows it immediately,
but a sensible person hides the insult.

Proverbs 12:16

When you are irritated, you are being a fool. When other people insult you, when they bug and frustrate you, and you react to that irritation, you're a fool. In God's Word a fool is a person who rejects the very existence of God (see Ps. 14:1; Prov. 1:7). And isn't that what you do in that moment of irritation—reject God and his rule in your life and put yourself on the throne, serving your own feelings? When that happens all you can do is repent immediately. Confess that you have sinned against God, and then apologize to the person whose vicinity you were in when you sinned. Irritation isn't a godly characteristic; it's a character trait of a fool. Do you want to be a fool?

As a God Girl you have a different requirement on your life than people who don't believe. You are called to be holy as God is holy (see 1 Peter 1:16), to think of others as better than yourself (see Phil. 2:3), and to be slow to anger (see James 1:19). In following all these calls you choose to slay the very part of you that demands others serve you and demands their kindness and sympathy as a requirement for your obedience to God. This **conditional obedience is pure idolatry.** It accepts God's law only when your own law has first been met, and it puts you on the throne just above God. Ugh!

It's not hard to get frustrated, and to act on that frustration is only human, but if you want freedom from your sinful nature to live a new way of life, then you have to know that God's commands on your life can be followed. And they can be followed because God would never command the impossible; that would be cruelty. But he does promise to help you, through his Holy Spirit, to do everything that he asks of you, and all you have to do is call on that power, will to obey, and trust God to create a new heart in you, one that no longer serves yourself but serves him fully.

Careless words stab like a sword,
but the words of wise people bring healing.

Proverbs 12:18

*Y*ou don't have to have a knife in order to stab someone. Words can do the same amount of damage internally. When you talk without thinking of God first, your carelessness makes you a fool. The wise person chooses words that heal, words that are consistent with the God she believes in. When you say whatever you are feeling, you get careless because feelings major in self and not others. But God says you are to care less about yourself than others, and that's the source of all wisdom. Humility—the thought that life isn't all about you—brings wisdom and kills pride. It makes the effort to consider the heart, mind, and even soul of others, and so it chooses its words wisely.

If you want to stop your foolish talk, then don't talk. **Silence isn't usually offensive, except when someone is expecting you to speak.** But keeping your mouth shut when your deepest desire is to speak your mind is wisdom. It might be hard to talk less, and if it is, then think about not speaking at all. Take one day of speechlessness to teach yourself self-control. Don't let your tongue control you any more, but show it who's the boss and teach it to come under the authority of your God.

Whoever walks with wise people will be wise,
but whoever associates with fools will suffer.

Proverbs 13:20

*Y*our friends say a lot about who you are. What kind of people they are not only tells other people who you are but changes who you are too. **You can't be friends with someone without being changed by them**—maybe only in subtle ways, but changed all the same. **Your soul is highly influenced by whatever it is exposed to the most.** You can find out how wise or foolish you are by looking at the lives of your friends. Sometimes it's hard to look at your own life and see what kind of person you are, but it can be easier to look at them. If what you see when you look carefully at them is something you don't like, then it's time to make a change or suffer the consequences.

In God's economy, friendship is a really important thing. What's at stake is not just an aspect of your social life but your faith. Friendship binds two people together; it makes them more and more alike. They learn from each other. If you think your friends are learning more from you than you are from them, don't be so sure. It's usually the lowest common denominator that is reached in relationships.

As a God Girl you have to choose to surround yourself with the wise people of this world, people who believe and trust God. They might be less than perfect, but they have to want perfection. They have to serve the Father and want whatever he wants. Then and only then can you be sure that you are not a companion to fools.

A person may plan his own journey,
but the LORD directs his steps.

Proverbs 16:9

T he God Girl's number one goal is to know Christ. Because of
that she never believes that the things that happen to her are
just coincidence or luck, but she believes that everything that
she is dumped down into is meant to teach her more about God. The
God Girl has to think like this, looking for God's hand in everything,
because if she doesn't she'll just keep experiencing the same kinds
of things over and over again until she gets it.

**A lot of believers give the enemy more power than he really has
when they give him credit for things he had nothing to do with.**
Instead, you should think about everything that happens to you as
allowed by God and therefore useful for your spiritual growth. Then
you don't give the enemy more credit than he deserves, and
you don't waste the chance to obey on running away or sitting around worrying yourself to death about the enemy's
hand in your life. Forget him—God's hand is bigger!

A lot of girls are controlled by fear, stress, and worry.
They grow up thinking thoughts that are inconsistent
with faith. They act on those fears and make decisions based on them, and because of that they are
always controlled by the god of their emotions,
not the God of all creation. But the God Girl isn't a
fearful girl because she has faith in the God who is
all-powerful, all-knowing, and always present. She
knows that nothing happens by chance and that her
days are numbered not by fate but by God. When a
girl knows this truth and lives by it, she grows into a confident and
fearless woman who, unlike the rest of the world, is free from the
chains of worry and fear.

Pride precedes a disaster,
and an arrogant attitude precedes a fall.

Proverbs 16:18

When you fall, look back and see what's behind you. What was your stumbling block? Where did you trip? Most of the time it's in the area of pride. When pride pops up it makes your pathway uneven and treacherous. Pride promises a lot to the person who feels it. It promises protection and success, and even salvation. It says that the thing you want for yourself is exactly what you need. Pride talks about your brains or your brawn, and it tells you that you are the most important person in your life. Pride focuses on the weaknesses of other people, on their bad parts instead of their good. But God has no patience for pride, and when it's in your life, he promises trouble. Pride comes before the fall because pride removes God as Lord and all hope for success. **Pride is worship of self, but humility is worship removed from self and turned toward God.** Humility is rewarded, but pride brings destruction (see Prov. 18:12).

When you look at your past and see where you have fallen, can you spot the pride that came before the fall? Can you see where your own sense of self—either your fear for yourself or thinking too highly of yourself—brought you low? Self-loathing is also a sign of pride. It's a pride that demands perfection, as if you were on par with Jesus himself, and so it hates the human part of you that is so weak. **Be careful that you don't make being good more important than loving God.** When you make loving him number one, there is nothing you do that he won't forgive, nowhere you have fallen that he can't lift you up from if you will just take his outstretched hand. Don't be so proud that you reject his gift. Don't be so disgusted with yourself that you obsess about you instead of about him. But let go of self altogether and serve the one who can save you. Then you will be free from pride and learn the value of true humility.

Pride precedes a disaster,
and an arrogant attitude precedes a fall.
Better to be humble with lowly people
than to share stolen goods with arrogant people.

Proverbs 16:18–19

*H*umility is the foundation of all godliness. It is the beginning of all righteousness, and so it's crucial to the God Girl. But what about when you are humiliated by a bad or prideful person? When you're faced with the sin of someone else's pride, your first instinct isn't holiness. The natural human reaction is retaliation or revenge. In fact, **other people's sin can become an excuse for your sin if you're not careful.** "But she started it!" or "How dare he!" you say, and game on! When they sin, your sense of fairness kicks in, and the last thing on your mind is meekness and obedience, and that's how things get started—fights, arguments, bitterness. Troubled relationships start with a lack of humility, which keeps us from finding peace when others are sinning. It's as if your mind decides that it's not fair that you have to be good when they're being so bad. But that's human thinking, not godly thinking. If God's law depended on the actions of others, then even the pagans would be considered obedient (check out Matt. 5:46–48). But God's law depends not on what they do but on who he is.

In any relationship it's crucial for you, as a God Girl, to know what God commands instead of relying on what other people do. In every battle you have to choose what God wants you to choose, even if the result will be your humiliation. It seems counterintuitive, but mean people are changed not by your retaliation but by your prayer. So go to God in prayer instead of going to *them* in anger. Trust that his law is good even if it seems unfair. And you will find yourself with more peace than you know what to do with.

A joyful heart is good medicine,
but depression drains one's strength.

Proverbs 17:22

*D*on't let other people's issues become your own. When you have friends who are depressed, stressed, or just plain bummed, you don't do anyone any good by taking on those emotions yourself. I call it co-miseration and it doesn't help anyone. All it does is let their misery dominate the relationship. If someone has fallen into a pit, who's more helpful—the girl who jumps in the pit and cries out with them, or the girl who stays out of the pit and lowers a rope? In the life of the God Girl, your faith and hope should be the dominant force, at least for you.

"Co-miseration" doesn't help anyone to see their way to God's grace or to be set free from the lies that depression tells them. But your compassion and prayer do make a difference. You don't need to condemn the person for their feelings—just don't catch them. After all, the event is not what's hurting the person; how they have chosen to think about it is what's causing them all the anguish. **You are not showing them any kind of love or kindness by joining them in their misery.** If you're changing how you think as Paul talks about in Romans 12:2, you can't fall back into that destructive pattern of negative thinking just because someone else is there. Change the way you think; renew your mind continuously. Jealously guard your mind to keep it pure. Be a kind ear to listen to others' pains, but don't take their negative and unproductive attitudes onto yourself.

A person with good sense is patient,
and it is to his credit that he overlooks an offense.

Proverbs 19:11

Patience overlooks stuff that would offend the average **girl.** It takes the attacks of evil people and difficult circumstances without losing its cool or getting angry. Patience doesn't want revenge. It isn't quick to be irritated or moody. Patience is a calm boat on a wild sea. It isn't tossed about by the wind of emotions, reacting to the actions or words of others. Patience is a virtue because it conforms to God's law. The person bent on loving God and doing what pleases him is the person who wants nothing more than to practice patience.

Endurance is another word for patience, but it can have a better connotation, because it sounds like it proves your strength more than patience, which can sound weak and passive. After all, you hear a lot about endurance races but never about patience races. But just like patience, endurance needs you to stick it out and be obedient instead of giving up and resorting to taking things into your own hands. And endurance comes with a promise. You can see it in James 1:3–4: "You know that such testing of your faith produces endurance. Endure until your testing is over. Then you will be mature and complete, and you won't need anything." So be patient, God Girl. Practice endurance by resisting the temptation to return evil for evil, and decide instead to trust the God who commands you to overlook an offense and to endure even if the test is hard.

Laziness throws one into a deep sleep,
and an idle person will go hungry.

Proverbs 19:15

A re you spiritually lazy? It's easy to be so busy and so energetic in life that you have nothing left for spiritual stuff. But if you want more faith, more hope, more peace—if you want more of God and his presence—then you can't afford to be lazy. Your soul will starve if you let yourself be spiritually lazy (see Prov. 19:15).

Spiritual laziness starts when you don't have the energy to love God with all your heart, soul, mind, and strength. And it keeps going when you are too worn out or exhausted to get up and do what you know God is asking you to do. When you see a need and you don't fill it, when you hear a cry for help and you're too busy to answer, spiritual laziness will distract you and comfort you for the moment. But **when you stay in bed an extra half hour instead of getting up early to spend time with God, you miss out on an opportunity to hear from him.** When you skip reading your Bible to go out and have fun, you miss the chance to have more of him in your life. Every time you fall into the trap of spiritual laziness, you are refusing to feed your soul, and as a result your soul gets weak and fearful. Guard your heart, your mind, and your soul by becoming aware of your tendency to choose the easy way instead of devotion and discipline.

Whoever shuts his ear to the cry of the poor will call and not be answered.

Proverbs 21:13

Are you guilty of mistreating the poor? You have the things and money that they need, but you never deliver it to them because you are so used to looking at everything you get as being for your own good. **Can you be trusted with delivering what is needed to God's people?** When you take a look at God's Word, you see that your stuff is not your own and was meant to be shared with people who need it more.

But how can that happen when you have so little? You're not rolling in it. You're lucky to get what you need for yourself. Well, think about the widow who gave away her last two coins. Jesus said, "I can guarantee this truth: This poor widow has given more than all the others. All of these people have given what they could spare. But she, in her poverty, has given everything she had to live on" (Luke 21:3–4). As a God Girl what you do today determines your path tomorrow. Learn while you are young to give to the poor. Don't hoard what you have. It'll all mean nothing to you in the kingdom of heaven. So give, give, give, and be happy.

Sensible people foresee trouble and hide from it,
but gullible people go ahead and suffer the consequence.

Proverbs 22:3

R ed flags are red for a reason: they warn about danger. **When you see or even sense a red flag in your path, stop everything.** It's not wise to see trouble coming and keep on going anyway. As a God Girl you're supposed to be loving, kind, generous, and thoughtful but not gullible or easily taken advantage of. It's biblical to turn the other cheek to people who persecute you and hate you, but it's foolishness to see trouble coming and to keep on heading in the same direction, as if a red flag means "go" instead of "stop and turn the other way."

The God Girl is as cunning as a snake and as innocent as a dove (see Matt. 10:16) because she doesn't let herself be easily deceived, but she is innocent of the guilt of disobedience. Jesus didn't want his disciples to look for opportunities to be persecuted and martyred (see Matt. 10:17), but he didn't want them to fear persecution once it came either. It's always best to avoid attack when you have warning. But once it hits, don't freak out, but stand and know that God's way is the best way.

Rescue captives condemned to death,
  and spare those staggering toward their slaughter.
When you say, "We didn't know this,"
  won't the one who weighs hearts take note of it?
  Won't the one who guards your soul know it?
  Won't he pay back people for what they do?

                                    Proverbs 24:11–12

*B*e fearless. When someone you know doesn't know about salvation, you can't just keep quiet. You need to be courageous enough to speak, even if it means you're gonna lose your friend. Helping those who are staggering toward slaughter isn't a chance to prove yourself right or to win them over to your way of thinking; it's your chance to send out a rescue line. It's your chance to prove to yourself and to God that other people matter to you as much as they matter to God. You can't plead ignorance, claiming that you didn't know that they didn't know. If you really think about what they do and say, you'll have no question about their heart, because out of the heart comes everything people say and do (see Matt. 15:16–20). If they don't honor God's Word, if they don't talk about it in general conversation, if they pick and choose the parts they like, or if they reject any or all of it, then you know the state of their heart. Can't you tell an apple tree by the fruit that grows on it? You wouldn't look at a fig tree and say, "I think it's an apple tree, but I'm just not sure." You'd walk over, look at the fruit, even taste it, and see for sure what it is.

You can't plead ignorance about the faith of the people in your life. You can know about their salvation when you pay attention to their words and their actions. So always make sure that your own words and actions match up with what you claim to believe. And be sure that when you talk to people who don't have the wisdom to know the love of God, you share that love in a way that expresses it to them but doesn't force it on them.

Do not brag about tomorrow,
because you do not know what another day may bring.

Proverbs 27:1

ou don't know what's gonna happen tomorrow. You might hope for something to happen. You might have plans, dreams, and ideas, but you can never know for sure what will happen. So it's silly to brag about what you're going to do tomorrow when you don't even know for sure if God will let it happen. **Bragging makes you seem arrogant to those who listen, because those who brag are proud of themselves and their beautiful future.** They find satisfaction in showing off and presenting a touched-up picture of who they really are.

You have to remember that God is the one who decides if you're gonna live or die, go here or go there. All you can do is prepare, plan, and then pray that his will be done—not your fantasy or hopes and dreams but his will and plans for your life. Then you can start to be more and more certain that tomorrow will hold just what it should, no more and no less, because you want only what he sees fit to give you. With this way of thinking, when things don't happen like you wanted them to, you don't freak out. You can be content in any and every situation, being sure that God works everything together for your good, no matter how bad it looks.

It's always best to make plans with the hand of God in mind. Then refuse to brag or to worry, because both are a giant waste of time and energy.

Surely the prayer of someone who refuses
to listen to God's teachings is disgusting.

Proverbs 28:9

*H*aving a hard time hearing God or being heard by him? It might just be because something has wedged its way between you—something in you that you won't even admit to yourself. Sin that you consider acceptable in your life, in other words sin that you find comfort in and refuse to fully acknowledge because you're afraid of having to do something about it, will put a wall between you and God. No prayers will pass it and no hand will reach through it.

And the job of tearing it down is yours. **If you want your prayers to make a difference,** if you want the airways to be clear and the communication to be strong,

then **you have to ditch your** *sin* **right now.** You can't claim to be too weak to do anything about it. That's a lie, and there's nothing true about it. Sin stopped being your master at the point when you said "I do" to the God who hung on that cross. So act like it. Agree with God about truth, and refuse to listen to the lies this world might tell you. When your focus is on God and his will, your prayers will be powerful and effective (see James 5:16).

Whoever covers over his sins does not prosper.

Whoever confesses and abandons them receives compassion.

Proverbs 28:13

*N*ot one person has God's approval" (Rom. 3:10). No one is perfect. We all mess up and get it wrong, and there's nothing more ugly, nothing more ungodly than a person who says, "I haven't done anything wrong," and refuses to admit his or her mistakes.

Confession can feel as uncomfortable as being stripped of all your clothes and forced to run naked through a crowd of people. But confessing when you do something wrong is the foundation of all faith. Without confession you wouldn't be saved, because your confession is what first brought you to your knees and brought Jesus to your heart.

Confession of sin is crucial to the life of the believer, and so is apologizing when your sin hurts others. The fact is that when you apologize, you don't actually look vulnerable; you look strong. **The strong girl is the one who can control herself enough to risk embarrassment or disdain from others in order to be godly.** The strong girl isn't afraid of the wrath of people, but only of God. And the strong girl puts the feelings and needs of others first and refuses to be ruled by the fear of others finding out she's an imperfect person.

An apology turns away wrath. It turned away the wrath of God when you offered it to him, and it will turn away the wrath of the people you've wronged when you offer it to them. Apologizing when you've been wrong restores relationships. It builds trust and strengthens love.

A quick apology is like pulling a splinter out of your finger: it gets the pain over with, eliminates the danger of infection, and lets the healing begin. So be quick to apologize, and you will discover that truth never disappoints and confession is the foundation of all things pure and godly. Bring your darkness into the light, think about your sin, and let the words "I'm sorry, please forgive me" be your friend.

Whoever trusts his own heart is a fool.
Whoever walks in wisdom will survive.

Proverbs 28:26

You can't judge God's nearness or distance by how you feel. If you feel like God is far away, know that your feelings have nothing to do with where he is. If you feel like you have fallen from grace, know that your feelings are not what decide your state of grace. Your feelings have little or no impact on truth. The truth is a constant, it doesn't change—but your feelings do, so how could they be a good indicator of truth?

Don't let your feelings determine your happiness.

They're not even a good indicator of that! You can be miserable or happy in the same situation depending on how you choose to think about the situation. Don't let your feelings define your position in life or your thoughts about God because your feelings aren't always set on the truth of God's Word. Wisdom isn't the child of emotions. But healthy emotions have their birth in wisdom. The more of God's truth you allow into your mind and heart, the stronger you will become emotionally. The secret of contentment in life is knowing who God is and what he wants. Faith in who he is will serve you much more than faith in your own feelings.

*A person's fear sets a trap for him,
but one who trusts the LORD is safe.*

Proverbs 29:25

Fear of anything or anyone other than God is sin. People are afraid because they don't have the blood of Jesus in their veins. Worry and fear come from doubt, so how can anyone who trusts Jesus be filled with worry and fear? If you are a God Girl, by definition you are a believer, not a doubter. Doubt and belief cannot peacefully coexist. One will always conquer the other. Fear and worry are the symptoms of doubt, so they should be rejected in favor of faith.

If you tend to fear, think about this: the same God who saved you from your sin can save you from whatever it is that you are afraid of. Are you more devoted to the voice of fear or the voice of God? In order to be free, you have to say no every time fear talks to your soul. Just say, "I trust my God," and leave it at that (see Prov. 29:25). Fear might never stop knocking at your door, but you don't have to answer ever again. Lock the dead bolt and cover the peephole.

Fear is a blatant disregard for the work that Christ has done for you. Don't call him a liar. Take his hand and trust him to hold you up as you climb the cliff and cross the canyon.

Every word of God has proven to be true.
He is a shield to those who come to him for protection.
Do not add to his words,
or he will reprimand you, and you will be found to be a liar.

Proverbs 30:5–6

The only thing you can be certain of is God's Word. Your hunches, your dreams, or your visions can't be counted on 100 percent of the time. Only God's Word can. So when you say, "God told me," I say show it to me in Scripture. Otherwise you run the risk of "adding to" his Word. And a lot of time what you're adding is just your own desires and passions that are so powerful that they feel like the very voice of God. But every "word from God" must be tested. **God still talks to his children today, but his words will never, ever contradict his written Word, the Bible.** When you get a "word" from God, don't talk about it with everyone; just take it to *the* Word and look for more of what you heard there. Does it contradict what's written in Scripture? Does it center on serving self? Is it all about your happiness and fulfillment? Then there's a big chance it isn't from God. **God's focus is your holiness and not so much your happiness.** When you think you've heard from God, pray that God would reveal more to you through the wisdom of your counselors and friends. But don't be so eager to share your dreams and visions with the world just yet. They'll see them soon enough if they were really godly visions.

It can be easy, in all the excitement of your dreams, to want to act on them immediately and see them come true now. But that can get you ahead of God. Slow down. If it is his will, then it will be done on his timeline, not yours. Rest with confidence in his ability to bring to pass whatever it is he would bring to pass, and don't try to lead God in the direction you want to go. Stick with his Word and find your path by doing what is written in the Scriptures.

Don't give me either poverty or riches.
Feed me only the food I need,
* or I may feel satisfied and deny you*
*   and say, "Who is the LORD?"*
* or I may become poor and steal*
*   and give the name of my God a bad reputation.*

Proverbs 30:8–9

*D*o you consume more than you need? It's a simple question about a simple topic: stuff. How much stuff—clothes, food, and toys—do you use that you technically don't need in order to survive? When you overconsume, it's because of your focus. We tend to focus on what we consume and consume to the degree of our obsession over a thing. In other words, if you love books and read them ravenously, your focus is knowledge. Or you may eat anything and everything because your focus is comfort or satisfaction.

When someone consumes more than they need, they run the risk of actually denying God by making what they consume more important than he is. The author of this proverb asked God to make him neither rich nor poor. Can you imagine praying for something like that? "Lord, don't give me lots of money so I can buy all the things I want." What a prayer!

Think about the impact of your consumption on your relationship with the Father. Where do you put most of your thoughts? What occupies most of your time, your energy, your heart? Have obsessions, those things you can't live without, replaced God on the throne of your heart? If so, they are little idols, and they won't be tolerated by a holy God. If you want more of his hand and presence in your life, then take a look at what you consume and see if you don't spend too much time and energy on the things around you instead of the God above you.

Speak out for the one who cannot speak,
for the rights of those who are doomed.
Speak out,
judge fairly,
and defend the rights of oppressed and needy people.

Proverbs 31:8–9

While on earth, Jesus never stood up for himself, only for his Father. A lot of times he slipped away from a violent crowd and kept silent when being taunted, but he never stood up for his rights or argued to save himself. And you are called to do the same kind of thing: to stand up for the Father and for his children but not to worry about yourself (see Matt. 6:34; Phil. 4:6–7). When people hate you, you are supposed to turn the other cheek (see Matt. 5:38–42), but when you see someone who is being treated badly, you have to stand up for them. As a God Girl you can't sit quietly by while other people suffer. You have to say something or do something to change what's happening.

The world is full of oppressed and needy people who need the children of God to stand up for them and to take on their case. You might feel powerless and not know where to start, but all you have to do is to look around you. Whatever helplessness you can find, judge fairly: "Is this something that needs to be fixed?" and "Can I do something to help?" If the answer to both of those is yes, then it's time to take action. And when persecution comes to your life, pray that God would send someone to rescue you and to speak for you, and you will be cared for by the very hand of God (see Luke 21:36; Heb. 13:6).

*I have seen everything that is done under the sun. Look at it! It's all point-
less. It's like trying to catch the wind.*

Ecclesiastes 1:14

*D*o you wanna be rich and famous? How do you think that
would change your life? Would it make you happier, more
at ease, more hopeful? The truth is that a lot of us look for
our reason, our significance, in the hope of fame. It's easy to believe
that it would be heaven on earth, or at least a ton better than your
ordinary life. But if you think being famous would be the bomb, then
read Ecclesiastes.

Solomon was the richest and most famous guy on earth. He was
the king. He could buy or build, take or own anything he wanted.
And since he had it all, he used his dough and fame to try to buy
happiness. He owned everything he wanted to own and had the
luxury to spend a ton of time just looking for fun things to do on this
earth, or "under the sun," as he put it. He did find temporary pleasure, but he realized in his old age that it was all pointless—that none
of it really mattered. All his parties and purchases, all his popularity
and his ability to get other people to do whatever he wanted them
to do was a total zero when he looked back on it all. In the end he
figured out that nothing under that big ol' yellow sun would make
him happy and content the way God could.

It's easy, even as a God Girl (or in Solomon's case, a God Guy),
to make pleasure your number one goal, but as Solomon found out,
it doesn't really satisfy you. **Life is about more than your happiness
or even your comfort.** The most important things in
life are spiritual, not physical. When you find this out,
you'll find everything you've ever needed.

Who can eat or enjoy themselves without God?

Ecclesiastes 2:25

True happiness, or joy, as the Bible calls it, isn't dependent on what happens to you or around you. If it were it'd be just manufactured happiness, a fake imitation of the real thing. True happiness is something that comes right from God. When you concentrate and rely on his Spirit's presence in your life, you will get more happiness than you ever knew was possible.

It's easy to find happiness in things and people and even easier to lose all hope of happiness when those things and people disappoint you or fail you. But the girl who doesn't rely on the stuff or situations around her to find joy is the girl who has found all she needs.

Like Paul, you can find the secret of being content, or happy, in all situations if you're just willing to draw your happiness from the well of living water instead of from the imitation of life here on earth (see Phil. 4:10–14). When trials come, when boredom sets in, happiness can still be yours when you take into account the Word of God and its truth in your life. **A girl who never lets God's Word be too far from her mind and refuses to let one day go by without looking for him is a girl who knows the secret to true happiness.** God promises true happiness to anyone who is willing to make him Lord of their life and then to continually focus their mind and heart on him daily.

When you make a promise to God, don't be slow to keep it because God doesn't like fools. Keep your promise. It is better not to make a promise than to make one and not keep it.

Ecclesiastes 5:4–5

When you know you are supposed to do something but you don't do it right away, that's not obedience but disobedience. In order for it to be obedience, you have to do it immediately, not later on when you "have time." A lot of people know what they are supposed to do but take their own sweet time doing it so that they can do something else first. But just knowing the truth is worthless if you don't act on it too (see James 1:22–25).

Procrastination isn't a biblical value; in fact, in spiritual matters it is completely unbiblical and leads to sin, that is, disobedience. When your commander orders you to march and you stay seated, saying, "I'll do it in just a minute," you are not following orders but disobeying a direct command, and there's gonna be a price to pay. When you promise God you'll do something—whether it's obeying his Word, honoring him, loving him, or serving him—and then you're slow to get to it, you're a fool.

It can be easy to put God at the middle or even bottom of the list. There are pressing things that need to get done, and God doesn't press; he whispers. So your promises to him can be easily forgotten or saved for later, but each time that you wait on doing what you know you need to do spiritually, you move further and further away from the lover of your soul, and you set yourself up for trouble. Keep your promises quickly, or make no promise at all. What have you promised to God and to yourself regarding him? Take control of your life and do what you know needs to be done today, and you will discover the blessings that come from a life bent on obedience.

Remember your Creator when you are young.

Ecclesiastes 12:1

What do you want in your spiritual life? What's your goal when it comes to worship? Your relationship with God was designed for something, but are you matching up with that design?

When you want things for yourself, when you come to him just for peace or blessings, or when you want him to make you feel complete or happy, you miss out on the whole purpose for your salvation: for you to love him. Your faith didn't save you so that you could get all you want but so that you could get back to a right relationship with the Father. That relationship isn't about getting but giving. Think of it like this: the two greatest commandments aren't about your peace or your happiness but about stepping outside yourself and loving God and your neighbor, not yourself (see Matt. 22:34–40).

You weren't put here on earth to develop your spiritual life so that you could "arrive" and then just lie back and rest. No, you were made for much more, and that much more starts with a shift in your goals. **What you want each morning when you get up will determine who you become every day.** The God Girl makes her goal not her own emotional well-being but knowing her God—remembering her Creator while she is young (see Eccles. 12:1). When he is your goal, everything else falls into place, and then no one can hurt you, slander you, or damage you. Nothing others do will faze you when your goal is not to feel good, or even to be happy, but to know God more. Each morning when you get up, tell yourself, "Today my goal is God himself—not happiness or peace or even his blessings, but him and him alone."

Look at you! You are beautiful, my true love!
Look at you! You are so beautiful!

Song of Songs 1:15

*T*rue love can't hold itself back. When you're in love, your heart wants to tell the world, because it feels like if you don't it's just gonna burst. Love notes, love songs, and love poetry all come from a heart filled to overflowing with adoration and passion. But after a while it can be easy to forget to tell the people you love what you love about them. Life gets in the way, times get tough, tempers flare, and suddenly you aren't speaking all lovey to each other anymore. But love needs to be talked about; it needs to be given in the form of verbal appreciation and adoration. We have to tell the people we love why we love them, and tell them often. Song of Songs is an example of this, and we need to do the same thing when it comes to our love for God.

In the life of faith, the God Girl wants to tell her God how much she adores him. She wants to tell him how much he means to her, not only to worship him but to remind her own heart of all that he is. If she doesn't do this, she can quickly forget all about his good-ness and holiness. As a God Girl you have to concentrate on the goodness of God. You have to **remind yourself how you've been touched by his kindness, his provision, and his power** and tell him every day what his presence in your life means. The God Girl knows that the power of love rests in her ability to speak words of love.

God's love for you is expressed in his Word and in the life of his Son, the Word made flesh. Don't miss his love songs, love letters, and love gifts. Know love and know him. Speak love and be known by him.

Young women of Jerusalem, swear to me
by the gazelles
or by the does in the field
that you will not awaken love
or arouse love before its proper time.

Song of Songs 2:7

A lot of girls' hearts have been given to famous boys on stage and screen, but that kind of love is a one-way street. It's called unrequited love, and it's a kind of a lie. A lot of well-meaning girls have convinced themselves that what they feel about a boy is so strong that it must be true. They dream of him and fantasize about his love. Then, over time, when he never calls, they start to think that maybe God lied or maybe they did something wrong, but nothing could be further from the truth. Love is a totally amazing experience, but it also has to be grounded in faith—and not faith in a feeling but in a God who never promises romantic bliss but most definitely promises holiness.

When all your energy is focused on how *you* feel, your focus is selfish, and true love isn't selfish. True love is not about being adored or romanced but about loving your neighbor, or in this case your significant other, as yourself. It's about thinking of others as better than yourself (see Phil. 2:3) and sometimes even about loving your enemies.

There is a season when love is ripe, and it is important that you know your season. Don't let feelings lie to you. **Feelings can't be commanded, but actions can, and God commands love, so it must be an action.** God's Word never orders us to be fulfilled or to find our dream but to learn the secret of being content no matter what the situation.

Feelings of love are sure to come, but it's what you think about them that's gonna prove how true they are. Don't let your life be about obeying your feelings instead of obeying your God. Feelings can be fun, but they aren't always trustworthy, so take every feeling captive to the Word of God and be careful not to call it love before its proper time.

So I said, "Oh, no!
I'm doomed.
Every word that passes through my lips is sinful.
I live among people with sinful lips.
I have seen the king, the LORD of Armies!"

Isaiah 6:5

When you confess, be specific. Don't just say, "I'm a sinner," but give details. God doesn't need your confession to know what you did, but you need to say what you did was a sin, not that you are a sinner—of course you are! But call a spade a spade, as the saying goes, and fess up all of your stuff. When you are in the presence of God, you will know you are a sinful creature, but if you are afraid to look at him and to get to know his Word, then you'll have a hard time finding any specific sin to confess.

When God brings some kind of sin to your mind, confess it immediately, and then don't be surprised if he starts to bring more ideas of your mistakes to mind. Don't freak out—it's a good thing. It's like house cleaning: it needs to be done or your house will get overrun with junk. Confession takes a lot of work and honesty, but don't avoid confession any more than you avoid washing your hair or clothes. It's easier to ignore your spiritual mess than your physical mess, but you can't do it any longer. **If you don't have something to confess every day, then you just aren't looking at yourself.** So get real, dig into God's Word to know what's right and what's wrong, and get right today.

Then I heard the voice of the Lord, saying, "Whom will I send? Who will go for us?" I said, "Here I am. Send me!"

Isaiah 6:8

God is always speaking but only a few are ever listening. Silence in the spiritual realm isn't the result of God's distance but of ours. God is forever asking, forever sending, and forever saving, but only those who are interested in his presence and listening for his voice will ever know it. In this case, Isaiah wasn't "called"—he was listening when God was calling anyone who would listen. Isaiah had his mind and ears on God and was ready and willing to do whatever needed to be done. He wasn't waiting for a specific call; he was just waiting for God to speak. God spoke and Isaiah answered: "Here I am. Send me!" (Isa. 6:8). Were there others who could have answered? Probably, but Isaiah didn't hesitate to answer, and because of that, events in his life were set into motion that changed the course of history.

Your purpose in life isn't something you need to dig deep to discover. It isn't hidden and difficult to find. It is to know God, to listen to his voice, and to do whatever he commands. And nowhere is God's voice heard more clearly than in his Word. You can be sure of his voice when you read it in the pages of Scripture. All you have to do is make it a part of your life, your actions, and your thoughts. As you do, God's will for your life will become evident. If you have to make a choice between two things, the question you need to ask is, "Would one choice be against God's will as seen in his Word?" If the answer is yes, then you know which choice to make, because sin is never an option.

If you want more of God, more guidance, and more direction, then learn his Word. Make it your goal to be alert to his voice and to stand up and say, "Here I am. Send me."

The LORD is waiting to be kind to you.
He rises to have compassion on you.
The LORD is a God of justice.
Blessed are all those who wait for him.

Isaiah 30:18

*Y*ou are tired, exhausted, and running on empty. Have you ever thought about why? Does your day start with prayer or a rush to get out the door? Are you waiting each morning at the Father's feet to find out what he wants you to do today? The Lord waits for you to come to him—how long have you kept him waiting?

Fatigue is a fact of life. Living well requires work, but not always the kind of work the world pushes off on us. Rush from here to there, join this group, take this class, do this thing, and suddenly your life is anything but peaceful. But what's worse is you have no time to wait on God. You have too much to do to wait. And you start to get into the habit of doing everything yourself. **You become a "take charge" kind of girl, and suddenly God is left out of the equation.**

If your life is overbooked, then unbook yourself. Cut back. Do less. If you don't have time to spend alone with God each day, then you are too busy. Period. Nothing is so important that it has to be done at the expense of spending time waiting to hear from God. The God Girl takes charge of her calendar and doesn't let it take charge of her. She knows that doing *things* isn't as important as being in God's presence, so she makes room in her life for that. Nothing is so important that you can't say no to it, except the call of God on your life. If you are exhausted, then it's time to reassess your priorities and to find a way to give the things you believe are important a more important place in your life.

Jacob, why do you complain?
Israel, why do you say,
  "My way is hidden from the LORD,
    and my rights are ignored by my God"?

Isaiah 40:27

*D*o you ever feel like doing good is a giant waste of time because no one ever notices? Or worse yet, they think you are being bad when you are being good? You get no respect, and it's no fair. But never mind if you don't get the respect you deserve. Never mind if you work hard on something and never get the credit for it. Don't look for fame and approval from people. Don't scratch and fight to be recognized. You aren't working for people but for eternity, and your reward won't be now but later. It's much better to invest in eternity than in today.

As a God Girl your only goal should be doing the will of God, not getting approval from other people. You have to trust God to bless you for the things you do to serve him here on earth. He promises blessing to those who do good. When he says you will get your reward for whatever you do, he isn't lying. You have to trust the economy of God—**everything you do will either build your inheritance in heaven or tear it down.** Work for blessing by sowing goodness and mercy, by serving in peace and in hope, and by trusting him, rather than people, for your reward.

The strength of those who wait with hope in the LORD
will be renewed.
They will soar on wings like eagles.
They will run and won't become weary.
They will walk and won't grow tired.

Isaiah 40:31

Impatience is not a virtue. When you look at a situation in your life and decide that it's moving too slow for you and you're gonna take matters into your own hands instead of waiting for God, you turn your back on the God who was going to do it for you or through you. For a while this approach might work, and you might get things done. The attention you wanted might come your way, the dreams you had might be coming true, but if what you did was in your own strength and not the strength of the Lord, then your energy is gonna run out and your success is gonna turn to failure.

When you think you need something in this life, it's almost second nature to dive in headfirst and get things done. You take charge of your life and even the lives of others and do what you can to ward off loneliness, suffering, and what you think are the mean acts of mean people. But maybe the loneliness and suffering that would come by waiting on God to meet all your needs are just what your soul needs.

To wait on God means to trust him with every part of your life—especially the parts where you have to be patient. Patience is a virtue because it teaches your heart not to rely on its own understanding but to trust in the Lord (see Prov. 3:5). When you wait on God, your eyes aren't on yourself but are looking upward in hopeful anticipation of his next move. When that's your position, you're gonna see his glory and his love start to work in your life. Eyes focused on God might see trials and even danger, but they aren't overwhelmed with fear. They are never weary and never fail because they always see God's tender, loving care and ability to meet all your needs.

Who has determined the course of history from the beginning?
I, the LORD, was there first, and I will be there to the end. . . .
Don't be afraid, because I am with you.

Isaiah 41:4, 10

*H*ow hard is it to hear God? How hard is it to even know he's listening and watching your every move? Hard sometimes, huh? That might just be because you don't know his voice. He's talking, but maybe you're confusing his voice with something else.

The truth is that a lot of times God talks through circumstances. Nothing happens to you that doesn't first go through his victorious hands. No matter how tragic the situation you're in, you have to get into the habit of listening to God's voice in the rumbling of circumstance. If you can stop and say, "Talk to me, God—I want to listen," and then really listen instead of worrying, whining, or complaining, your life will become amazing. Nothing will ever again be meaningless. Nothing is out of God's control, and nothing is so miserable that God's hand can't lift you up out of it. The more you listen and expect to hear his voice, the more you will know its sound.

Life isn't like a series of events that God watches from a distance but more like a movie with a beginning, a middle, and an end; a hero, a villain, and a tragedy. For those who believe, the ending is sure to be a good one, and the middle can be pure adventure if you are only willing to believe that God is talking. Believe and trust that what he says is true: he will strengthen you and help you; he will support you with his victorious right hand (see Isa. 41:10). Let these words be your strength, especially when all seems lost. Never forget that God is always involved.

He was abused and punished,
but he didn't open his mouth.

Isaiah 53:7

You've been misunderstood. Slammed. Lied about. Something is going around and it isn't true. Your choice? Vindication. "I have to explain myself. I have to get them to understand," you say to yourself, and so off you go to fix things, manage the situation, get people to understand. And suddenly God slips from the throne of your life and up you crawl to take your rightful place.

Screech. "Stop this ride, I wanna get off!" It's time to take a lesson from Jesus and get back on track. Listen, he wasn't in the habit of explaining everything when he was walking on earth. Almost unimaginably, he left misunderstandings to correct themselves—or better said, he left it to God to work things out in the lives of the people who misunderstood him, lied about him, or generally hated him. Isn't his example good enough for you? Or are you willing to imitate the perfect one?

Sure, it won't be easy, but godliness rarely is. **As long as you are looking for vindication in the eyes of other human beings, you are going to be completely distracted from God.** And that distraction will affect your heart, your mind, and your body. Get your focus off the world and onto God. What people think or say has no bearing on eternity. Don't give them more power over you than they deserve, but choose to make your investment in the eternal and let the King work out the temporary for himself.

> *The Lord is not too weak to save*
> *or his ear too deaf to hear.*
> *But your wrongs have separated you from your God,*
> *and your sins have made him hide his face*
> *so that he doesn't hear you.*
>
> Isaiah 59:1–2

*D*o you have a sin in your life that you just can't walk away from? If your answer is yes, then don't be surprised that God isn't answering your prayers. Don't be surprised that you have drama in your life. When sin becomes so important to you that you won't give it up even though you've spotted it, then you've let that sin become more important than God.

God doesn't answer the prayers of people who are unrepentant, choosing to hang on to a sin or two instead of getting rid of them all. You have to be careful not to say, "I've tried to stop it, but it's just too hard." That's like saying, "I know sin is bad, but it's worse to walk away from it than to keep doing it." That's calling God a liar and arguing the case that you and your sin are totally unique and so cannot possibly be separated.

Look for those areas where you struggle and see if you aren't refusing to drop the hand of sin and reach for the hand of God. A lot of people say that it's too difficult to stop a particular sinful habit, but as a follower of Christ you can't use that excuse. According to him sin is no longer your master, but he is. So when you disagree you are saying he is wrong and giving the sin in your life the role of master. Remember, you can't serve two masters. So choose today who you're gonna serve.

I have posted watchmen on your walls, Jerusalem.
They will never be silent day or night.
Whoever calls on the LORD, do not give yourselves any rest.

Isaiah 62:6

he strong Christian is the one who has a life filled with prayer. Prayerlessness leaves a believer weakened and fearful. When things aren't happening in your life, when hope is lost, when emotions run wild, the first place to look is your prayerlessness. When a God Girl prays, she calls on the name of the Lord and he listens. She makes it clear to herself and to her God who is the most important person of all and places more emphasis on communion with him than on pleasure, busyness, and distraction. **Prayerlessness is one of the most common sins in the life of a believer.** But when you don't pray you don't worship the God you claim to serve. Prayerlessness can derail even the strongest believer. If your life isn't producing everything you imagined it would, then look at your prayer life. The amount of time you spend speaking with God, pleading with him, and seeking his mind directly affects your success in every area of your life.

When a God Girl prays, really prays, she finds doors that were slammed shut opening in front of her. She finds life changing around her and within her. She releases the power of the Holy Spirit in her life and begins to find more hope and peace than she ever dreamed existed. You can't afford to accept prayerlessness in your life. Fight to devote your mind and time to the pursuit of communion with the Creator of the universe and lover of your soul.

This is what the LORD says:
I remember the unfailing loyalty of your youth,
the love you had for me as a bride.
I remember how you followed me into the desert,
into a land that couldn't be farmed.
Israel was set apart for the LORD.

Jeremiah 2:2–3

*A*re you still eager to please God, or are you more interested in him pleasing you? Are you driven by a desire to serve him, or are you whining because things aren't going your way? Your soul will never be happy when it has forgotten what God wants from it, and that is your presence and adoration. How much of that do you give? How much do you work to do what pleases him and to give him a good rep with your friends and family?

In Jeremiah 2, God is asking his people why they have walked away, forgotten they loved him, and gone after other gods. He can remember a time when they adored and trusted him, but somehow they have gotten away from that passion, hope, and love. Do you notice a difference in your life? Has your passion for God grown or diminished? Can you remember a time when you didn't care about anything but him? **If you have gone backward instead of forward in your love relationship, then you will more than likely feel bad right now, and that's good**—it means you are distressed, and godly distress causes you to change or repent (see 2 Cor. 7:10).

Today is your second chance to get back to your first love. Plan time today, tomorrow, and all week to devote to remembering what he has done for you, to adoring him, and to just being in his presence.

Whom can I speak to?
Whom can I give a warning to?
Who will listen?

Jeremiah 6:10

*W*hen God talks, do you listen or change the subject? Hearing from God isn't always a good feeling. A lot of times it's a pain and nothing you want to hear. It can be like a rude awakening to get an unwanted reminder of your own imperfection, and the easy response is to say, "So what?" "That's just how I am," or "Nobody's perfect." But the better way to handle a correction, whether it comes as a heavenly tap or as a rude slap from an unloving human being, is with humility and sanctification in mind. Brushing off correction or admonishment is never a good idea, so the smart girl thinks it over and compares it with God's Word to see if what she's hearing sounds like a message from God. Nobody grows in godliness without facing the ugly truth about themselves from time to time. So don't get all depressed or freak out, but reset and think about taking a new path, a new way of thinking or acting.

The prophets of the Old Testament warned God's people of their sinful ways, but even though they spoke for God, they were most often rejected and feared by the people, who didn't want to be told they were doing anything wrong. **It's human nature to run the other way when someone starts to point a finger at you, but that doesn't make it godly.** As you read the books of the prophets, look at how easy it was for the people to choose their sin over God's correction, but also look at how God never gave up on his people.

Not everything that everyone tells you is a word from God, but the God Girl looks at correction as a chance to find out more about what pleases God and to really look at her own motives and desires. When you are corrected, your best response is always to be honest about your motives and choose not to blame the person who's correcting you but to try to find some truth in their words.

If you will speak what is worthwhile and not what is worthless,
you will stand in my presence.

Jeremiah 15:19

One of the best signs of your faith is the way you talk. Talk like a believer and people will know you are a believer. But if you talk like a pagan—if you use the name of the Lord like a cuss word, if you are foul mouthed, or if you worry or complain a lot—people will find it hard to believe you have any faith at all.

Sarcasm is not the kind of language used by a God Girl. It hurts people and it is unloving. Talking about yourself most of the time is self-obsession and shows others that you are more important to you than God or anyone else. Sure, you feel like you need to express yourself and be understood, but really, is that what God commanded—"Talk a lot so others know all about you"? Doesn't sound like God, does it? When you are compelled to dump every thought out on anyone who will listen, something is wrong with your spirit. It's a sign that you've lost touch with the reality that God and only God can ever deliver you and save you from your misery and stress. **It is emotionally and spiritually dangerous to think that dumping on another human being is the answer to your problems.** Most of the time you end up spending too much energy concentrating on the bad stuff in your life and not enough time concentrating on the godly things around you.

The God Girl's best option for faithful speech is to just keep silent unless you absolutely have to speak. Remember, God's Word commands us to love our neighbors, love our enemies, make disciples, and do a lot more that requires us to talk. So ask yourself, "Is the gospel part of my day-to-day speech?" Talking just for the sake of talking can cut away at your higher purpose. If you become what you think and talk about the most, then what are you becoming?

I know the plans that I have for you, declares the LORD. They are plans for peace and not disaster, plans to give you a future filled with hope.

Jeremiah 29:11

*H*ave you ever heard how God took the day off? He got so tired from running the world and listening to everyone's prayers that he just clocked out. He didn't make the sun rise or set; he didn't set the wind in motion. The ocean flooded and the sky fell. It was a disaster. Never heard about that day? That's because it never happened. If God took the day off, more than a few things would get messed up.

Have you ever thought that God took the day off from hearing you? Felt like he was clueless about your life and your needs? How reliable you think he is all depends on your definition of God. If you think God is all-knowing, all-present, and all-powerful, then by definition he can't take the day off. How could he be omnipresent (everywhere all the time) and take the day off? Not possible. You'd have to change his name to "Bob" or "god" with a little g. The only reason he doesn't "feel" present is because you chose to believe he's AWOL—absent without leave.

You want God to hear you? Then all you have to do is believe. Faith requires belief. Belief that he does have a plan for you. **Belief that he's there and he's working everything out for good.** Belief that he knows best. When you have faith, suddenly you'll find that even bad stuff is good stuff in your life. **What looks like disaster is actually protection.** And what feels like failure is actually pure success. God says that his wisdom will look like nonsense to the world (see 1 Cor. 1:18), and the truth is, it will look like nonsense to you if you aren't willing to believe and to trust that he can make good out of anything and everything that happens to you.

When you look for me, you will find me. When you wholeheartedly seek me, I will let you find me, declares the LORD.

Jeremiah 29:13–14

*D*oes your worship require a day off? Does your devotion need a vacation? The day of rest, also known as the Sabbath, wasn't designed to give you a break from worship or from doing good. It wasn't given as a day to sleep in, to overeat, or to play in the sun. It's not God's plan for you to take a break from doing good, from worship, or from devotion and Bible study.

As a believer you may often think about how exhausting devoting your life to God can be—so exhausting, in fact, that you need to take a break occasionally. But is that true, ya think? Or could it be a cleverly disguised ruse of the enemy to get you off track and focused on yourself instead of God? Where do you think the believer finds true renewal and rest—in the distractions of this world, or in the presence of God? **Can you as a God Girl truly say that devotion to him is so taxing that you need a break?** In a true love relationship, the lovers don't want time away but want more time in each other's presence.

Do not forsake your first love by claiming that loving him is too tiring, too demanding, and unrewarding. Instead trust him who you have loved. Trust the lover of your soul with your time and attention. If you freely devote yourself to him daily, giving him your very best, surely he will reward your pursuit (see Jer. 29:13).

"All of them, from the least important to the most important, will know me," declares the LORD, "because I will forgive their wickedness and I will no longer hold their sins against them."

*G*od made a covenant, or an agreement, with the Israelites and they broke it (see Jer. 11:10). They messed up royally! But God didn't give up on them; in fact, he gave them a second chance, a new covenant. But can you imagine if they wouldn't agree to it because they just couldn't get over their past mistakes? Sounds ridiculous, but how many times do you say, "I just can't get over what I did"? When you can't get over your sin or accept God's forgiveness, the past can haunt you and keep you living in your mistakes and traumas. It can make you keep reliving the very thing you should be done with: the past.

Your past was never meant to be your present, but it should inform it. God lets you remember your mess-ups and your misery so they can be a light for the future. If you're brave enough to step out of the past and only look at it as a guide to the future, then you can be free to live in the present without the chains of your mistakes. **Holding on to yesterday as if it's a part of today is craziness.** God has offered you a second chance. Grace is his gift to the sinner in you—will you reject it today and choose to live in your sinful past? Or will you trust that he's big enough to help you get over your mistakes? Let go and **refuse to continue to relive yesterday,** and you will let God redeem your past. God is relentless in his love for you, and he will continue to call you back to him no matter what you have done in the past. The only thing that stands between you and forgiveness is your inability to accept his forgiveness, not your inability to forgive yourself. You don't need your own forgiveness—God's is all-sufficient. So accept it and move on. He is ready and waiting.

*We will obey the L*ORD *our God to whom we are sending you, whether it's good or bad. Yes, we will obey the L*ORD *our God so that everything will go well for us.*

Jeremiah 42:6

When you get no answer from God, it isn't a sign that he has walked away. When your feelings lie and tell you that he's shut the door on you, don't believe them. **What you feel about God and what you know about him can be totally opposite,** but that doesn't make what you feel more reliable than what you know. Think about it like this: **God might have bigger things at stake than the thing you are asking for right now.** Since he rules the world and keeps his promise to provide for and protect you, you have to know that what you ask might be insignificant compared to what he is doing right now. So why do you cry when your prayers don't come true, as if you had a right for your wish to be fulfilled? Wouldn't you rather have the best for your life? And who do you think knows better what that best is—you or God?

So don't worry when you can't feel him.

Feelings are irrelevant at times like these. The only thing that matters is that you hang on tight to his Word and that you tell yourself and anyone who's listening that you're not going anywhere. Even if it kills you, you're still gonna believe. It is this kind of faith in the goodness of God instead of your own feelings that will help you make it through even the hardest things.

Growing up can put a strain on your emotions. They can easily get out of control if you let them have any kind of power in your life. As a God Girl you shouldn't give in to your feelings or give them more significance than they deserve. Feelings are here today and gone tomorrow. They are picky and a lot of times just plain sinful, so don't protect them like a sweet little kitten but discipline them like a child. And when you do, they'll just get more and more in tune with the will of God and less and less bossy and demanding.

Are you looking for great things for yourself?
Jeremiah 45:5

Is your main goal happiness or holiness? God's goal is one of them, even at the expense of the other. Can you guess which one? If you're asking God for things and not getting them, then you might not be asking in line with God's will. *Things* are not what God wants for you; holiness is. And a lot of times that comes when you don't get what you want. Your lack has the ability to draw you closer to God and make you rely on him as your everything.

God's Word promises to give you what you ask when you ask for what he wants. Ask yourself what you want from God and why. Is it something that would make you more holy or more happy? If you're more concerned with happiness, then you might want to rethink your wish list. Think about what you're asking God for and how you could start to want more of what he wants for your life. God's goal is always to strengthen your relationship with him, not to increase your comfort, popularity, success, or happiness. He wants to give you great things—far greater than you think—but it all has to do with your holiness and relationship with him.

So look at his Word and see what he wants for his kids. Think about his gifts, his life, his love. Think about what you want and what that says about you. Do you concentrate on the things of heaven? Are you content with the things God has given you, or do you need more? Can you find hope in your situation knowing that God answers prayers not according to your will but according to his divine and perfect will? Practice trusting that because God is truly good, he will always give you what is the very best for you right now.

The reason I can still find hope is that I keep this one thing in mind: the LORD's mercy.

Lamentations 3:21–22

D o you live by your emotions? Do you yell when you're angry and fight back when you're hurt? As a follower of Christ you were never meant to blindly follow your emotions. That's what you did before you met Jesus. So **why do you still get bossed around by your emotions** at times instead of listening to the voice of God?

Do you bow to your emotions just out of habit or weakness? Or do you sometimes feel cheated because you didn't get out of a situation what you thought you should have gotten? "That's not fair!" you say. "I deserve more." Someone didn't do what you wanted, so you are angry. Someone didn't give you what you thought you were going to get, so you are sad. Frustrated expectations lead you down bad emotional paths, and more often than not you follow them.

But what if you could be free from your emotions' control and back under the control of Christ—wouldn't your life be better? Wouldn't your self-control improve and your emotions calm? After all, that's what he promises: "Come to me, all who are tired from carrying heavy loads, and I will give you rest" (Matt. 11:28). He'll give you rest from what led you here and there, up and down. Rest from yourself.

A life completely turned over to Christ is a life where emotions complement but do not control. You have to choose who you are gonna follow, your emotions or your God. For all human beings there will be heartache, grief, and great loss, but if you're willing to choose God, then your emotions will start to come under your control and bring depth to your life instead of misery. Like Jeremiah, you can express grief and despair, but never to the point that it distracts you from who God is and what a life lived for him ultimately means.

Tell them, "This is what the Almighty LORD says."... Don't let the things they say frighten you. Don't be terrified in their presence, even though they are rebellious people. Speak my words to them whether they listen or not, because they are rebellious.

Ezekiel 2:4, 6–7

Is being nice always the godly choice? Sometimes we're nice just to keep the peace. Your friend asks you if you think she has a problem with gossip, and while you know she does, you say "no way" so that she won't gossip about you. Or you have a friend who is mean to other people, but you don't say anything because you don't want to fight. **When you are nice in order to protect yourself,** look out, because **you might just be putting yourself before God.** Sometimes you, like the prophet Ezekiel, have to speak up, and that might mean ticking people off. It's so much easier to just be nice and avoid the conflict altogether. But **when sin is involved, being nice and not saying anything that would offend is contributing to that sin,** even joining in.

As a God Girl you need to be fearless in speaking God's Word. That means speaking the truth even when people don't want to hear it. They'll be expecting you to "love" them, meaning let them live in denial of their own sin. But that's not loving them; it's fearing them. You aren't to fear anyone but God.

This isn't a free pass to go around criticizing everyone but a call to be honest when honesty is requested. When your friends ask your opinion on something, you have an obligation to tell them the truth, even when it might hurt. But you don't have to run around getting onto everyone's sin; that's like throwing pearls to pigs (see Matt. 7:6)—they just aren't interested. But when you have an opening or even an invitation, don't pass it up. Speak God's Word and risk the agitation and even anger of others so that you might serve God rather than yourself.

He said to me, "Go in, and see the wicked, disgusting things that the people of Israel are doing here." So I went in and looked. I saw that the walls were covered with drawings of . . . all the idols in the nation of Israel.

Ezekiel 8:9–10

God hates **idols**. He calls them wicked and disgusting. An idol is anything that leads you to obsession and anything that you look to for answers, for hope, for peace, for comfort, or for anything else God wants to provide for you. We all have 'em; we just don't know it. That's because they've become such a part of us. A lot of times they control us so much that we can't even distinguish them from our own personalities. They control what we think and what we do. **They say things like "You deserve more than that," "You've got to get what you want," and "Life isn't fair."** They make big demands on our hearts and our lives, wanting us to serve them at all costs.

You might not recognize the voices of your idols, but chances are they are there, deep inside you. In order to love and serve God, you have to refuse to serve your idols. You can't have two gods; it doesn't work that way. In order to spot your idols just ask yourself what you think about the most, what you can't live without, and where you lack self-control. As you explore these areas of yourself, you will more than likely find places where something other than God controls you, and there you've found your idols.

Don't become enemies with God by following idols. Dare to break free today. Reject, renounce, and refuse your idols. It's the only way to serve God, and it will be the answer to your bondage. Nothing can control the God Girl who has her mind set on pleasing God and God alone.

I appointed an angel to guard you.

Ezekiel 28:14

I t is easy to look around and think that you are all alone, but don't be so sure. There just might be angels watching you right now. Just because you can't see them doesn't mean they're less real. Contrary to what some people might say, they aren't the ghosts of people who have died and now serve as messengers of God. They are angelic beings created to do God's work, and part of that work is watching over his people (see Ps. 34:7). There is more to your life than meets the eye. God promises to guard those who fear him with an invisible protection. Even though sometimes your life might look like a lonely disaster, as a God Girl you've got to remember that you are never alone—you have the Spirit of God inside you and his angels beside you.

Loneliness is a lie that pulls you inside of yourself to find emptiness and despair. When you look at your loneliness and resent it, or when you think you are too bad to be loved, you sin by calling God a liar. His promises are too many to list here, but his Word is clear that we are not alone. Millions like you walk this earth and share the same struggles every day, and millions more watch you from heaven (see 1 Cor. 10:13; Gal. 6:2; Heb. 12:1).

When you start to feel bad about your life, stop and look for things in your life that prove God is there. And if you can't find evidence in your life, then look to the lives of the millions of believers all over the world. Look beyond the physical world and trust the truth of Scripture when it points you to the invisible world that is all around you.

I will forgive them for all the times they turned away from me and sinned. I will cleanse them so that they will be my people, and I will be their God.

Ezekiel 37:23

God is a God of justice. That means he doesn't let evil or sin win. In the end both require a price be paid, and that price is death. But God doesn't want you to die, so he made a way out for you. The way out is called repentance—changing the way you think and act and turning to God.

You might feel like you've done something so bad that you can't be forgiven even if you change your ways, but that's not true. People from the beginning of time have been sinning just as badly as you, and time and again God has proven nothing is so bad that it can't be forgiven, except completely rejecting him. Even the Israelites, who turned their back on the God of their ancestors and worshiped other gods, were taken back over and over again by the same God who will take you back. Of course, they did suffer the consequences of their sinful choices—disease, attack, slavery, and even exile— but still God was their God, and still he promised to take them back. Ultimately he sent his Son as a guilt offering so that no one would have to die but anyone could have eternal life, and that includes you.

Don't let your life slogan be that you're "just too bad to be forgiven" or "just too bad to be loved," because that's just not true. You are too loved to be forgotten and too prized to be given up on. But to be forgiven you've gotta confess and repent—a simple yet challenging task. So don't argue with God about your sinfulness; just agree with him and then accept his outstretched hand by saying, "Thank you." Today you are one step away from freedom. Take it now and get on with the better things God has waiting for you.

If our God, whom we honor, can save us from a blazing furnace and from your power, he will, Your Majesty. But if he doesn't, you should know, Your Majesty, we'll never honor your gods or worship the gold statue that you set up.

Daniel 3:17–18

When God shows you something, you can't let your common sense talk you out of it. Common sense is natural and faith is spiritual. When God's way totally contradicts your common sense, who are you gonna trust? For Daniel, it would have made more sense to join the crowd, but his faith said different. If your common sense can't make sense of your faith, which wins out? It's easy in those great mountaintop moments to say, "I trust him and I'll do whatever he says," but what happens when you come down into the valley where it's all cold, dark, and damp and everything you see argues against what you learned on the mountain?

When God shows something to you, it won't stay just an idea for long. Soon your vision is gonna be tested, and to prove its truth you'll have to do what you know is right even when everything in you screams, "This doesn't make sense!" If you can hold on to what you heard God tell you and stay connected to him and his Word, your faith will quickly become a part of your very soul. It won't be just a good idea but will be your way of life.

Is your faith being tested? Then think about the idea that this test will either prove God right or steal your faith. Jesus said, "Whoever doesn't lose his faith in me is indeed blessed" (Matt. 11:6). You have to trust God's faithfulness no matter what test you come up against. The tests aren't going to stop; they have to come in order to make your faith real. So keep fighting for the truth. Don't let your common sense or anybody else's sway you. Faith is a total trust in God that refuses to believe for a second that he will fail.

Three times each day he got down on his knees and prayed to his God. He had always praised God this way.

Daniel 6:10

*P*rayer is to your soul what your pulse is to your body. A doctor can tell the condition of your heart by checking your pulse, and you can check the condition of your soul by checking your prayer. What percentage of your time does God get from you? How much prayer is too much? If you truly believed in the power of prayer, could you ever get enough? Would any effort to find the time for it be too much? The girl who believes in this power is the girl who finds more value and strength in the presence of God than in sleep, rest, or play. Instead of considering prayer a drudgery and a difficult discipline, she sees it as a joy and a necessity to her very soul. She finds in it the strength and ability to do more than she ever could without it.

The enemy's goal is to keep you from communion with the Father.

When you put off prayer for another time, you obey the enemy's secret whispers. Don't let your life be controlled by his deceit. You cannot live without prayer—it is your lifeblood and the only thing that will set you free from the chaos of life.

Daniel had a choice to make: he could obey the king's decree not to worship God or defy it and risk certain death. Knowing his God and his own need for prayer, he chose the better path (see Daniel 6). If you want to become as devoted as Daniel, then promise to wake up 30 minutes earlier every day and talk to God. Confess your junk, plead with him about those you love, and tell him how much you adore him. Do this for a week and then check yourself. Is life better, easier? Are you happier? When you find that you are, you will have found your strength in prayer.

I will go back to my place until they admit that they are guilty.

Hosea 5:15

*C*onfession is a requirement for forgiveness because it cleanses your soul. It's the same as with your body: if you don't clean your wounds, you will never heal. When you get a big, bloody cut, the first step is to stop the bleeding with some kind of bandage, but what then? Do you just wrap it up and go on with your life, or do you hop in the car, drive to the hospital, and go through the pain of letting them take off the bandage and clean the wound? Even though it doesn't sound like much fun, you've got to open it up. If you don't clean your wound, every little speck of dirt that might have gotten into your body through the gash can lead to infection. The small, invisible attackers of bacteria can easily go unnoticed and be ignored, but eventually they will flare up and attack not only the area of the wound but your entire body. And it's the same with your soul: it has to be cleaned and protected from small sins that can work their way into your bloodstream. Confession is the antibacterial cleanser for the job. "If we confess our sins, he forgives them and cleanses us from everything we've done wrong" (1 John 1:9).

So what about your unconfessed sins, those small bacteria that infect and cause trouble? A girl who covers over her sin is bound for a life of chaos and pain. God promises that he won't give those who do that much success (see Deut. 28:15–68), and in fact he also says he will ignore their prayers (see Prov. 28:9). As a God Girl you have to confess daily. Every day look over your life and agree with God that sin is sin. As soon as you confess, it's forgiven and you are all cleaned up, saved from infection. So admit your guilt and God will be your protection and guide. Then when you search for him, you will find him.

The day of the LORD is near,
and it will come like destruction from the Almighty.

Joel 1:15

God isn't happy when his people sin. And when things get really bad, God does something about it. In the Old Testament God used things like plagues, invasion, and destruction to get his people to wake up and look up. The prophet Joel wrote to the people of Israel about all the miserable things that had been happening to them and would keep happening to them because of their sin. But he wrote not to condemn them but to show them a way out of their misery. The way out he wanted them to see was simple, and it applies to us even today: it is repentance, prayer, and fasting. God wouldn't hold anything against them if they would just be willing to stop what they were doing, turn around, and be serious about turning back to him. God wanted his people to make pleasing him more important than pleasing themselves and even their appetites.

God didn't want the attacks on Israel to be looked at like haphazard events, having nothing to do with their choices or their sin. He wants his people to know beyond a shadow of a doubt that nothing happens outside of God's control. And when he lets destruction come on his people, it's a call for them to sit up and listen. When hard times come your way, don't worry over them, but look to God and find out how he wants you to react to them. Is he trying to get your attention? Is he letting all this stuff happen in order to purify you or strengthen you? Not all destruction comes from your sin; a lot of it is because of the sin of other people, but that doesn't change your responsibility to ask, "Where is my sin and how can I turn around and get things right?" **God uses everything in your life for your good when you are willing to trust him and to turn your life over to him.**

Do two people ever walk together without meeting first?

Amos 3:3

*A*mos 3:3 explains that when two people are friends, it's because they believe the same things; they have something in common. Two people don't walk together unless they've met, talked, and agreed they both want to go the same direction. But what happens when one of the two leaves the path of faith and refuses to walk in godliness? At this point one goes in one direction, toward godliness, while the other goes in another direction, toward sin. Then the friendship is in trouble.

When this happens it can be easy to deviate from what you know is right just because you want to make your friend happy and keep walking together. But you have to remember that your ultimate goal is God and not the whims of a friend. The God Girl has to stay on the path of righteousness as she loves her friend, even if that means loving that friend only from a distance. She must refuse to change her path because her ultimate goal is to make God happy, even at the expense of friendship.

When you make a decision about what kind of friend you're going to be, decide to be one who doesn't just act on feelings but lives by the facts of God's Word. Know that when you walk with someone and call them friend, you show your agreement with them. **If your friend isn't living a godly life, then you might be on the wrong path too.** You can't be friends for long and not end up on the same path. Take a look at all your friendships from God's perspective, and then fearlessly love them or leave them according to God's call on your life.

Search for the LORD and live!

Amos 5:6

*S*earch for me and live," God says to you (Amos 5:4). Have you strayed from God? Done wrong in his eyes? Go back to him and live. When you look at some of the ways God punishes sin, you might think he's dangerous and not to be trusted. Thinking about all the wrath he has poured out on the earth can be scary. But the message that keeps repeating itself throughout the entire Bible is God's love for his people even when they mess up. Even when you mess up, he still loves you and offers you a way out: "Search for me and live."

If your life is in a dark place, if you feel dead inside and don't know what to do, turn around and go to God to live. **When you risk leaving the things of this world in your rearview mirror and heading as fast as you can toward God, you risk pure bliss.** The way to get your life back on track is not hiding things under the rug but bringing them into the light so that you are free to run unencumbered back to him. Don't worry about not being prepared or needing to get things right first—his love has no prerequisite. Know that whatever the condition of your heart today, you can go back to him and live.

Don't gloat over your relative's misfortune
or be happy when the people of Judah are destroyed.
Don't brag so much when they're in distress.

Obadiah 12

Somebody else's failure can never be your success. When you see someone who has failed and you say to yourself, "See, I am smarter than she is" or "He deserved it," all you are doing is bringing judgment on yourself, not on them. In Romans 2:1 Paul explains it this way: "No matter who you are, if you judge anyone, you have no excuse. When you judge another person, you condemn yourself, since you, the judge, do the same things." Their sin, whatever it might be, is theirs to deal with, but as soon as you make it an excuse for *your* sin, you bring the problem home with you. And in most cases focusing on their sin can lead to your pride.

You have to learn to let God deal with others the way God will deal with them without being happy when they suffer. The most important thing for you is your relationship with God, not with people. Whatever you might think about another person can never lead you to break God's commandments. When all you want to do is obey him, suddenly you are free from the strain of worrying about human failure and attack because you want only what God wants. And all of a sudden you're getting happy when other people do well and sad when they fail. And that's a sure sign you're becoming a disciple who attracts people to God's side instead of being just another catty girl who pushes them away.

You will be treated as you have treated others.
You will get back what you have given.

Obadiah 15

If God treated you the way you treat other people, how happy would that make you feel? God is a God of justice. That means that he doesn't just let sin go, and he also doesn't care how mean other people are to you; he'll never let that be your excuse for sin. In Mark 11:25 Jesus says forgiveness is only for people who have forgiven others. It's easy to love only the people who love you and never hurt you, but big whoop—even nonbelievers do that. It's a natural human response, but the God Girl doesn't act on her emotion alone, but on truth.

God's command is for his children to love at all times. That doesn't mean to love sin, in ourselves or others, but it does mean that love isn't reserved for the lovable. It means that sometimes we have to act in love even though we feel like doing the complete opposite. After all, God loved us even when we didn't love him. He loved us even though we totally rejected him with our sin. He gave his Son for the world even though he knew the world wouldn't accept him. The God Girl wants to love like God loves, so that makes her want to love people who don't deserve it and to obey no matter how much it might cost.

Is your love a godly love? Do you demand respect? Or do you try to do to others what you would want them to do to you? Treat others with the same love that God has shown to you, and the love in your life will only grow stronger and deeper.

From inside the fish Jonah prayed to the LORD his God. Jonah prayed:
"I called to the LORD in my distress,
*   and he answered me.*
From the depths of my watery grave I cried for help,
*   and you heard my cry. . . .*
I will sacrifice to you with songs of thanksgiving.
I will keep my vow."

Jonah 2:1–2, 9

*G*od provided a giant fish for Jonah as protection from a watery grave. That cold, stinky, wet fish wouldn't have been a nice place. Jonah would have been terrified, sure he was going to die. But being a prophet, Jonah knew something about God. And after the initial shock wore off and he took a look at the situation, he did the most important thing he could do: he thanked God. Yep, he thanked God from inside his fishy prison.

Thanking God in the midst of your stinky fish and suffering will save you a lot of pain. Nothing happens to you that God cannot and will not use for your good (see Rom. 8:28). When you believe that and trust him, you will be free to live without fear or worry. You'll be free to rest in a peace that goes beyond anything that you can imagine (see Phil. 4:7). No storm, no trial, no destruction can get to you unless God puts it there to rescue you from your choices.

In the belly of the fish Jonah had something to learn. And he wasn't set free until he learned it. If you're trapped and want to get free, you have to learn what God wants you to learn. What lesson are you refusing to get? What work won't you do? Decide to just do it and then thank him. Pray to him and offer him your life, your will, and your praise. Then you will see things start to happen. If God can save a despicable city like Nineveh (see Jonah 3), he can save you. Just accept his rebuke and his forgiveness and move on to the blessing he wants to give you.

The sun beat down on Jonah's head so that he was about to faint. He wanted to die. So he said, "I'd rather be dead than alive."

Jonah 4:8

*S*elf-pity says, "I can't do this." It says, "This is too hard." **Self-pity takes God off of the throne and puts you and your self-interests in his place.** And self-pity makes decisions based on feelings instead of faith. This isn't an acceptable way of thinking for the God Girl. God wants you to decide the worth of your life based not on your circumstances but on his faithfulness. You can be sure that nothing can get you out of his hands, and so whatever happens to you or around you won't be the end of you, any more than it's the end of God.

As a God Girl you can't allow a hint of self-pity to get you off track from trusting the truth that God has everything under control. No challenge, no situation, no pain, no calling is too difficult for you to get over and through in faith instead of fear and self-pity. But no one finds God's glory till they stop staring at their miserable life. When negative thoughts start to creep in, your mind starts to whine and complain, and you tell God, "I can't do this," just remember that he made you able to do it. You can and you have to. So instead of saying, "I can't do it," say, "Why not? Why shouldn't I suffer, since suffering is here to make me more like Jesus?" (see Phil. 3:10).

When you feel self-pity you start to think of yourself as a freak, a girl whose life just can't be fixed, but that's never true of the God Girl. God can use anything for good (see Rom. 8:28). You can survive anything, and if you trust God, you can grow and be happy even in the midst of suffering and trials.

You hate good and love evil. . . .
Then you will cry to the LORD,
but he will not answer you.
He will hide his face from you at that time
because you have done evil things.

Micah 3:2, 4

I t can be hard not to pay attention to the world with all of its amazing sights and imaginative ideas, but every time you get all wrapped up in the world, you open yourself up to turning away from God. And suddenly you find yourself living not in him but in the world, and your prayer life suffers. See, **God says he won't listen to people who love the world, which means those who put all their hope in it and get obsessed about it.** The problem with obsession is that it means all your thoughts are caught up in getting the one thing you obsess about, even to the detriment of other things and people. When you obsess you take a giant step toward hating good and loving evil (see Micah 3:2), since evil is anything that draws your attention away from God in order to control you.

If your prayer life is weak and you never get the answers you want, then maybe the answer is in where you are living: in the world or in faith? So think about your week. What do you do and think about most often? Is your life all wrapped up in Jesus and his Word, or do you spend the majority of your strength just keeping up with the world?

Prayer is your access to the Creator of all. It's your way to ask and to receive from the one who provides everything you need for life and for happiness. If you could have continual access to the God of the universe, why wouldn't you take the chance and run with it? The only thing you lack in your prayer life is your allegiance. Turn your back on the world, deny it, and head straight for the arms of God. Learn to live there, without giving the world a vote, and your prayer life will explode.

Who is a God like you?
You forgive sin
and overlook the rebellion of your faithful people.
You will not be angry forever,
because you would rather show mercy.
You will again have compassion on us.
You will overcome our wrongdoing.
You will throw all our sins into the deep sea.

Micah 7:18–19

*A*re you absolutely convinced that God can do anything he says he will do? If you are, then you have faith. If not, then you do not have faith; you have doubt. If you want to be forgiven for the junk you've done, then you have to believe in God's forgiveness. You have to believe that no matter what you did, it's done, over, finished and that you're forgiven—not because of how you fixed it or what you did but because you believe him.

God promises to make you cleaned up, spotless, righteous, **if you'll just believe** that he can do that. **When you worry about your past sins,** think about them all the time, and say stuff like, "I just can't get over it," **you don't believe; you doubt.** Did you know that only believers get forgiveness, not doubters? It's so simple that a lot of people miss it. Just believe in his forgiveness and you've got it. Don't believe and you've missed it. How simple, yet how difficult!

So here's how it's done: when you mess up, agree with God that you sinned. Tell him point blank that you sinned against him, not anybody else. Then thank him for his forgiveness and promise you'll never do it again. If you can do that, then you've got it. Plain and simple.

See, forgiveness is grounded in faith, not works. It's not about you but about him. All you have to do is have the guts to believe. Can you believe?

The LORD is patient and has great strength.
The LORD will never let the guilty go unpunished.

Nahum 1:3

Life isn't fair. Seems like it oughta be, but it isn't. Sometimes bad people are luckier than good people. They torture and even kill people, and life seems to go their way. They seem to have success in everything they do, even though they do it with an evil heart. But as a God Girl you can be sure of one thing: God doesn't let evil go unpunished. He doesn't look away and just allow bad people to win. Sure, it may look like it right now, but in the end everyone will have to pay for the evil that they do.

In the days of the prophet Nahum, the city of Nineveh was the greatest and most powerful city in the land. It was the capital of Assyria, and they ruled a lot of the world. The people who lived there were known for being bloodthirsty even to the point of burning children and cutting off the hands of their enemies. They had overthrown Israel and turned Judah into a vassal state. Now the same Nineveh that Jonah had reluctantly warned to repent was being given another opportunity to do the same thing, but this time Nineveh would refuse to change, and in the end it would be completely destroyed, never to be rebuilt again.

In the New Testament Jesus teaches us that we are to love our enemies and do good to those who hate us, and at times this can seem like sheer insanity. But you have to remember that although you aren't allowed to get revenge, God is a God of justice, so he's not gonna let evil be rewarded for long. **When bad people win at your expense, don't complain;** just thank God for the amazing gift of Jesus Christ and the forgiveness he offers for your sins.

The LORD Almighty is my strength.
He makes my feet like those of a deer.
He makes me walk on the mountains.

Habakkuk 3:19

God can and will be your strength. He will give you the ability and the power to do hard things if you will just trust him. God has given you a promise, and that is that he will give you strength and feet like those of a deer and help you walk on mountains (see Hab. 3:19). Climbing a mountain isn't easy. There are brambles, loose rocks, and crevices. Your feet can get stuck and you can trip, skin your knees, and hurt your hands. Your body can be tormented by climbing up the mountains that fill your life. But if you are only willing to let him, he will help you to leap across large crevices, to climb swiftly without faltering, and to rise to mountain peaks where you can see the world from a totally new perspective.

Are you tired of being lost in the valley, unable to see the open sky above or the lay of the land beyond? **Do you want the freshness of the mountaintop,** the rush of the climb, and **the protection of feet as sure as a deer's?** Then pour everything into loving the one who loves you. Refuse to find your hope anywhere else. Walk away from things and people who control you. Turn your life over to the God who saves. Dig into his Word, beg him for his presence, and vow to serve him and him alone for the rest of your life, and you will have feet like a deer as you climb higher and higher out of the valley that surrounds you. Never fear, even if you walk through the dark valley of death, but turn to him and know that he will protect you and make your way straight. He will smooth out the rough patches and effortlessly give you the ability to overcome any treacherous way you may find yourself on.

The Lord your God is with you.
He is a hero who saves you.
He happily rejoices over you,
renews you with his love,
and celebrates over you with shouts of joy.

Zephaniah 3:17

The believer should never think that God is not involved or paying attention to her life. When you believe, you know that he is always present, and not only present but totally interested in and concerned with your well-being. His Word confirms his love for you. Even if your doubt and distraction help you to miss the truth, it's still true that if you're far from him, he's not the one who walked away—you are.

If your God can't save you, then he isn't God.

If you doubt his ability or desire to take care of you and love you, then you are doubting his very being. As a God Girl you have to believe that God is concerned with your life and cares about you. Even when your world looks horrific, your soul is never lost, and your heart shouldn't be either.

Remember all that he's done. Rehearse it over and over in your head. Read his thoughts and his plans for you in his Word. When you do you can make his Word a part of the way you think and therefore a part of how you feel as well. Don't forget your first love. When you come back to basics and let the cares of this world fade into the background, you'll find everything you need by just trusting in the God of the Bible no matter what the world looks like around you. Don't look anywhere else for him when he's right here calling you near. Trust that his Word is true and his intentions are holy, and you'll find more hope and peace than you ever thought possible.

This is what the LORD of Armies says: Carefully consider your ways! You planted a lot, but you harvested little. You eat, but you're never full. You drink, but you're still thirsty. You wear clothing, but you never have enough to keep you warm. You spend money as fast as you earn it.

Haggai 1:5–6

*A*re you let down by your life and what you have or don't have? You do everything you think you need to do in order to be happy, but you aren't satisfied. Everything and everyone seems to disappoint you. You look for more but can't find it. And then when you do find what you were looking for, you still aren't satisfied. Why?

An unsatisfied life comes from a lack of agreeing with God, not a lack of cute stuff. When you decide to agree with Christ no matter what happens, you'll find more than the world could ever offer, but as long as you think that the riches of this world, all the fame it has to offer, and the comfort it promises are what you want and need, what you plant will never produce the success you want to be yours.

The answer to all discontentment is to think carefully before you act. What would be the holy choice? If your first thought and reason for acting is based on the world's ideas of right and wrong, then you can be sure that the result will not be God's best for you. It's easy to think like the world around you and just accept things that seem to make sense to you, but in order to be content, the believer has to look at things differently—that is, with Scripture in mind. Run everything you think and accept as truth through the filter of God's Word, and don't let the lies of this world color your faith. The truth can set you free from a deceptive world and let you see things for what they really are. Truth heals, and the truth is found nowhere but in the pages of God's Word.

I will bring this third of the people through the fire.
I will refine them as silver is refined.
I will test them as gold is tested.
  They will call on me, and I will answer them.
    I will say, "They are my people."
      They will reply, "The LORD is our God."

Zechariah 13:9

The grass is always greener in the neighbor's yard. Why does it seem like you have a "blah" or even miserable life and everyone else's is so great? Life isn't always fair, at least not to the human eye. But remember, in order for gold to be purified and refined, it has to be heated to extreme temperatures. All the dross, or bad stuff, is then lifted to the top so that it can be skimmed off as the heat rises. It's next to impossible to find your own dross when life is good. But when troubles hit and the heat goes up, then your dirty parts are easier to see. And that's when you can start to scrape off all that junk once and for all. As you are refined by the trials of life, you start to turn to the one who can save you, the one you need more than anything or anyone else, and your life is cleansed and made new.

So don't fear the fire. Don't worry when life goes wrong, but look to Jesus and see what he wants removed. When your focus is on improvement and purification instead of worldly questions and worries, your ability to rise above and even overcome adversity grows. **No trial is a waste of time when your focus is on pleasing** God instead of yourself. When you see suffering as God's tool for your sanctification, it suddenly doesn't control you or scare you. The goal of the God Girl is humility, thankfulness, and praise, and when you practice those things in your life, the power your trials used to have is gone.

This is what the LORD of Armies says: A son honors his father, and a servant honors his master. So if I am a father, where is my honor? If I am a master, where is my respect?

Malachi 1:6

*W*hat does it mean to honor the Father? How do you give him respect? You look to the life of the Son, Jesus, who honored and respected God better than anyone. In his life you can find the way to do what God wants and to give him honor and respect. One of the most important truths about the life of Jesus is that he never made decisions to serve himself. He was never self-determined or self-willed, but he was one with the Father. That means it wasn't about him but was about what God wanted of him. And Jesus wants the same for you. He wants you to be one with him as he is one with the Father. But what does that mean?

Being one with Jesus means that you will never be slighted or offended by what people say or do, because you know that life isn't about you. Life is about him, and that gives you freedom from shame and embarrassment, because nothing you do is about you, but everything is about doing the will of God. When you submit to the will of God and lean on him, honoring him and humbling yourself as Christ humbled himself, you become one with him, and when you are one with Christ himself, you are free to live with all the power with which he lived.

Don't stand on your right to do this or that. Don't work at godliness with your self-will, but rely on him, trusting that if you honor and respect him, he will lift you up. As you become one with Christ and you stop making life about you and start making it all about him, the life you've wanted will be yours. You will experience more peace, more hope, and more joy than you ever dreamed of, and all because of your insistence on giving honor and respect to the one who deserves it.

"Since the time of your ancestors you have turned away from my laws and have not followed them. Return to me, and I will return to you," says the LORD of Armies.

Malachi 3:7

In an ungodly world it can be easy to start to think of godliness as extremism. When you see the world around you living life however it wants to live, it's easy to then look at God's Word and say, "That's just asking too much." And that's exactly what happened to the Israelites after they returned from exile. They started to let things slide, to become less and less worried about obedience and more preoccupied with the easy life. They still loved God, or so they said. They prayed to him and worshiped him, but they also worshiped other things like their dreams and wants. They started to question God's love for them and their definition of sin. And so their faith kind of fell apart, and God had to send the prophet Malachi to warn them that things were going to get bad because they walked away from their first love.

Centuries after Malachi wrote his book, the same kinds of things are still going on in the lives of believers across the world. A lot of believers look just like culture around them, and they give God's grace more weight than his judgment and wrath. A lot of us see salvation as our free pass to live like the rest of the world. But this side of the cross we still have to understand God's justice. He doesn't change his law like the world changes. He doesn't turn a blind eye to the sinful choices of his people. Nope, he promises justice.

Read the book of Malachi, and as you do, don't just think about the life of the Israelites, but think about believers today and even about yourself. Where do you walk away from truth and accept the world's ideas of right and wrong? Where do you think about grace as your free pass to forgiveness? And what does God expect of his children, even today? The Old Testament wasn't just written for the olden days; there's good stuff in it that is for today as well, so read it with the cross and the present in mind.

You have said, "It's pointless to serve God. What do we gain if we meet his standards or if we walk around feeling sorry for what we've done? So now we call arrogant people blessed. Not only are evildoers encouraged, they even test God and get away with it."

Malachi 3:14–15

Sometimes it seems pointless to obey God. Whether you do right or wrong, it's all the same, isn't it? It's easy to think so when you're tired of doing what's right.

But the more you think like this, the more the payoff of sin seems more appealing than obedience. Many famous people claw their way to the top, and we call them blessed. They disobey God's commands and we envy them. Their success makes it look like their sin goes unpunished, but that's a lie. They might look successful on the outside, but on the inside they're empty.

Choosing the right path instead of the easy one is never a mistake. The life of a God Girl is not an easy life. You are going to see other people doing a lot of things that you want to do but can't. And because of that it's going to look like they're getting away with more. But the easy life isn't the definition of success. God's Word says you are to find happiness in the trials, not in the easy life. Happiness (or joy) comes from knowing that God's way is the only way that will bring you permanent joy.

The prophets got on God's people because of their belief that the world and all its little gods were more valuable than God. They wandered off and got distracted with pretty things, happy things, and hopeful things. They turned away from God's law and picked up other laws or just made their own, and in the end they suffered. Let their error serve as a warning for your life. Refuse to serve the world, but serve God with all your heart, soul, mind, and strength. When you do, your life will have all that it needs—in fact, even more than you ever dreamed (see Eph. 3:20).

Then the Spirit led Jesus into the desert to be tempted by the devil.

Matthew 4:1

The most obvious temptation is the temptation to do wrong things, but what about the temptation to do good things for God? Have you ever been tempted to be great in the eyes of God? Have you ever thought about how amazing it would be to save the world with your gifts or to become the best in some area of ministry? This kind of temptation is tricky because it looks all noble and good, but at the heart of it is a teeny-weeny bit of pride, and that pride puts the focus on you instead of on God. We've got Christian "stars," those people in the faith who've made it big. They even have fan clubs. But that should never be your goal. When it is, Satan uses your dream of fame to distract you and to make it all about you.

After Jesus was baptized, immediately he went out into the desert to be tempted. Do you remember how he was tempted? He wasn't just tempted to do wrong but to do God-like things that proved he was who he said he was, like command the angels and turn rocks into bread (see Matt. 4:1–11). Maybe once you were saved you became tempted to do great things too so that you could prove yourself, get the glory, be successful, or have a greater purpose. So don't look at temptation as just a chance to do bad things, but look at your heart and make sure it doesn't want to be worshiped just a little bit. Make sure it doesn't want glory or fame. Don't let it lead you to try to take the attention off of Jesus. Everything you do as a God Girl should be to bring glory to God and not to yourself.

Blessed are those who recognize they are spiritually helpless.
The kingdom of heaven belongs to them.

Matthew 5:3

You must understand that your biggest spiritual blessing comes when you are completely broken, empty, worn out, and poor. Until you get to that point, God can't do anything in your life, because you think that you can do it yourself. You get access to his power when you admit that you're powerless. As long as you are rich with pride or independence, God won't be able to do anything for you. When you reach the point where you are spiritually hungry, the kingdom of heaven belongs to you, according to Jesus. When you admit that you can't do it all by yourself and that you need the Lord, then you have the power of his Spirit within, and when you admit that you aren't the answer but he is, then you have access to all the power in the universe.

When you insist on doing all the work yourself, when you give and give but refuse to take, and when you insist that your hope lies in something you do or don't do, that's pride. But when you humble yourself and let go of any idea that you can fix things or make yourself holy, then you come face-to-face with the one who can make you holy. **The only thing that ultimately will make you holy is God himself being shown in your life through your obedience to his will.** When you do the will of God, you grow in strength and are fed spiritually. His will is to be your spiritual manna (see Exod. 16:4, 31). And when it is, you too will say, as Jesus himself said, "My food is to do what the one who sent me wants me to do and to finish the work he has given me" (John 4:34).

Blessed are those who mourn.
They will be comforted.

Matthew 5:4

*D*on't let your defeats in life become your destruction. It's easy to let the world take your failures and convince you they represent your life, but failure for the God Girl is a blessing, not a curse. Over and over again the Bible says that you are blessed when you are a failure and when you are hurt and hated for your faith (see Ps. 119:71; John 12:24; James 5:10–11). So how could a blessing mean your destruction? Failure is only negative if you let it define you. As a God Girl you are defined not by your success in life but by your God. He might be using you through your failure on this particular thing— who are you to doubt him? Trust that your failure will be used for good when you refuse to dwell on it in misery and angst. Learn to see it for what it is: the providential hand of God in your life, guiding you out of disaster and into his arms.

The next time you feel defeated, don't let the lie that "this is the end" become your truth. Nothing could be farther from the truth. Defeat shouldn't be the end of you but should be the beginning of your reliance on God and your faith in his ability to save you. That's a reason to be happy. Think of it like this: only people who really need God ever get to experience him. So the next time you are defeated, look up and smile and say, "Thank you. Now I know how much I need you, and I won't let this defeat be the end of me, but let it be the beginning of more of you in me."

Blessed are those who show mercy.
They will be treated mercifully.

Matthew 5:7

When people do bad things, you want justice. You want them to pay for what they did. It seems only fair that bad acts should be punished, but the truth is that your job isn't punisher. In fact, God makes it clear that your job is the total opposite of that. When God chose you, he chose you to become more like him (see Eph. 5:1). It's a tall order but an order all the same. And one of the most amazing traits of God is his ability to give mercy to people who have sinned against him. And he wants you to do the same—to show mercy when people do you wrong. "But they don't deserve mercy!" you scream. True. In fact, that's actually the definition of mercy: not giving people what they deserve.

Mercy sounds good when it's coming your way, but handing it out can be tough. But that doesn't make it less important. Mercy isn't just a recommendation for the God Girl; it's a necessity. If you want mercy, you gotta show mercy. So don't let what other people do wrong take your mercy away, but use it as your chance to practice loving other people the way God loves you. Loving people who are hard to love has its reward: love "ties everything together perfectly" (Col. 3:14). So do what God asks you to do even when it makes no sense at all. Look for chances to show the world the same kind of compassionate mercy God has shown you.

Blessed are you when people insult you,
persecute you,
lie, and say all kinds of evil things about you because of me.

Matthew 5:11

*N*o one can insult you. Sure, they might try to, but no one can insult you or hurt you emotionally unless you let them. See, the insult or the attack itself is not what hurts you, but how you think about the insult determines if you will be hurt or not.

It goes like this. When you feel attacked you can choose two different responses to take away the sting: (1) you can choose to just ignore what they said, or (2) you can turn the tables and try to put yourself in their shoes, asking, "What must they be feeling to say what they've said?" But they can't hurt you unless you choose to take in what they said and internalize it as if it had any impact on your life at all.

What affects your emotions is never what happens to you but your *interpretation* of what happened to you. See things from God's viewpoint and suddenly no one can slam you and no one can hurt you anymore. Freedom belongs to the God Girl who can stop thinking about things from a human perspective and start thinking about them from a godly one.

If you love those who love you, do you deserve a reward? Even the tax collectors do that!

Matthew 5:46

Love, according to Jesus, isn't picky. It's not just for the lovable ones, but it's gotta be given to the unlovable as well. **If you only love those who love you back, then what good is love to a world that is dying?** Jesus put it this way: "If you love those who love you, do you deserve a reward? Even the tax collectors do that! Are you doing anything remarkable if you welcome only your friends? Everyone does that!" (Matt. 5:46–47). Love doesn't exclude people who don't love you back. It includes them all, even your enemies. Jesus made that clear when he said, "But I tell you this: Love your enemies, and pray for those who persecute you" (Matt. 5:44).

So what do you think? Can you do it? Can you love someone who is out to get you? Someone who wants to hurt you? If not, Jesus asks, then what good is your love? The God Girl loves others not because of who they are or what they do but because of who God is and what he has done.

When you learn to look at life from this perspective, what people do to you or around you doesn't hurt you like it used to. When your number one goal isn't getting the attention you want but giving the love God commands, you can no longer be pulled down or hurt by anyone. God gives you the answer for bullies, mean girls, angry people, and the cruel world, and that answer is love. Just love. Love them. Hurt when they hurt, pray for them, care for them, and give to them, but above all love them as if God demanded it, because he does.

So I tell you to stop worrying about what you will eat, drink, or wear. Isn't life more than food and the body more than clothes?

Matthew 6:25

E ver heard a little kid whining to his parents? Little kids fuss and complain when things don't go like they want them to. It's their way of letting their parents know they're unhappy or anxious. You might think that a little complaining about your life is just your expression of your feelings or a cry for help, but it's more than that: it's saying you need to get your own way, and it is a pathway to sin. See, when you whine and complain, you point out the bad stuff and start to analyze it. You end up reliving the pain over and again and imagining how much harder it is going to get, and that leads to worry. And when you worry, you make decisions without God because you don't trust him to work in your life. **Worrying denies the power of the God you claim to worship. That's why worry is sin.**

Jesus never worried about anything. He never stressed or complained, because he was never trying to get his own way—he only wanted what God wanted. You will win over worry when you decide that you don't want anything more than what God wants for you. And you *have* exactly that. If God wanted you to have more, he would have given it to you. If he thought you were prepared for more, he would make it happen. But what you have right now, today, is what you need. And your situation, your problem, or your lack is never too much for God to handle. A wise girl knows this, and so she trusts that "God's will be done" is the best way to look at life. Don't let worry define you, but define yourself by your faith!

If your child asks you for bread, would any of you give him a stone? Or if your child asks for a fish, would you give him a snake? Even though you're evil, you know how to give good gifts to your children. So how much more will your Father in heaven give good things to those who ask him?

Matthew 7:9–11

When a child asks for bread or for fish, he's not asking out of turn. He's not being greedy or selfish; he's just asking that his needs be met. What good parent, then, would refuse a reasonable and unselfish request from their child? None. And God is the same.

You can know that God will hear you and that he will give you what you ask when what you ask isn't out of turn—in other words, when it's within the realm of need for your life or your faith. If what you ask is in agreement with God's will, then you can be sure God will give it to you. He promises to give you what you ask, but not when you ask with sinful motives or a sinful heart. If your prayers aren't being answered, then take a look at your life. Are you asking for God's kindness on something when you are unwilling to offer kindness to someone else? Are you hoping God will be merciful to you when you are being irritable or unkind to someone else in your life?

If you want God to hear your prayers, then you need to be as good of a kid as he is a good parent. Do whatever he asks happily. Don't refuse to obey him and then wonder why your prayers are having no effect on your life. God promises to give you the "good" things that you ask for. Are you asking for good things out of a good heart? Or are you living a life of disobedience hoping that God won't notice when you ask him to be good to you? Your prayer life is under your control. You can choose today whether your prayers will be powerful or ineffective. Choose power by choosing to agree with God and acting on his will.

You know how to give good gifts to your children. So how much more will your Father in heaven give good things to those who ask him?

Matthew 7:11

*I*s there something that God has promised in his Word that he has not yet done for you? Are you beginning to mistrust him, or at the very least your ability to hear him?

If God is slow in bringing to pass one of his promises to you, there's a reason for it. Like a good father who knows what his kids need and when they need it, the Father above knows exactly what you need and when you need it. Sometimes not getting the thing you want is exactly what you need, but with your limited perspective you don't know that. That's why it should be such a relief to know that you have a Father God who can be trusted. Everything good that you have comes from him, and **everything bad that you have in your life he has allowed in order that it might bring some glory to him.**

Now, the only wild card in this situation is you. Will you stand on the truth of God's Word, acting upon it and living it, and so prove yourself? Or will you reject truth because what you want is slow in coming? A God Girl's faith must be grounded in the kindness and infallibility of the Father. When you can trust him, then you can be set free. And that freedom will be the doorway to spiritual growth and maturity.

Every girl has moments of fear when she wonders, Does my Father really care? Will he always be there? Every girl needs a rock, a solid foundation that will never shake, and though her earthly father may never be any of those things, she has a heavenly Father who will always be those things. This should bring you a lot of joy! He can be trusted. He is not a liar; you can trust him with your heart.

Everyone who hears what I say but doesn't obey it will be like a foolish person who built a house on sand. Rain poured, and floods came. Winds blew and struck that house. It collapsed, and the result was a total disaster.

Matthew 7:26–27

Sometimes you are waiting for a sign from God because you really want to do something but you aren't sure if it's his will or not. You wait and you wait, but you get nothing. People might be telling you you're crazy and telling you to just drop it, but still you wait because you need a sign. When that's the case, you need some help. And you get help by finding out what others who know God well think and by digging into God's Word. The hitch might be not that your plan is bad but that you've failed to do something that you were supposed to do. Sometimes you are paralyzed by a choice because there's another more basic, more mundane command that you are ignoring.

For example, maybe you want to do something really bad and your parents are trying to tell you that you shouldn't do it. What do you do? Go to God's Word and you'll find the answer. This might sound like the last thing in the world you wanna hear, but the answer comes down to his basic command to honor your mother and father. If your parents are saying one thing and you are disobeying them in order to "find God's will," then you're never going to hear from God because you are being disobedient. You always have to obey God first before looking for an answer to your dilemma. Only after you obey his very basic commands, the very words written in Scripture, can you expect to hear from him when it comes to your dreams.

Whoever doesn't take up his cross and follow me doesn't deserve to be my disciple. The person who tries to preserve his life will lose it, but the person who loses his life for me will preserve it.

Matthew 10:38–39

A lot of times the things you do to "save" your life actually destroy it. When you cut, purge, or abuse yourself in any way, you falsely believe that this act might just fix you or save you. Unfortunately the exact opposite is true: these things are sure to give you pain and suffering. It's a good trick of the enemy to get you to take a lie and make it your reality. But it's a gift of God to break up those lies and show you the real truth that will set you free.

The truth is that you don't find your salvation in one more cut on your leg or pound off your stomach. But when you try to find your life you lose it, and if you lose your life for Christ's sake, you find it (see Matt. 10:39).

To lose your life for Christ means that you are so concerned about serving him, loving him, and telling others about him that your feelings can't dissuade you or get you off track. When you give up your need to be anything other than his disciple, you find more life than you could ever imagine.

The greatest thing you can do isn't to soothe your suffering but to offer it to God. Jesus didn't run away or try to soothe his pain; the gospel required that he endure suffering for you. And you can't hide or medicate your pain with the lie that hurting yourself will bring you any kind of salvation at all. Salvation comes from the wounds of Jesus. Nothing you do can improve on that. Jesus promises that if you give up your life by giving up your need to stop the pain, you will find your life. The lies you believe are not giving you what they promise. Walk away now and turn to the cross, and you will find your salvation.

Come to me, all who are tired from carrying heavy loads, and I will give you rest.

Matthew 11:28

When your world starts to fall apart, don't get deeper into the mess by going deeper into you. Studying your past or the people from your past isn't what God calls for in order for you to find the rest that you need. "Come to me," says Jesus, not, "Go back to your past and figure out what is affecting you now." Coming to him is how you get over the things that haunt you. Jesus and Jesus alone can set you free from the worries and fears of yesterday. God wants you to live a life that is complete in Christ. Nothing else is needed. No magical incantation, no remembering of events will set you free—if that were the case, then Christ wouldn't be sufficient. But that's not true. He's all-sufficient. His Spirit has the power to heal, to set you free in an instant, and all you need to do is come to him.

When you wrestle with your past, you take a detour. God's will is not that you should fix life but that you should have a new life in him. All the old is gone and the new has come (see 2 Cor. 5:17; Col. 3:10). So don't waste your strength on figuring out your emotional baggage; just give your load to the one who wants to take it, and rest in the fact that it is finished. You don't have anything to work out other than your trust in him who makes you new.

Come to me, all who are tired from carrying heavy loads, and I will give you rest.

Matthew 11:28

Exhaustion can never be an excuse for sin. When your fatigue "makes" you jealous that other people get to rest, you look away from God. Don't look at the lives of the people around you to find an excuse to resent your own life. The life of faith isn't the easy life. God's Word never commanded vacation days or rest from doing good, only stuff like perseverance and endurance—kind of the opposite of a sunny getaway on a tropical isle, huh? A lot of people throughout history have worked to the point of exhaustion serving God. In fact, you might say that most of the great things in history were done by people who were worn out.

You'll find the rest you need not on vacation but in the arms of the Father. Christ left us with this promise: "Come to me, all who are tired from carrying heavy loads, and I will give you rest" (Matt. 11:28). There is rest for your weary soul. There is a place of refreshing, and it can be yours today. Don't let the cares of this world overwhelm you. And don't tell yourself that you have to get away in order to find rest. You can rest right where you are, in the middle of your work, at home, with your family, here and now—no need to get away. You can find the peace that goes beyond anything we can imagine (see Phil. 4:7) right now. Every morning God hands out the peace that day needs, offering it to you like manna from heaven. He doesn't give you enough to store it up and make it last the whole month or even the week, but he asks you to come to him every day and find just what you need to continue on in strength and in hope.

Come to me, all who are tired from carrying heavy loads, and I will give you rest.

Matthew 11:28

What does it mean to find the kind of rest talked about in Matthew 11:28? Have you found it, or are you lost in the stress of a particular problem? God promises to take that problem from you, but you have to be willing to hand it over. He's never going to take it by force. The longer you hold on to it and refuse to let go, the longer you make God wait. Part of believing in God is believing God's Word is true. And nothing is truer than the truth that God can and will handle your burden for you. But turning it over to him means more than just giving it up; it means giving it up and taking up his yoke. You make an exchange—your burden for his. He promises that his is light.

So what is his burden, his yoke? It's simple. It's his commands. Give up your problems and start concerning yourself with doing just what he asks. It's easy, really. He promises it is, and that's because he helps you. He walks beside you and gives you the strength, his strength, to do it. The burden you are carrying right now is not his will for you. He wants you to be free to leave the heavy lifting to him. So let go and look to his Word for your marching orders. Know that when you do, life will get a whole lot easier and your burden a whole lot lighter.

You poisonous snakes! How can you evil people say anything good? Your mouth says what comes from inside you.

Matthew 12:34

What's your stress vocabulary? When you stub your toe, what comes out of your mouth? When you drop your plate, what do you say? What kinds of words do you use when things don't go so well and times get stressful?

The Bible says that what comes out of your mouth is what's inside you. Of course, how you talk seems to change based on what you're feeling at the time, so the best gauge of your heart is to see what comes out of your mouth when the tough times hit. Do you complain about it or pray about it? Do you worry with your words or hope with them? The funny thing about words is that your ears hear whatever you say, and the more they hear something, the more your mind starts to believe it. So if you cut yourself down when things go bad, you reinforce how bad, weak, or stupid you feel. But that's not what God wants from your mouth. He wants your mouth to be used to glorify him. Do you think that complaint, fear, worry, or panic glorify him? The answer is pretty obvious.

So what's the answer to your stress vocabulary? Stress preparation: study God's Word. Learn the verses that will help you through the tough times. When you memorize them, they can be the first thing out of your mouth when trouble hits. And pray more. Don't let the sin of prayerlessness get you off track by pushing the thought of God out of your mind.

The more God you get into your life, the less stress will come out of your mouth.

But the worries of life and the deceitful pleasures of riches choke the word so that it can't produce anything.

Matthew 13:22

*D*id you notice what Jesus said will choke the word out of your life (see Matt. 13:1–23)? Is it the devil? No, he doesn't give the devil that much credit. What will kill the truth of God's Word in your life is the worries of life—worries about things you wish you had, what people think of you, your look, your image, and your friends or lack thereof.

Worry tells God that you don't trust him to take care of the practical parts of your life.

Sure, you trust him for salvation, but for food and clothing? Nope. When you were a child you trusted your parents to provide what you needed. You didn't worry about what you had or didn't have, because you knew all you had to do was to ask them and your needs would be met. But now that you are older you wonder, Will there be enough for me? Will it be what I need? Worrying is accusing God of not taking care of his own. It's calling him a delinquent father and looking for insurance to protect you in case of disaster.

But the God Girl has assurance, not insurance. She has the assurance that God will never leave her and will always provide for her. The God Girl is the most content girl on the planet because she knows she has exactly what she needs, and that's why she doesn't allow worry to choke out the seed of God's Word in her life.

Remember that **your fears and worries say more about your belief in God than they do about your lot in life.** Freedom isn't just about rebuking the devil and his hold on your life; it's also about seeing the truth about the thoughts in your head. Practice seeing worry for what it is—a lie about God's goodness—and choose to trust your faithful Father instead.

Then Jesus said to his disciples, "Those who want to come with me must say no to the things they want, pick up their crosses, and follow me."

Matthew 16:24

The stuff Jesus said while he walked this earth was, and still is, radical and even offensive to our ears. Deny yourself and take up your cross? What a thing to say! Aren't we supposed to look out for number one and stand up for ourselves? His words made no sense to the natural mind. He encouraged things like forgetting about self-protection, self-interest, and self-promotion. **Jesus asked people to consider themselves significant only insofar as they were slaves to the master** (see Matt. 6:24). And he said that out of that way of thinking comes all kinds of good stuff like love, blessings, and wisdom (see Matt. 7:24–27; Luke 11:28; John 9:31; 15:10).

Before Jesus got here, humans had to offer animal sacrifices for the forgiveness of sins. The blood of an animal would clear them of the wrong they had done. But now, on this side of the cross, you have a permanent sacrifice for your sin: the blood from the lamb they call Jesus. But not only that—you now have the power that was not available before to get it right the first time, and that comes from the Holy Spirit that God has sent to you. If you'll trust him, he'll give you all the power you need to do just what needs to be done.

When he taught, Jesus pushed the envelope and said things like that anger is just as bad as murder and lust is just as bad as adultery. He set such a high standard because God, through his Holy Spirit, now lives in you. He has set up residence. You are his temple, the place he stays, and your life is now a living sacrifice. Your life is no longer your own but has been given to him, and that is why your life needs to be focused not on yourself but on the God you live for.

Those who want to save their lives will lose them. But those who lose their lives for me will find them.

Matthew 16:25

*D*on't try to rewrite the past in your mind by going over and over it again and again. When you start to get all self-conscious about something you did or said or what someone said to you, you start to get introspective. You start looking deep inside and struggling with yourself about what happened. When you do that you get more *self*-conscious than God-conscious. Pretty soon you start to feel all kinds of self-pity, woe-is-me kind of stuff, and that's a sin. That way of thinking says, "I don't deserve this," and focuses on your lack of what you want instead of the abundance of all God has given you, and that gets you into trouble. When you think about it, it's an ungrateful heart that majors on self-pity.

The thing you need to do is to get over it. Let other people be who they're gonna be. Let them think what they're gonna think, and don't hold on to the problem as if thinking about it over and over will somehow make it better. When your mind is on Jesus and his Word, that takes the place of self-consciousness. And you're no longer a victim of your surroundings but a confident and peaceful God Girl who doesn't let the worries of this world distract her from what really matters.

Then Peter came to Jesus and asked him, "Lord, how often do I have to forgive a believer who wrongs me? Seven times?" Jesus answered him, "I tell you, not just seven times, but seventy times seven."

Matthew 18:21–22

orgiveness is something you can give. You just have to realize that people are trying to do the best they can. What someone has done or said to you is never as important as what God has done for or said to you.

It is true that you can't always trust people. They are human and they make mistakes. But you can always trust God, and his position is clear on this: forgiveness is good for you. It comes with a spiritual gift, the gift of freedom. **If you can't get over what someone has done or said to you, then you can't be free from it.** It's gonna keep on haunting you and bugging you until you let go of it. And you can't be too sure that God wasn't using this particular insult or attack to further his kingdom in some way. After all, he himself hardened Pharaoh's heart when he sent Moses to ask Pharaoh to set his people free (see Exod. 9:12). Why would he do such a thing? It may have been to show the people his power and to prove his devotion to them no matter what the obstacles. We don't always know why God allows certain problems in our lives, but we do know that if he allows them, it is for a very good reason.

When people don't do what you want them to do, practice forgiveness and the art of getting over it. Holding on to pain is useless; it only keeps the pain close at hand. So let it go and be willing to offer forgiveness when others ask for it and to get over things even if they never apologize.

His master replied, "Good job! You're a good and faithful servant! You proved that you could be trusted with a small amount. I will put you in charge of a large amount. Come and share your master's happiness."

Matthew 25:21

What are you good at? Are you a good listener? A good promoter? Are you a good problem solver? A good teacher? What do you do well that could help a hurting world?

When you have a talent that can improve the lives of those around you and you don't use it, you lose it. In other words, God promises in Matthew 25 to increase what you already have whenever you invest it for the good of his children. When you use your talents to serve God, you will find yourself with more than you ever imagined. But if you refuse to use the talents he's given you for good and instead you just let them rust or be used for evil, look out—the results could be disastrous. **God didn't give you your talent so that you could just go and bury it out of fear of rejection or failure.** He gave it to you so that you could go out and do all that you can to invest it in the lives of those in need.

Don't feel talented? Everyone has talent in something. Figure out what you are good at. Take a personality test or spiritual gifts inventory. Find out who you are and what you do best, and then do all you can to use those skills to serve others.

When Jesus came near, he spoke to them. He said, "All authority in heaven and on earth has been given to me. So wherever you go, make disciples of all nations: Baptize them in the name of the Father, and of the Son, and of the Holy Spirit."

The backstory behind making disciples is not the needs of unsaved people but the authority of Jesus. He said, "I have authority, *so* wherever you go, make disciples." That "so" means his authority is the reason. He didn't say, "They have needs, so wherever you go . . ." Jesus wants you to tell people about him wherever you go because of his authority, not their needs. This command isn't reserved for the missionary who decides to go somewhere to help a people group. Jesus is talking to everyone about the places they go every day—"wherever" they go.

Jesus' authority comes from God the Father and is important because **his authority can rescue people from everything bad in their lives.** His authority is the power people need to be set free, and knowing that, why would anyone keep quiet about it? If you could heal people of their disease, why would you keep the cure a secret? You wouldn't. You would share it with everyone. And it's the same with the gospel. The message of what Jesus did on the cross is just what the world needs to be saved.

Your only role in others' salvation is just the talking. After that, the rest of it is up to God. So don't be afraid to do your part: talk the gospel. Know it and then tell it. You don't have to argue or debate; just share it and then let God work on their hearts. Just remember that if no one had told you, you'd still be lost and wandering, unsure about your destiny, life, and your role in it. Let the world know the good news of what Jesus has done for you.

Jesus said to them, "Come, follow me!"

Mark 1:17

*A*re you a follower or a leader? When it comes to your life, who is in the lead? You or Jesus? In the Bible the disciples (Christians) were called "followers." A follower is someone who believes the Word of God, is saved by his sacrifice and filled with his Spirit, and imitates Jesus. But just look at the word for a minute: *follower*. A follower isn't out in the lead saying, "Come on! Let's go!" A follower isn't picking the path and then trying to convince the leader he should go where she wants. A follower goes behind. A follower does whatever the leader says and goes wherever the leader leads.

When you pray, are you in front of God directing him to where you want to go next, or are you behind him asking where he wants you to go next? It's really easy to try to direct God when you pray. It's easy to forget who's God and who's the follower. But do the words "stumbling around in the dark" mean anything to you? Does that ever sound like your life? Well, maybe that's because you've run ahead of the light. If you would fall back and follow the light, like walking through the dark with a flashlight in your hand, then you would be able to see better and stumble less.

Follow Jesus. Don't look back at him and say, "Are you keeping up?" Fall back and follow. Rest. Be calm. Wait. And move out as he moves out. When you follow God instead of trying to lead him, your steps will be more confident and firm.

Jesus was angry as he looked around at them. He was deeply hurt because their minds were closed. Then he told the man, "Hold out your hand." The man held it out, and his hand became normal again.

Mark 3:5

When there is something in your life that needs to be done, a change that has to be made, a direction that needs to be taken—ask God to help you and he will. But the important thing to know is that God doesn't do the work *for* you. He does the work *with* you. That means that you have to get up and move. You have to make the change, and as you do, he changes you.

Jesus told the man with the withered hand, "Hold out your hand," and as soon as he did, he was healed (Mark 3:5). He believed God and reached out his hand because of that belief.

God promises victory, but only after action.

Is there something in your life you don't like, something you know needs to be changed? Maybe it's a nasty habit or a bad character trait. Whatever it is, it's your turn to move. If you want victory over the trials that come at you, then don't wait around for change—get up and get going! You are a co-laborer with Christ, which means you have to do some of the work. Don't get lazy thinking God will do it all. You have to hear his command "Get up and walk" (Matt. 9:5) and then trust him enough to get up and move.

The scribes who had come from Jerusalem said, ". . . He forces demons out of people with the help of the ruler of demons."

Mark 3:22

In Mark 3:20–30, people are calling Jesus the devil. They are saying that the fact that demons are being released from people means that Satan is letting them go. They are blaming all of Jesus' work on Satan, and this is so obviously blasphemy (any word or action that insults or devalues God).

But what about when you blame stuff in your life on Satan? When you say stuff like "The devil is doing this or that to me," could you possibly be blaming Satan for something that God needs to let happen in your life?

Remember, God disciplines those he loves. And **sometimes discipline can look like an attack from the enemy.** You have to beware of giving Satan too much credit. When you do you can miss out on what God is trying to do in your life. Not all bad things are really bad—a lot are actually happening for your good. They are purifying you, teaching you, and leading you back to God. So don't be too quick to blame everything bad on the enemy. He doesn't have that much power over you. So don't give the Holy Spirit any reason to be upset with you (see Eph. 4:30) by giving the bad guys credit where credit isn't due.

He couldn't work any miracles there except to lay his hands on a few sick people and cure them. Their unbelief amazed him.

Mark 6:5–6

I trust God, I just don't trust myself." When it comes to your life and the needs you have, do you believe God's Word? Do you trust everything he says, but because you know yourself, you just aren't sure you'll get things done?

It's easy to be certain about who Jesus is and his power but still be unsure about yourself. But be careful of thinking like that. The truth is that you aren't unsure about yourself—you know exactly what you can't do. What you really are doing is doubting Jesus. When you fear your future and worry about what you will do, what you will wear, and how you will survive, you aren't just doubting yourself—you're doubting him. When you think you just can't do something or survive something, you have to confess your doubt—not your doubt about your own abilities but your doubt about God's abilities. You have to say, "God, I confess that I don't trust you. I haven't truly believed your Word, and I am completely stressed out because of it. Please forgive me and help me to trust that what you say is true and that you are God, the one who provides and meets all my needs." Just like Jesus couldn't work many miracles in his hometown where so many doubted him (see Mark 6:1–6),

God can't work any miracle in your life until you believe that he can and will.

Jesus asked him, "What do you want me to do for you?" The blind man said, "Teacher, I want to see again." Jesus told him, "Go, your faith has made you well."

Mark 10:51–52

You do not have because you do not believe. Jesus tells you to ask for anything in his name and it will be yours (see John 16:23–24), but if you don't have faith in him to do it, then you won't even think about asking. It's your faith in him that will change your life, heal you, and take out the old and bring in the new. But when you choose worry over faith, you cut the very rope that was there to pull you up, and you stay in the messy goo of your worry and helplessness.

It's super easy to doubt God's ability to help you when you look at your past and think, *I've always had this problem.* When it's a recurring issue, your mind starts to believe it's an irreversible problem, and so you are afraid to ask God to change it. But you have to remember that God likes doing what seems absolutely impossible. If you want to become like Christ, if you want his will to be done in your life, if you seek God with all your heart and boldly walk into the throne room of your Father, he will take away your worry and finish the work that he started in you when you were saved. Be like Bartimaeus—have no fear, just believe.

Jesus went into the temple courtyard and began to throw out those who were buying and selling there. He overturned the moneychangers' tables and the chairs of those who sold pigeons.

Mark 11:15

The temple was considered the holy place where God would come to meet his people. Jesus was very protective of the temple when he walked this earth. The Jews had started to use it for a marketplace instead of a holy place, and when Jesus saw it, he was ticked. He flew into a total rage, turning over tables and scattering their precious stuff all over the floor. He just wasn't going to stand for his Father's temple being used by the people for their own good. It was meant to be reserved for the uses of God alone (see Mark 11:15–19).

When Jesus left this earth and sent the Holy Spirit to live within us, we no longer needed the temple to meet God because now our bodies would be the temple of his Holy Spirit (see John 14:26; 1 Cor. 6:19). That was a game changer. Suddenly people didn't have to go to a certain place to be with God because they had God with them always.

So what does all this mean for your body, the new temple of the Holy Spirit? What kind of a temple are you keeping? Have you used your body for your own good? And would Jesus be pleased, or would he be kicking over tables and taking names? You have to **beware of making your body a temple for your own pleasure and your own service,** because when you do, it's just a matter of time before there will be consequences. No one owns your body but the Lord Jesus Christ, period, end of story. He has instructed you to take care of the temple, not to act like you own it yourself or to share it with a guy other than your husband. When you put everything under God's command, your temple will be as clean as a bleach factory after a tank spill—clean, disinfected, and pure.

Jesus answered, "The most important is, 'Listen, Israel, the Lord our God is the only Lord. So love the Lord your God with all your heart, with all your soul, with all your mind, and with all your strength.' The second most important commandment is this: 'Love your neighbor as you love yourself.' No other commandment is greater than these."

Mark 12:29–31

*H*umility is a part of every act of faith. Only in humility can you love God with all your heart, soul, mind, and strength, and only in humility can you love your neighbor as yourself. You can't love if your spirit is easily caught up in pride. How hard is it for you as a fallen human being to humble yourself and love others regardless of how you feel or what they've done or failed to do to you or for you? Nearly impossible, but that was what Jesus asked of all who heard his message. No commandment stands higher than these two: love God and love others. Love is the very nature of God and the supreme call for all his children.

Following God's Word—believing it and more importantly acting upon it—is a humbling experience. It's a weird twist of fate to find out that, in the words of Christ, "Whoever wants to become great among you will be your servant. Whoever wants to be most important among you will be a slave for everyone" (Mark 10:43–44), but you can trust this is true. You can be sure that God will oppose the arrogant but favor the humble (see 1 Peter 5:5).

That's why it's important to take the first step of humility seriously, and that is the humbling act of accepting the death and resurrection of Christ, understanding that your sin put him on that cross and that because of the way he suffered, you are now set free. **It is a good practice in the life of the God Girl to preach the gospel to yourself every day.** Read the accounts found in the Bible to always keep the truth fresh in your mind so that you can live in true humility, astounded by the amazing love of such a powerful God and touched by his relentless pursuit of you as part of humanity.

He said, "Abba! Father! You can do anything. Take this cup of suffering away from me. But let your will be done rather than mine."

Mark 14:36

*N*othing is wrong with asking God to take your suffering from you and to give you peace. But in the same breath you have to let him know that if he doesn't do what you ask, you still want whatever he wants. That's a hard statement to make, but that's what you say whenever you pray, as Jesus did, "Let your will be done" (Mark 14:36).

God **has a reason for everything he allows in your life, even the suffering part.** That's why we are commanded to be happy when we suffer (see James 1:2). Jesus knew what kind of suffering was soon to come for him, and it overwhelmed him to the point of sweating blood (see Luke 22:44). Nothing has been that hard for you, ever! But let Jesus be your example, knowing that even if your suffering is almost unbearable, you can trust that God's will for you in that suffering is the best will there is. When you are willing to suffer as Christ was willing to suffer, you will gain more faith, hope, and endurance than you could get any other way.

Suffering isn't your enemy or the worst thing that could happen to you. In fact, **it's not even inconsistent with happiness.** If it was impossible for happiness and suffering to coexist, then God would be a liar (see 1 Peter 1:6). No, suffering has tricked you into fearing it. The truth is that suffering isn't something that has to trample you like a wild horse but is something that you can climb on top of and ride to freedom. Suffering doesn't have to overwhelm you, but it can help you grow and make you a whole lot better.

Love your enemies. Be kind to those who hate you. Bless those who curse you. Pray for those who insult you.

Luke 6:27–28

The Mosaic law says this oldie but goodie: "an eye for an eye, a tooth for a tooth" (Exod. 21:24). Getting even and standing up for yourself by giving as good as you got were allowed in the Old Testament days. But then along came the Christ and his radical message that turned this ancient way of thinking on its head. He started telling people to *love* their enemies and even to be *kind* to those who hated them (see Luke 6:27). What a shocking message! Imagine a world where everyone acted this way, where everyone loved other people better than themselves. Heaven, maybe? But in the reality of earth, Jesus' teachings seem to make no sense; in fact, they sound downright insane. What about self-protection, defending your rights, and the all-important issue of fairness?

A lot of things in this world might make sense to you. Like Martha, you might worry about getting everything done (see Luke 10:38–42). Your eyes might be on the present problem and not the eternal God. But as a God Girl **you can't allow the urgent to come before the essential.** The essential of your faith, as taught by Jesus himself, is to " 'Love the Lord your God with all your heart, with all your soul, with all your strength, and with all your mind.' And 'Love your neighbor as you love yourself' " (Luke 10:27). You can't hate your enemies and obey Jesus. Not gonna happen. Nope, the answer is love.

As you study the life of Jesus, look at how Jesus loved his enemies, but don't confuse that with how he rejected *God's* enemies. And as you read Jesus' words, think about what a shock to the system his renegade message would have been to his listeners—and in fact, what a shock it is even today.

Give, and you will receive. A large quantity, pressed together, shaken down, and running over will be put into your pocket. The standards you use for others will be applied to you.

Luke 6:38

One of the big messages we see in the life of Job is patience in suffering. Job learned that both good and bad come from God, and that was how he was able to make it through the worst time of his life. Because he looked at things with a godly perspective, his suffering wasn't in vain. And in the end Job was rewarded for his patient trust in God and given more than he had ever had: more kids, more money, more things.

But don't look at Job and say, "I'm going to be happy in my suffering because I know that I'm going to be repaid double for all I'm going through." That isn't learning to live in patience and longsuffering—that's greed! It's true that God rewards you for your obedience. His Word even says that he will give you more based on what you give and how much that sacrifice hurts. "Give, and you will receive" (Luke 6:38). And his Word says you harvest whatever you plant (see 2 Cor. 9:6). All this is true and amazing, but **to suffer with the hope that you will double your loss in return for your efforts is not faithfulness but greed.** So do good, accept life's trials with patience, and trust that God will bless you in the way that he sees fit.

Each tree is known by its fruit. You don't pick figs from thorny plants or grapes from a thornbush. Good people do the good that is in them. But evil people do the evil that is in them. The things people say come from inside them.

Luke 6:44–45

God tells us that we can judge a tree by the kind of fruit it produces. So if you see a tree with big red apples all over it, you know it's an apple tree. But fruit isn't just a part of the five food groups; it's also a term used to describe the actions of people. The Bible talks about the fruit of the Spirit: those things that grow in the lives of people who live by the Spirit. They are love, joy, peace, patience, kindness, goodness, faithfulness, gentleness, and self-control (see Gal. 5:22–23). When you see this kind of fruit in a person's life, you are seeing the evidence of their faith. And when you see things like complaining, fighting, hate, anger, jealousy, and bitterness, you are seeing the fruit of a life that isn't centered on things of the Spirit.

In your life you will meet all kinds of people who go to church, read the Bible, and insist they believe in God, but as you watch their lives you will see from their fruit that they are living more for their sinful nature than by God's Spirit. **If the people you are** attracted to or already **friends with have some ugly fruit growing in their lives,** then you be the judge: **Are they good for your faith?** Will they benefit your spirit or drag you down?

God lets us have a glimpse into the spiritual lives of others by teaching us about the fruit of his Spirit. And though we can never know if another person is saved, we can definitely know if they are living a life that we want to be a part of. What kind of fruit are you growing? And what kind of fruit do your friends show in their lives? If you want more of God in your life, then find people with the fruit of the Spirit growing strong in their lives, and serve him together.

As they were sailing along, Jesus fell asleep. A violent storm came across the lake. The boat was taking on water, and they were in danger. They went to him, woke him up, and said, "Master! Master! We're going to die!" Then he got up and ordered the wind and the waves to stop. The wind stopped, and the sea became calm.

Luke 8:23–24

D o not sail on the sea using your own will as the wind that directs your course. If you don't let go and let God be the wind in your sails, then at the first storm that comes, you're gonna freak out. Will the sails hold? Will the boat tip over? Will you crash on the rocks?

When you are your own guide and you make things happen yourself, you have no one to turn to when the winds get strong and the waves start to churn. Your faith didn't get you there, so your faith now can't seem to save you when the going gets tough. But for the God Girl who lets God direct her path, even the most cruel storm is nothing to fear. That's because she has put all her faith in the one who commands the winds, so she knows that this storm has come for a reason, and therefore she's not going to fear.

Don't be caught in the wide open sea without an anchor. Trust God with all things, and then when the storm comes, you will be steady. Take the time now to **prepare for the storms by learning God's Word** and, more importantly, putting it into practice in your life. When you are willing to do what God says to do without complaining, then you are ready to weather any storm, no matter how heavy it might be.

He answered, "'Love the Lord your God with all your heart, with all your soul, with all your strength, and with all your mind.' And 'Love your neighbor as you love yourself.'"

Luke 10:27

Is your love selfless or selfish? Selfish love demands something in return. Love, acceptance, kindness, concern—something. It gives, therefore it wants to get. Selfish love is always thinking, "What's in it for me?" And it's always asking, "Why should I love you when you won't love me back?" But selfish love isn't really love at all, because true love thinks nothing of itself but focuses on loving others in order to serve them and Christ, who is our example of selfless love.

Unconditional love is something we all want as human beings. We want to be loved no matter what we do, but how often are we willing to return love the same way? We make demands and set rules on our love, but true love doesn't make demands. It is given freely and abundantly. The only rule when it comes to giving love is that

love for a human can never come before our love for God. Our love should never try to replace the Holy Spirit but should flow from his presence.

How many times do you give kindness and then scream when you get anger in return? How many times do you give advice and then complain when it isn't followed? Do you resent it when you give understanding and compassion and receive nothing of the kind in return? The love you give to others should never be conditional on what you get back but should come from knowing the God who first loved you. You should be compelled by his love, not the response from other people. You should be defined by his love, not the actions of others. When your focus is not getting but giving, then your love will grow, and through that all other virtues will flow.

I can guarantee that although he doesn't want to get up to give you anything, he will get up and give you whatever you need because he is your friend and because you were so bold.

Luke 11:8

The Bible is the story of God's unrelenting love. Over and over again God's people turned their backs on him. Repeatedly they forgot him. And over and over again he made ways to bring them back. There are gonna be times in your life when you get confused about God. "Does he love me?" "Is he listening?" "Is he even there?" But you can't let that confusion overwhelm you. You have to get back into the Word of God to find his promises and to be reassured by all the times that he has fulfilled them. He'll never leave you. And if you feel like he has, then remember the parable Jesus told about the guy who wouldn't open the door when his friend came by (see Luke 11:5–8). The friend was relentless, he wouldn't stop knocking, and to get him to stop the guy finally opened the door. Jesus told this story to tell you, "Don't give up. **God is listening, he is there, and your only job is not to give up when everything in you says he's not gonna come to the door.**"

Something beautiful can be found in persistence in relationship to faith. Don't ever let how you feel at the moment erase the fact that God is always there and always ready to listen. He might not be speaking right now, but that doesn't mean anything to the one who knows his promises. Just keep on going after him. Keep on knocking, and the door will open up and he will be there.

They look for a miraculous sign. But the only sign they will get is the sign of Jonah.

Luke 11:29

*H*ave you obeyed God and not had it turn out the way you thought it would? Have you done what he commanded and then been burned? When doing the right thing ends in the opposite of what you expected, does that mean that your obedience was wasted and there must have been a better option?

A lot of times you will be called to do some crazy things as a believer. Jonah thought preaching to the Ninevites would be crazy (see Jonah 1). Jesus says to love your enemies and do good to those who hate you (see Matt. 5:44)—huh? Sounds dangerous. Turn the other cheek—and get your feelings hurt? Submit—and be controlled? Preposterous! When you do these crazy things, a lot of the time nothing good seems to come of it. So over time you decide God's way just isn't working for you, and the next time you are hurt you retaliate instead of loving. When they say something you don't like, you criticize or refuse to do what you are told to do. You no longer do everything God asks but only what seems smart.

The real issue isn't whether doing the right thing has failed you but how you define failure. If your definition of failure is "not getting what you wanted," then yes, obeying God might lead to failure. But a more **accurate definition of failure is "not doing what God commands you to do."** So if you are obeying God, what looks like a total failure may actually be success in the spiritual realm. The God Girl knows that no matter what the outcome, her obedience will always produce godliness and therefore success, even when all things seem to say otherwise. When the promise seems to be broken and when the answer seems to be no, still she obeys, because she is aware of her eternal reward and spiritual destination. God promises that obedience will not disappoint, and she believes him.

He told the people, "Be careful to guard yourselves from every kind of greed. Life is not about having a lot of material possessions."

Luke 12:15

Greed is about wanting more than you need. It's about saying, "I have to have it right now, and nothing else will do." **When you use more than you need, eat more than you need, or buy more than you need for life,** you'd best beware your tendency for greed. How many times have you told yourself that you had to have something that wasn't essential for life? When you complain that you don't have something that isn't a requirement for living (like food, water, shelter, and essential clothing are), you only prove that you are a slave to yourself. You've let the habit of giving in to the demands of your wants dominate you. And when that happens, it gets harder and harder to break the bondage of self. The word for that condition of thinking more about yourself than others is *selfish*, and it is neither pretty nor biblical. In fact, the exact opposite is true: Scripture repeatedly calls the God Girl to a life of dying to self rather than serving self.

The only way to get free from yourself is through taking a new master, Jesus himself. When you choose to create the habit of becoming a slave to his Word, you set yourself free from your old taskmaster, your greed. Don't let what you think you "need" control you. The only thing you really need outside of food, water, air, and shelter is God himself. Once you look to Jesus as your ultimate master, you can be free.

A rich man had land that produced good crops. . . . He said, "I know what I'll do. I'll tear down my barns and build bigger ones so that I can store all my grain and goods in them. . . ." But God said to him, "You fool! I will demand your life from you tonight! Now who will get what you've accumulated?" That's how it is when a person has material riches but is not rich in his relationship with God.

Luke 12:16, 18, 20–21

It's time to de-accumulate. How much stuff do you own? More than you need? Are there places in your room where you haven't looked in months, maybe even years? It's easy to get so wrapped up in things that you don't even realize how many things you have. How many shoes are enough? How many pairs of jeans? Greed tells you to hold on to things because you might need them one day, but what if someone needs what you have today? If you have things you aren't using, get rid of them. Give away, sell, or throw out ten things this week.

When you're free to give away things and to declutter your life, you're free to be more concerned with things of God than things of this world. Material possessions, the things you own for a short time here on earth, don't last, and they don't improve your life for eternity. As a God Girl you can't let the things of this world become more important to you than doing what God wants. When your stuff becomes too important, that means that stuff may have taken his place in your life. Think about the fact that there are two categories of things in this world: stuff and God. While stuff can be useful for life, it can easily take control of your life and demand your allegiance. When stuff is your obsession, then stuff has to go, because God should be your only obsession. What stuff is crowding out God in your life? What can't you take your eyes off of? When you find it, get rid of it. Don't let stuff get in the way of your relationship with God. Unstuff your life today.

Sell your material possessions, and give the money to the poor. Make your-selves wallets that don't wear out! Make a treasure for yourselves in heaven that never loses its value!

Luke 12:33

*F*ollowing Christ is not going to cost you something; it's going to cost you *everything.* Everything in you that isn't a part of the life of Christ in you has to be purified, cleaned out of your life. And purification hurts. Your heart and body may violently object when something you love is taken away. But the pain of giving up all that isn't Christ in you shouldn't be something to fear but something to look forward to. Because with each part of you that you give up, you get a part of him. And the more you get, the more you become like him.

Giving things up in order to come closer to God, to obey his Word, and to refuse to serve yourself any longer isn't just holy, it's healthy. The truly strong and successful girl is the one who has nothing to prove to anyone but God. She is the one who has said no to all the world has to offer and yes to all that heaven holds and even demands.

When God shows you something that's got to go, be quick to get rid of it. Don't whine about how much you'll miss it, don't wonder if it's really God asking you to give it up, just give it up with the belief that a heart turned over completely to him is a happy heart. And your faith will be rewarded, guaranteed!

None of you can be my disciples unless you give up everything.

Luke 14:33

What does it mean to love Jesus more than your own life? Not a lot of people really know the answer to that Q. It's human nature to think of yourself first, and thinking of someone else first is downright divine. After all, it's *your* feelings that race through your body, *your* eyes that see the world, and *your* heart that feels the pain of rejection, worry, fear, loneliness, and even love. With all these feelings and experiences, it's hard to focus on something other than yourself, yet that's what Jesus wants you to do—to think about him more than yourself. He wants you to love him with *all* of your heart, not just a part of it.

Anything in your heart that isn't holy is not from Jesus and is direct evidence that you love your own life more than his. But don't freak—that doesn't mean you're a lost cause; it just means you're human. Thank God that his grace is freely given to those who realize the error of their ways! So check your life and find those areas of unholiness that make your life miserable or broken. Find out where you need healing, and then decide that your desires aren't as important as his.

Let go of anything that puts focus on your own life rather than the life of Jesus in you. Make him,

his Word, and his character the most important things in your life, and let him know it. Imitate him. Believe him and look at your life through his eyes instead of your own. When you do, you will find that your life and your spirit calm down and all becomes right with the world.

Everyone who honors himself will be humbled, but the person who humbles himself will be honored.

ame is not God's goal for your life. God isn't concerned about making people famous and adored. It's tempting to measure how successful you are as a person by how popular or famous you are, but that's not God's measuring stick. His own Son wasn't born a king or even a rich man but a poor carpenter's son. He didn't run around with a marketing guy or a PR girl, looking for the limelight; he looked for the hearts of people.

When you are really in love with God, you don't look for the attention of the world but you look to give God all your attention. Don't let fame become your goal. In your life, God should always be the famous one, because he's the one people need, the one they crave. God's goal is to humble you, not to feed your big fat ego. People without the Spirit of God can't understand how to resist the call to fame and popularity, but when you have the Spirit in you, he gives you the strength to be perfectly happy when you are perfectly unnoticeable. Don't try to draw attention to your holiness or your amazing prayer life, but work to put all the attention onto him so that whatever you do, you will do it all to the glory of God.

When Jesus heard this, he said to him, "You still need one thing. Sell every-thing you have. Distribute the money to the poor, and you will have treasure in heaven. Then follow me!"

Luke 18:22

*H*as God ever asked you to do something hard? If not, then you probably just weren't listening. At some point Jesus will ask you to do something that seems impossible, like "sell everything," and you'll have to decide whether to take him seriously or to just walk away sad because you know you can't do whatever he's asked.

The life of faith is not going to leave you the same. It's gonna change you, and change can be frightening and hard. But unless you do those hard things, you won't prove your faith. If you walk away like the rich man, sad that God asked too much of you because you really wanted to obey—but not that much!—then you have failed to believe. And when you fail to believe that what God asks of you is the best thing for you, you fail to receive the best that God has for you.

Jesus will never run after you. If you refuse to do the hard things he asks you to do, he's just gonna let you go. He doesn't force himself on anyone, and that's not because he's too arrogant or spiteful; that's because he loves you enough to let you make up your own mind. And he wants you to love him enough to choose the hard way instead of the easy one.

The next time you know God is asking you to do something hard, make yourself do it. Don't let your heart talk you out of it, but summon the will to do whatever he asks, especially the hard things, because that's where your faith is formed. Death isn't easy, but dying to yourself is a requirement of faith. Risk the pain of doing the hard things today and you will soon see the fruit of your faith.

We were hoping that he was the one who would free Israel.

Luke 24:21

If you are feeling depressed about life, it may be because you don't trust in God's providence or his power in this world. Depression is often a result of either getting what you want and realizing it wasn't what you thought it would be or not getting what you want and being upset about it. Either way, that's all about you, not God. But it isn't something you have to live with. Unless you're dealing with a real medical condition, like clinical depression, **feeling better about life just has to do with reassessing what you want.**

When you can change your focus from loving what you want to loving whatever God wants to give you, then depression starts to fade away. When you trust that God is truly involved in the lives of those who love him, then you don't need to be all depressed because suddenly you see things through new lenses. You see life—the good, the bad, the ugly, all of it—as a gift from him, one that you might not understand just yet but trust that one day you will appreciate.

Depression and moping around about life are often symptoms of spiritual sickness, and you can change your attitude if you are willing to trust God and look for him relentlessly. Take your focus off of what you want, need, or demand and put it onto looking for God and finding him in the middle of your mess and your emptiness.

The woman said to him, "Sir, you don't have anything to use to get water, and the well is deep. So where are you going to get this living water?"

John 4:11

H ave you ever felt like the well of your emotions was too deep for even Jesus to manage? Does your soul seem so out of whack, such a particularly depressing case, that not even Jesus himself can get to the bottom of things and heal you? Like the woman at the well, you think your troubles are too deep for him to give you any comfort. When Jesus tells you not to let your heart be troubled, you turn away from him and say, "It can't be done. My well of pain and agony is too deep."

But wait—isn't Jesus the Almighty God? When you say he can't help you, you are denying the Almighty part of his name. There's a reason for that name, and it's that he's, well, "all mighty"—not partly mighty or almost mighty enough but all mighty.

Sure, it's easy for you to go to him as Comforter or Sympathizer, maybe even Provider. But you just can't call him Almighty, can ya? **The reason a lot of Christians don't feel Christ working in their lives is because they have refused to recognize that he is the Almighty.** When you get into a particularly tough situation, don't mock the Almighty by saying, "Of course he can't do what I need. This is just too much for him to fix." Do you really think your problems are bigger than Almighty God? It may seem that way at times, but it's simply not true. So trust yourself to his care and give the Almighty back the power in your life. He has done some amazing things in history and he can do an amazing work in your life too.

Jesus said to the Jews, "I can guarantee this truth: The Son cannot do any-thing on his own. He can do only what he sees the Father doing. Indeed, the Son does exactly what the Father does. The Father loves the Son and shows him everything he is doing."

John 5:19–20

*J*esus never did anything except what the Father himself was doing. In fact, according to his own words, he did "exactly what the Father does" (John 5:19). There wasn't an ounce of "what about me?" in him. He never gave his "needs" a second thought because he was so sure of his Father and his Father's perfect will. And in the life of the God Girl, the same can and should be true.

When life is about anything but what God wants, it gets off track and messy. When you focus on your momentary good instead of your eternal good, you lose sight of what's really important, and like a girl on a bike looking backward instead of forward, you run off the road of faith and right into the nearest ditch. When you take your eyes off of the Father, you're unstable. Not only is your faith no longer grounded, but neither are your feelings or thoughts. And when those get off track, your life goes all kinds of crazy. To be so concentrated on the face of God that you only want what he wants might seem like a tall order, but it's the natural state of the believer. The easy life of getting everything you want never really satisfies; it just leaves you wanting more. The road to heaven is narrow and difficult (see Matt. 7:13–14). It wasn't meant to be so easy that you can say, "Look, Mom, no hands!" as you turn to the left and to the right and go anywhere but straight into the face of God. No, the life of the God Girl demands all of your attention. It will test and challenge you, but if you endure, if you rise above your own personal wants and set your thoughts on things above instead of things below, you're gonna win where you used to lose and be content where you used to be unhappy.

I am the bread of life.

John 6:48

Feast your eyes on this." "You'll get an eyeful." "Eye candy." All of these expressions make the eyes sound like the place on your face where you put your food, the mouth. And that isn't so far from the truth. You ingest things not just with your mouth but also with your eyes. Maybe that's what Jesus meant when he said, "I am the bread of life" (John 6:48) and "feed on me" (John 6:57). After all, you can't literally eat him. So what's with this choice of words?

When you feed on something, you get your strength from it. Eat vegetables and meat, and you'll get strength from them. Without food you get weak and cranky, and eventually you're too worn out to think or even move. Food for the mouth is necessary for life. But another kind of food is essential for the spirit, and that is the Jesus kind. In John 1, Jesus is called the Word, and that's also what we call Scripture: the Word of God. No coincidence here. You feed on Jesus by feasting your eyes on his Word, and that means the Bible.

When your emotional life is on edge, when you feel weak spiritually or your mind is weak and weary, feed it by drinking in the Word of God. Get your strength by devouring truth. When you do, the truth of the Word goes into your mind and through your heart until it nourishes you and teaches you all that you need to live a holy life, and that means a good life. When you devour the Word of God, instead of getting a sugar high or a little extra around the middle, you get things like peace, hope, contentment, and love. As your spiritual life gains nourishment through the Word, your soul is satisfied. So take a big bite and enjoy!

Streams of living water will flow from deep within the person who be-
lieves in me.

John 7:38

J esus didn't say, "Streams of living water will pool deep inside the person who believes in me." No, he's not talking about a green, stagnant pond, covered with lily pads and water skeeters, where all the goodness and blessing stays comfortably inside of you, unmoved by the current. He's talking about a river with a current of blessing and goodness that flows right through you and out to everyone around you.

Contrary to popular belief, Jesus' teachings were never about "finding yourself" but rather about the life that comes out of you. It's a life not for your own comfort and enjoyment but for service to the rest of the world. When you continually focus on yourself, you do the exact opposite of what Christ taught. **Nowhere in Scripture are you called to elevate yourself.** Instead you're told to live for others and not to think more highly of yourself than you should. Jesus' life is the model; he didn't live to find himself but gave all he was as an offering to the Father. And he died on that cross because he loved the world.

In your life that means that you can and should let what God puts into your life freely flow out into the lives of others. When you do, you will find your life is no longer stagnant and murky but is becoming a great source of living water—of hope to the world around you.

After some of the crowd heard Jesus say these words, they said, "This man is certainly the prophet." Other people said, "This man is the Messiah."

John 7:40–41

A lot of people say Jesus was a prophet or a good man but was not God. They'll listen to what he has to say and take some truth out of it, but they won't go so far as to believe that he was who he said he was. See, it's easy to believe only the human parts about Jesus, like recognizing his wisdom and his common sense, but it's another thing completely to believe that he is God, who became flesh and walked among us.

We as believers need to be convinced of who Jesus is. If we only give him credit for being a good guy, we miss out on his very nature and we reject God himself. As you read about his life, you have to decide if Jesus was a wise man with crazy tendencies or truly the Son of God. It's hard to call him just a prophet or a wise teacher when he also called himself God. But consider that each way he described himself points to his divinity: "the bread of life" (John 6:35, 48), "the light of the world" (John 8:12), "the gate" (John 10:7), "the good shepherd" (John 10:11, 14), "life itself" (John 11:25), "the way, the truth, and the life" (John 14:6), and "the vine" (John 15:1, 5). Yep, Jesus called himself God seven different ways. Saying stuff like this about himself made the people who didn't believe him angry enough to send him to the cross. As a God Girl, you need to know this God you serve and love.

Yet, when Jesus heard that Lazarus was sick, he stayed where he was for two more days.

John 11:6

You can't always fear the silence. When you feel like God is nowhere to be found, when you have no sense of his presence but others seem to be high on his love, don't worry. It doesn't mean there's something wrong with you. Love isn't about feeling amazing all the time, and silence doesn't mean he's not paying attention to your prayers.

When Lazarus was sick, Jesus didn't come to see him. He stayed away for two days. And in those two days Lazarus died. To the human eye it looked like Jesus didn't care, but the truth is that he cared very much and he was very aware of all that was going on. Jesus' silence was meant not to torment but to teach. Can you trust him even in the silence? **A lot of times out of that silence can come a bigger revelation than if he had answered you right away.**

When you are absolutely certain of who God is, his silence doesn't scare you because you trust him. He's not frantic, he's not running around trying to fix things, but he's calm and patient and trustworthy. So don't fear the silence or your lack of a sense of him. Just keep on believing and keep on trusting that he has heard your prayer and that because of that, you know he will provide for your needs.

I've given you an example that you should follow.

John 13:15

Defeat isn't always the end, and in fact a lot of times it's the very beginning of life. After all, **Jesus kicked the power of sin by the defeat of his own body.** His victory came not through glory but through pure humiliation and apparent defeat. Even if the path you are on seems hostile and bent on your destruction, that doesn't mean it's the end for you. The hard parts of your life might just be the foundation for your victory. The God Girl never has to fear humiliation or failure because she is sure that God doesn't just use the pretty things of life to bring glory but uses the ugly things as well. He didn't send his Son to earth to wear a crown. He sent Jesus to walk the earth without a place to call home, with nothing but the clothes he wore, and with a mission that would bring all the shame of the world onto his back. And the worst possible situation became your salvation.

While the disciples looked on from a distance, their human eyes saw the end of everything they had imagined about their Jesus. They questioned what they had seen for the past three years. They wondered how they could have been so wrong. That's because they only saw with earthly eyes and didn't see the glory that would come from the suffering of their Savior in the next three days. But at the end of those three days their eyes were opened, and suddenly they found not only the strength to believe but also the strength to suffer no matter how horrific the pain because they could see beyond their present pain and into a far greater and more significant future.

Don't let your pain be your destruction, but make it your salvation. Rise from the ashes in victory. Hold tight to the truth you know about Jesus. And never let go of the cross.

I'm giving you a new commandment: Love each other in the same way that I have loved you. Everyone will know that you are my disciples because of your love for each other.

John 13:34–35

Loving isn't just a suggestion; it's the command on which all other commands are based. As a believer, you have nothing without love—but that doesn't have anything to do with the love you are getting; it's all about the love you are giving. It is super duper important that you love other believers, and a lot of times that means giving in, losing, and turning the other cheek. If you are unwilling to do those things, you are unwilling to love. Love is selfless; it chooses to give no matter what it gets in return. When Christians love only people who love them, they don't prove to anyone anything about who God is. They only prove their hypocrisy. It doesn't make sense to accept the love of God, who doesn't owe us anything and who we turn away from daily, and then refuse to love others when they hurt or reject us. Christian love is a sign to the world that God is greater than our needs and feelings and a sign of his great power in our lives.

If your love defines you, then who are you? Do you look like the God who loves you or like the world that surrounds you? When you understand the power of love and God's command to love, then you will truly be set free from the chains of rejection, fear, and loneliness. Then you will be able to see everything in the light of love, and out of that will come blessings for you and for those you love.

Take heart—love never fails. It might be rejected and it might give you pain, but that doesn't make it less valuable or rewarding to your soul. The God Girl will be known by her love. And the love that she offers will impact the hearts of not only those who receive it but also the girl who gives it.

I will do anything you ask the Father in my name so that the Father will be given glory because of the Son.

John 14:13

*Y*ou don't need prayer in order to live, but you do need prayer in order for Christ to live in you. If you don't eat food, you starve your body, and if you don't pray, you starve your spirit. Prayer isn't about asking so that you can get things for yourself but so that you can know God more.

You have to give Jesus a chance to do what he said he'd do: answer your prayers. But if you aren't praying, then how's he gonna do what he promised? You are a part of the deal. But think about what you ask for. Do you ask for more wisdom or more popularity? Do you ask for more faith or more things? God will give you what you ask for when what you ask for is what you need. And what the God Girl needs is more of the life of Christ in her. When you let that happen by praying, you're gonna find yourself with exactly what you want. When your will lines up with God's, the sky's the limit. That's why it is so important to study God's Word and to understand it for yourself. As you study and pray consistently, your life will become a vehicle for the power of the living God.

If you feel weak and ineffective, then it's time to pray. If you want more of God and his wisdom, then get to praying. Don't let your sin be a sin of prayerlessness, but be devoted to looking for the only one who can save you from everything that would hurt you.

I'm leaving you peace. I'm giving you my peace. I don't give you the kind of peace that the world gives. So don't be troubled or cowardly.

John 14:27

Is your life all calm right now, or is there some turmoil, some wavy seas? Where's the peace that Jesus left you? Where's the peace he said he gave you so that you won't be troubled? Wouldn't you rather have that than the mess you're living in right now? Good. Then take it; it's yours.

The peace you want hasn't been yours so far because you are concentrating on yourself instead of God. That's the secret of faith, ya know: concentrating on God, not on you. When you put your mind on you and your troubles, you are bound to be a wreck. That's because you don't have what it takes to calm the seas, but Jesus does (see Matt. 8:23–27).

So take your eyes off of your stuff and turn them onto him. Look God in the face and find peace. Don't worry about taking your eyes off the trouble as if you're taking them off the steering wheel of life—you aren't. Looking up instead of in is really the only way through the maze of life. You don't know what's around the next corner, but God does. You can't tell when this path ends and another begins, but God can. If you want peace, then peace is yours for the taking. Just give up fighting for it and focus on him.

Live in me, and I will live in you.

John 15:4

*J*esus commands you to live in him. But how do you do that? What does it mean? How do you live "in" someone? How do you live with anyone who isn't physically with you?

The way you live with Jesus and stay attached to the vine is through your thoughts. That means the more time you spend studying, reading, praying, and thinking of him, the stronger your connection will be. When you find there are times that he slips off your already full plate or you just don't have the strength to obey, you need to look at your thoughts. How much thought time do you really give to your God? Does he get ten minutes of uninterrupted thought a day? One hour?

Without spending a good amount of time thinking on Jesus, you will not live in him. Sure, you're busy. You have so many demands on you and so much to do, but without time spent with Jesus, you won't have the energy it takes to do it all. And you certainly won't have the power to handle the temptations that come your way every day. The truth is that you never have enough time to not spend time with Jesus. The more you have to do, the more time you need to spend with him. He is your source of strength. He is the one who will make you fruitful and productive. If you are feeling insufficient, then it's time to check your thought life. Are you living in him or leaving him for other "more important" things? You don't have the strength to do it all by yourself. You need to live in him in order to get done what you have been given to do.

He will come to convict the world of sin, to show the world what has God's approval, and to convince the world that God judges it.

John 16:8

When the Holy Spirit reveals sin in your life, it's natural to feel unworthy of the kindness of God. But you can't let feelings of unworthiness become more important to you than the gifts of God. It can be easy to condemn yourself, easy to be overwhelmed with feelings of guilt and then to make that the final word on your soul. But God has the final word on your holiness, not you. When he offers forgiveness, he offers it regardless of how unworthy you feel. Your feelings are no judge of truth. God's truth is the only thing that matters. To hold on to your unworthiness, then, is to sin. It's trying to make your rules trump God's.

One of the Holy Spirit's jobs is to convict you of your sin, which shows you how unworthy you are, so don't be shocked by the experience. Accept the truth of it and the truth that God sent Jesus as a ransom for your sin. Don't hold on to your unworthiness as if it's more important than the salvation Jesus gave you, because when you do, you worship your unworthiness more than you worship God.

I've told you this so that my peace will be with you. In the world you'll have trouble. But cheer up! I have overcome the world.

John 16:33

Ever feel like everything and everyone is against you? Is your life sometimes a battle? That's normal and even good. The natural state of things is not order and peace but mess and strife. Things naturally deteriorate, just like if you ignore your room, eventually the mess will overwhelm it. So don't be shocked when life gets hard; just decide whether you want to let the battle ruin you or improve you.

Your natural state is a mess too—sinful, not holy. **Nobody is holy because they can't help it.** They are holy because they stand and fight. They refuse to let the world win and make them into its likeness. Jesus made it clear: "In the world you'll have trouble" (John 16:33). When you feel like the world is against you, say, "No duh. What else should I expect?" Then decide if you will roll over and accept the attacks or refuse to let them knock you down. When you choose holiness, you choose to say, "Hit me with your best shot. I have a King who has overcome, so I'm not afraid." Every time your flesh cries out in fear but your mind chooses to believe God and to take him at his word, you are winning the continual battle for holiness. So remember Jesus' words: "I've told you this so that my peace will be with you. In the world you'll have trouble. But cheer up! I have overcome the world" (John 16:33).

Jesus told Peter, "Put your sword away. Shouldn't I drink the cup of suffering that my Father has given me?"

John 18:11

*P*eter was adamantly opposed to the suffering of Christ. He wanted Jesus to avoid it completely. But suffering can't be avoided; no matter how much you fight it, it's gonna come. Everyone suffers in this world. For example, a lot of girls suffer insults and meanness from other girls. But what's important isn't that suffering but the *result* of that suffering. Will you let it destroy you, or will you let God use it for your good?

Like the athlete who strains her muscles to make them stronger, sometimes you have to suffer in areas where you are weak so that your strength will be complete. God uses your suffering to draw you to him, to make you stronger, to purify you, and to produce endurance and character. When you can accept that, then suffering will be something you can not only handle but rise above. It won't have such agonizing power over you, because you will have become stronger because of it.

Suffering has a purpose in the life of the God Girl. It is never in vain as long as you pay spiritual attention to it so it can make you more holy. So when you feel like fighting your suffering or even the one who seems to be bringing it upon you, put away your sword and follow Jesus' example instead.

You will receive power when the Holy Spirit comes to you. Then you will be my witnesses to testify about me in Jerusalem, throughout Judea and Samaria, and to the ends of the earth.

Acts 1:8

When Jesus was arrested, all the men who followed him ran off like scared little boys. They went from following a rock star to following a common criminal, and it freaked them out. A lot of them started to question how he could die if he really was the Son of God. They hid out and tried to figure out what to do next. But then something changed, and those scared boys suddenly became brave and fearless men. What happened? They saw Jesus, that's what. Before Jesus came back to life, these guys were scared and hiding, trying to figure out where they got it wrong. But once they saw the risen Jesus, they were convinced he was God, and from then on nothing could stop them.

As a God Girl **you have to become convinced that Jesus is who he said he was.** Nothing in you can be afraid of being associated with him, like Peter was. When things look bad, when God's Word seems to be failing, the God Girl doesn't give up on him. She doesn't turn tail and run, but she stands strong and fearless because she has seen the risen King and given him her full allegiance.

Millions who have gone before you have decided that they would serve Christ no matter what happened. Take a look at Peter, the scared one who denied Christ three times (see Matt. 26:69–75). Now all of a sudden he's filled with the Holy Spirit and talking to everyone about Jesus, like a totally different guy. When Jesus becomes real to you and you see your life start to change because of his presence in it, your bravery grows and you want to tell everyone about him. The book of Acts is a good example of this. Notice how the early believers loved and took care of each other and how nothing, not even the threat of death, could derail them from their mission to tell the world about Jesus.

Peter and the other apostles answered, "We must obey God rather than people."

Acts 5:29

When given the choice between doing what you want and doing what your friends or even your enemies want, which do you choose? What about if what God wants is going to cost you dearly? What if it means people won't like you, or worse yet, they will hate you or hurt you? How do you decide who you're going to obey in those situations?

Your faith requires obedience. Any going the other way and doing what people want instead of what God wants is sin. When the apostles were told to stop talking about Jesus or else, they didn't give a rip about the "or else" part. They just did what they were meant to do: preach the truth. If you want to be sure to always choose God over anybody else, then you've got to find out what God wants you to do—and that starts with reading his Word. You might not be called to preach, but you are called to love your enemies, to give to those in need, and to respect authority.

Your life will be much easier and involve a whole lot less guesswork once you find out more about God's will for your life—his commands, his thoughts, and his plans. The Bible was written to instruct you on how best to live your life, so reading it shouldn't be a boring prospect. So dive in today and find out something you didn't know about God and his will for your life.

Suddenly, an angel from the Lord stood near Peter, and his cell was filled with light. . . . At that moment the chains fell from Peter's hands. . . . Peter followed the angel out of the cell.

Acts 12:7, 9

*D*o you feel trapped by doubt? Are you living in isolation and fear of what other girls are thinking or saying about you? When you feel like the walls are closing in and everything and everyone is against you in these ways, you have landed in an imaginary prison of your own making. The walls feel as real as any prison walls ever could be. You are as paralyzed and as stuck as you would be if someone had really locked a door and thrown away the key. But the walls aren't real. Like a mime in a box, you struggle to free yourself from the nonexistent cell. As you moan about your inability to get out of this mess, you reinforce the walls, the bars, and the cold hard floor where you restlessly sleep each night.

How tragic to sentence yourself to a prison that doesn't really exist. How crazy to believe all is lost and everyone is against you. Even **if everyone around you is against you, is your God all you need to sustain you no matter what, or isn't he?**

For the child of God, there is freedom. The walls can hold you only as long as you keep your eyes on them. Once you stop considering your difficulties and start considering God's truth, you will find an open door to walk through. To be free, all you have to do is recognize that nothing matters except the call of God on your life and that nothing happens to you unless God allows it in order to teach you something. Let go of your need to fear the outside world and walk free, just like Peter walked out of his prison on the night the walls shook and God set him free (see Acts 12:1–11).

I humbly served the Lord, often with tears in my eyes. . . . But I don't place any value on my own life. I want to finish the race I'm running. I want to carry out the mission I received from the Lord Jesus.

Acts 20:19, 24

When life starts spinning out of control, when you feel like you can't go on, and when nothing is going your way, there is something you can do: remember the bottom line. Review the facts—just the facts is all you need. Answer these questions:

1. **Is God who he says he is?**
2. Does he love you or not?
3. Is his will good or bad?
4. **Does anything happen to you without him allowing it?**
5. Does he truly work everything together for the good of the people who love him?
6. **Do you want God's will or your own?**

If you can honestly answer these questions, then you can get over any trauma in your life and get to the truth of the matter. After all, your feelings are just your simple interpretation of a situation, a lot of times without considering the facts of the matter. When you panic about life, you miss out on the bottom line—the truth about God and his role in your life. For a true believer, life is never spinning out of control and never near disaster. It is always built on the rock and safe under his wings. When you allow your emotions to become your sacred truth, you lose all hope and worry sets in. If you want to be free from fear and angst, you have to remember the facts. When you can look at your life through the reality of God's love and will for you, then you will find a whole new life full of peace and calm.

I fell to the ground and heard a voice asking me, "Saul! Saul! Why are you persecuting me?" I answered, "Who are you, sir?" The person told me, "I'm Jesus from Nazareth, the one you're persecuting."

Acts 22:7–8

There is nothing you can do that can't be forgiven except to deny that God is God. If you have made him Lord of your life, then you have forgiveness for all of your stuff. All of it! There is no dark corner, no seedy past, no horrible mistake that can't be wiped clean. If God could forgive Paul, who persecuted Christians, and turn him into a holy man who wrote much of the New Testament (see Acts 22:1–21), then surely your sin isn't too awful to be forgiven as well.

If you think your sin is too huge for the blood of Christ to cover, then you're saying that Christ died for nothing. But you know that isn't true. His death was sufficient to bring forgiveness to anyone who wants it, including you. You are not the most loathsome creature to ask for forgiveness. You are not a special case; you are a human case. And we are all the same: dirty, rotten sinners in need of salvation. Just agree with God that your sin was evil against him, and every part of your past will be forgiven and cleansed. That means you don't have to hold on to it any longer. You don't have to worry about it, regret it, or wonder about it. It's gone—as far as the east is from the west (see Ps. 103:12).

Once you accept his forgiveness, you will be made new. Your life can be redeemed to change the world, just like Paul's was. You can be freed from your old, empty way of life and set on a new path toward becoming the woman God wants you to be.

You will be his witness and will tell everyone what you have seen and heard.

Acts 22:15

What kind of a witness are you? Is your life proof that Jesus is who he says he is? Or are you less of a witness and more of a weakness? Your life may be the only Bible that the people around you read, so when you take God's Word and apply it to your life, they see what it says and what it does. But if you take his Word and hide it, then how will they ever know the truth?

As a God Girl you must be ready to be a witness to the saving power of Jesus and the life-giving nature of faith. Everything you do can and should be evidence of him. It might sound harsh, but your responsibility in life is not just to yourself but also to those in your circle who are watching you and need you to be the hands and feet of Christ. Don't worry if you have failed at that so far—today is a new day. The old is gone, the new has come.

So today make a fresh start and decide that everything in your life happens so that you can be a Bible to the people around you. How you react will be your witness. What you say and how you say it all will impact the kingdom. This isn't more than you can handle; it's what you were made for. Either Jesus is who he said he was or he isn't—how you act today will prove your answer to everyone who is looking! Be the witness you were made to be.

Both groups were expected to change the way they thought and acted and to turn to God. I told them to do things that prove they had changed their lives.

Acts 26:20

*W*hat are you doing that proves your life has changed? When you were saved, you became a new person. But sometimes you still resort to your old ways of thinking, acting, talking, and even believing. But that won't do. You can't hang on to who you were. The old you with all of its selfish ways used to guide your life, but now a greater God does that, so you have to let go of your old nature and hold on for dear life to the new nature. Prove to yourself, to God, and to others that you aren't the same person you were.

As a God Girl you are growing, changing, and forever becoming the new and improved you. As you grow up you have to choose between the old and the new. Are you gonna go back to your old ways, or will you keep moving toward a more holy way of life? Becoming more like Christ is a hard job, but it's a command (see Rom. 13:14; 1 Cor. 11:1). Don't let the world tell you that compromise is okay because holiness is too hard. You need to imitate his perfection, not respond to your flaws by saying, "That's just who I am, so deal with it." No, that's not who you are; that's who you *were*. Now you are a new person—changing, growing, becoming a better girl and an amazing woman.

Look at the life of Paul. He was a violent person, persecuting early believers (see Acts 26:11), but he changed when he was given a new nature in Christ. You have to do the same. You can become more like Christ every day. And when you do, your reward will be good stuff like hope, joy, and peace—everything that comes from obeying the Word of the living God.

No matter who you are, if you judge anyone, you have no excuse. When you judge another person, you condemn yourself, since you, the judge, do the same things.

Romans 2:1

*D*on't judge others for their weaknesses. If the only thing you can control is yourself, then complaining about the sins or weaknesses of other people is a waste of your time. No matter how much you whine about them to how many people, you aren't going to change them. All you're doing is sinning by finding fault and complaining. When you are constantly occupied with things beyond your control, you just end up feeling frustrated and bitter—not the holiest of emotions.

The sins of other people will get more and more obvious the closer you draw to God, but so will your own sins, so concentrate on those and leave the sins of others to them. Stop the wrestling with thoughts of how bad they are and confess that by just thinking such a thing, you show yourself to be worse than them, according to Romans 2:1.

You should find some comfort in this thought: no matter who you are or what you've done, this verse applies to the people around you as well. Just like we are told in Romans 3:9–10, everyone is under the power of sin, and that means that none of us should think any more highly or worse of ourselves than is proper. We find the most hope in all of this in Romans 8:1, which says, "So those who are believers in Christ Jesus can no longer be condemned." We are all down here in the same boat. And while we are to judge right from wrong (see 1 Cor. 2:15; 1 Thess. 5:21) and to avoid sin at all costs, we are not to spend our strength on judging others when there is plenty of sin within us that needs to be addressed.

*When you judge people for doing these things but then do them yourself,
do you think you will escape God's judgment?*

Romans 2:3

When something about another person disgusts you, look
out. When you judge them for their bad behavior, beware.
Judgment is God's job, just like revenge (see Heb. 10:30).
And to put yourself in the place of judge is to condemn yourself,
according to Romans 2:1. When your judgment nerve flares up, the
first thing you should do is look at whether the thing you so hate in
them might be the same thing that you do to God or to others. You
usually will be offended by and judgmental of the things in others
that you subconsciously see in yourself, and that anger that lies just
beneath the surface is where your resentment comes from.

**To decide what's right and wrong isn't a sin, and neither is point-
ing out sin. But when you judge another person without knowing
why they did what they did or having the whole story from the
horse's mouth, you're wrong.** You have to remember that your tendency is to sit in judgment of others and quickly find them guilty like
you're both judge and jury, and while their sin might be totally obvious,
you aren't ordained to try them or to condemn them (see Acts 10:42).
Certainly you have to judge whether their sinful actions should be a
part of your life or you should avoid them altogether, but that's just
making a judgment call, not being judgmental—see the difference?

As a God Girl you can and should correct other believers (see 2 Tim.
4:2) and help each other to spot the secret sins in life, but don't do it
with a judgmental heart. Human judgment resents the sins of others
and rehearses their sins over and over in disgust. And this kind of
judgment colors your feelings, occupies your thoughts, and leads to
sin. Don't be ignorant of the sins of your friends and family, but don't
condemn them either. What you need to do is to pray for them, correct
them, and share God's Word with them in love. And while you're at
it, ask God to show you if you have the same sin in your life.

Because all people have sinned, they have fallen short of God's glory. They receive God's approval freely by an act of his kindness through the price Christ Jesus paid to set us free from sin.

Romans 3:23–24

*G*uilt is not from God. When Jesus died on the cross, he took away your guilt. So guilty feelings are not telling you the truth. Conviction of sin? Now that's from God. He makes you feel convicted, like a little red flag is waving in your brain to tell you "Something ain't right here," but that's totally different from those feelings of guilt you are living with. God's Word is clear that not one person has God's approval (see Rom. 3:10). That means that no one can get God's love by never messing up or sinning, so you're lying to yourself if you think that you are a special case who should be perfect and never mess up. The truth is that everyone has turned away and is rotten to the core; no one does anything good (see Rom. 3:10–12).

But in the book of Romans, Paul makes it clear that sin isn't the end. Because of confession and repentance, guilt doesn't stick to the believer, and so **the God Girl can be free from the guilt of anything she has done.** When you confess with your mouth that you were wrong and God was right and you promise to turn from your error and go a new direction, you are no longer guilty—period, the end (see 1 John 1:9). Therefore **any guilt that you feel is just that: a feeling.** And don't you know that feelings can't be trusted? How many times have you felt something only to be proven wrong? Emotions can't be trusted, but God's Word can. You're believing a bald-faced lie if you think that you are still guilty once you've confessed your sin. Jesus came to set you free, not to keep you in guilt. His death and resurrection means that the one who has confessed and turned away from sin is no longer guilty.

*We know that suffering creates endurance, endurance creates character, and
character creates confidence.*

Romans 5:3–4

*A*re you a rescuer—forever helping people in need, saving
them from trials and temptations? If you find that you aren't
hearing from God or that you want more from your spiritual
life than you are getting, then it might just be because you are trying
to play God in the lives of your friends.

Suffering is a powerful tool in the hand of God. He uses it to shape
people and to move them toward him. If you feel a need to stop the
suffering of others and to give them advice that you have no right
to be giving them, then you might be putting something between
them and the voice of God. You can most certainly give advice to
others, but it has to be advice that you come to through discernment
and constant prayer. It shouldn't be off the cuff with the sole goal of
relieving the other person's pain.

Always get back to God's Word. Are they suffering because they
refuse to obey? Can God make something out of their suffering? What
do they need to learn from this experience? Don't always think that
your job is to help them get away from the trial. Sometimes the most
important thing is for them to stay in it and to fall on their knees in
complete surrender to the only one who can truly save them. Let
others need God more than they need you,
and stop playing God in their lives.

Certainly, sin shouldn't have power over you because you're not controlled by laws, but by God's favor.

Romans 6:14

*D*on't hate the sinner; hate the sin." You've heard it before, but how does that apply to you? Your sin is no excuse to hate yourself. You fail. You fall. You sin. And your sin is horrible. But there is a cure, and it's called the kindness or grace of God. It is powerful and effective. No sooner do you say "thank you for your forgiveness" than your sins are totally cleaned up.

Your sin is just your love affair with something other than God.

So the cure is deciding to agree with God, and that means hating your sin, or just calling a sin a sin instead of pretending like you aren't sure if it's bad or not. If you have to ask, deep down you know the answer. But you have to remember: don't hate yourself; hate the sin. What's so ugly is not you but the sin in you. It's the sin that's gotta be destroyed, not you. You can gain total self-control when you accept the fact that your sins are forgiven as soon as you hate them as much as God does and you promise to walk away from them instead of protecting them. You must choose to hate sin, because when you love your sin you reject God.

If you are tired of sin and tired of being unproductive for God, then start with the question "What do I love more, my sin or my God?" Only the right answer will set you free and bring you back into a position of soul integrity, where you aren't divided between your loyalty to God and sin, but instead you are consistent in your faith in the one who saves you from your sin.

Either your master is sin, or your master is obedience. Letting sin be your master leads to death. Letting obedience be your master leads to God's approval.

Romans 6:16

*Y*ou cannot serve two masters, but you will serve one. Whom do you serve? If you are a God Girl, then you are a servant of God, and not only that but his slave. A slave serves only the will of her master and nothing else. She is devoted to her master and her master's needs. An *employee* can serve two bosses, like having a day job with one boss and a night job with another. But as a God Girl you don't have that luxury. **You can't obey your master sin and your master God—you must obey one or the other.** Who is your master? Finding the answer is easy: do you give in to the call of God only, or do you sometimes serve other gods, such as the god of comfort, popularity, sex, or food?

If you serve another god, then you are not yet a slave of Jesus Christ. Slavery to him annihilates slavery to sin. Want to be free from the bondage of sin in your life? Then give your life, your choices, and your days over to the Master. Think of yourself as dead to sin, and it will no longer be your master. As a God Girl you don't have to be controlled by anything any longer. Your **freedom is found in calling sin sin.** Jesus' resurrection bought your freedom, and because of that you can have confidence that God is beside you helping you to break free from any power that threatens to control you (see Rom. 6:8–18). Yes, we all have sinned and will continue to sin, but sin doesn't have to be your master anymore. Determine that you won't let your life be controlled by anything but God and you will serve only him.

Now you have been freed from sin and have become God's slaves. This results in a holy life and, finally, in everlasting life.

Romans 6:22

*H*ave you been freed from sin? Or are you still in bondage? If a sin still controls you, then you have your answer. You're still a slave to something other than God.

When you are a slave to sin, you can't get out from under its control, and the result, according to God's Word, is death (see Rom. 6:23). But when you are a slave to God, the result is a holy, even everlasting life. See the difference? One pays you with death and the other pays with life. Jesus came to set the captives free, not to make them feel more comfortable while in captivity. The freedom he gives you is complete; it takes off the chains of sin and destroys its power over you. Does that mean you aren't going to sin anymore? Nope, but it does mean that sin can't be your master anymore (see Rom. 6:12–14). In other words, you might sin occasionally in an area you used to sin in, but you won't keep giving in to its call day in and day out, because you have found salvation from sin, a way out of it.

The Israelites were set free from slavery to the Egyptians, but when things got tough in the desert they wanted their slavery back (see Exod. 14:12). They liked the control more than the faith that they needed to survive in the desert. **Sometimes slavery is more appealing than trust.** It's definitely more familiar, and what's familiar can seem easier, **but slavery to anyone other than God is never really easy.** That is a lie, because when you're a slave to sin you're out of control and out of God's will.

Freedom can be yours when you realize that sin isn't your master anymore and that Jesus came not to just send you to heaven but to free you from captivity to sin.

I take pleasure in God's standards in my inner being. However, I see a different standard at work throughout my body. It is at war with the standards my mind sets and tries to take me captive to sin's standards which still exist throughout my body.

Romans 7:22–23

*H*as the truth set you free yet? Or is there something in your life that controls you, your emotions, your fear, your worry, and your happiness? The truth is that until you are willing to listen to the truth, you will be a slave to the lies you believe. At some point in your life you gave in to yourself. You yielded to something you desperately wanted, and as a result you became a slave to that thing you wanted. When you are enslaved to your whims, it becomes very hard to see your chains, because after all, you willingly put them on, and you hold the key.

At the point when you gave in to your deep desire or lust for something, you became a slave to that thing. And even though you might hate it now, nothing you do to try to get rid of it will rescue you. You don't have the strength to free yourself, but there is hope, and it's found in knowing the truth. You have to honestly look at yourself and the Word of God and find out where you are believing a lie. So if there is something in your life that enslaves you and you want freedom from that, read verses about that topic and discover where your mind is disagreeing with God's Word. Think about what you believe about that thing, and then search the Word to find out if that is truth or a lie. Freedom requires truth, and the truth will set you free (see John 8:32).

Those who live by the corrupt nature have the corrupt nature's attitude. But those who live by the spiritual nature have the spiritual nature's attitude.

Romans 8:5

What do you want in life? What you want says a lot about who you are. **If you could look at a piece of paper that lists everything a person thinks about, wants, and really loves, you could see the soul of that person.** So what's on your piece of paper? What is your focus in life, your obsession? If someone were to read your soul, what would they see?

If you aren't sure of the answer, then it's time to take an inventory. Find out what occupies most of your thoughts. Make a list. Keep a journal of the things you think about, want, and do. Write a small record of your soul. What is its focus and what takes up most of your mind space?

When you have the answer, then you'll see where changes need to be made. No one's thoughts are perfect, and no one spends enough time thinking about God, but that doesn't mean you should just accept the status quo. You need to decide that your thoughts need a little cleaning up. How can you take your thoughts and attention off of the world and turn them to God? When you start to replace the worldly things in your life with God, your life will start to change. What used to bother you, you won't even notice anymore. What you used to be afraid of will be nothing of importance. Change how your mind spends most of its time, and you'll change your life!

Those who live by the corrupt nature have the corrupt nature's attitude. But those who live by the spiritual nature have the spiritual nature's attitude. The corrupt nature's attitude leads to death. But the spiritual nature's attitude leads to life and peace.

Romans 8:5–6

In the life of faith the question is never what God's going to do but what you're going to do. God's Word makes it clear what he will do, but your choices aren't so certain. When you know there is something to be done, you have to be sure that you will do it. That means that you must turn your will to doing that one thing. No matter how hard it is, you have to decide to do it. Your actions follow your will. If you really just want to go play, then you're going to go play instead of praying or reading. Your mind speaks to you, quietly prodding you to do what it has already willed. So if there is some area in your life where you feel like you just can't do the right thing, then think about the fact that maybe you just don't want to do it. Sure, you know you should, but deep down you just don't want to. The reason is usually that there is some good payoff in doing the wrong thing; it's something you really enjoy and don't want to give up. It might be the worst habit in the world, but it gives you something you really want, even though you might be totally oblivious to it.

So take a deeper look at your bad habits and your will. What do your habits provide for you? Peace, hope, joy? Then remember that those things are what God promises to give you. Would you turn to something or someone else to give you what God wants to give you? When you see that the payoff of sin is more exciting to you than the payoff to obedience, you know you have to change that way of thinking. Dig into God's Word and find out the reasons why doing what God wants you to do really has a bigger payoff for your life. Learn about obedience and how God reacts to it. **If you want a habit to be gone, then you have to replace it with something of greater value to your heart.** What do you value, God Girl?

But if God's Spirit lives in you, you are under the control of your spiritual nature, not your corrupt nature. Whoever doesn't have the Spirit of Christ doesn't belong to him.

Romans 8:9

Sin is no longer your master once you have the Spirit of Christ living in you. That's because you belong to him; he's your new master. And that means that you aren't under the control of that sinful nature anymore but are under the control of your spiritual nature. So then why do you keep on sinning? Why do you keep doing the very things you hate?

We all have days when we fall into sin as if we've fallen into some kind of pit, but when the Spirit lives in you, you don't stay in the pit and make yourself at home there. You jump out immediately and decide to avoid that hole in the future.

When you find yourself in a pit but you just don't want to get out, that's when you're in trouble. That's called living in sin, and it's evidence that you aren't living for God. Sin happens, but don't let it be by your choice. Choose to get far away from it once you notice it in your life or in your vicinity. We all sin; we all mess up and do things we don't want to do or didn't mean to do, and that's why Jesus went to the cross for us. But knowing that you're sinful and expecting to sin are two totally different things. Have an expectation that, with the help of the Holy Spirit and spending time in God's Word, you will not sin. But when you do sin, lean on and trust in the Spirit of God that lives in you to master you. In your Spirit be a slave to God—do all you can to please your master, not expecting to sin, but also do not hold on to regret or be surprised when you do sin.

If you live by your corrupt nature, you are going to die. But if you use your spiritual nature to put to death the evil activities of the body, you will live.

Romans 8:13

*Y*ou have to keep reminding yourself what your purpose is in life. Your purpose isn't to be happy or to get what you want. It isn't self-realization or fulfillment. It's holiness. Even though holiness sounds like something just for monks or saints, it's actually for you too. When you read the Bible you learn that you get more holy by becoming more like Christ. Sounds like a tall order, but don't freak out—it can be done.

The way it happens is by the amazing act of dying to self. The act of dying to self is what ultimately fulfills your purpose here on earth. But dying to self is not about hating yourself or hurting yourself but about loving God and other people more than you love yourself. That's the dying part. When you make your life about more than you, it kills a part of you—but not a good part, a sinful part. It kills the part that is self-obsessed instead of God-obsessed. This dying to self reminds you that life is not about you but about him. And it sets you free to live a life filled with peace and hope and love. Those whose purpose is fulfilling themselves are forever in turmoil because when their lives are their main focus, they are out of touch with the hand of God, and anyone who is separated from his hand is living in discord and chaos.

As a God Girl you have a clear purpose: to love and honor God and to search for and crave holiness. Thankfully this is something you don't do alone but do alongside of God. The sacrifice of Jesus means that God can and will work things out between you and himself. It means that holiness can and will be yours when you are in agreement with God and working toward the same goal.

I consider our present sufferings insignificant compared to the glory that will soon be revealed to us.

Romans 8:18

Would you say that being happy is usually your daily goal? Who doesn't want to be happy, after all? Happiness is a good thing; it draws people to you and proves that your faith is unshakeable. But sometimes happiness can start to become an idol, especially when you tell yourself you can't handle life without it. How important is happiness to you? Ask yourself a few questions on the topic:

Would I rather be happy or holy?

Am I happy to be tested (see James 1:2)?

What kinds of sins have I committed in order to find happiness?

Is "because it will make me happy" ever an excuse for sin?

What does God have to say about happiness?

What does he have to say about endurance and suffering?

Why is happiness such an obsession?

What is the difference between happiness and joy?

Sometimes it's good to question yourself just to stay on track. When life starts to get you down, asking questions about your faith, what you believe, and what God says can really help you through the hard times. When it comes to your emotional state, what is most important to you says a lot about your faith. If you think you must be happy at all times, then consider Romans 8:18 and the insignificance of your unhappiness in the grand scheme of things. Happiness is a good thing, and we all want to be happy, but happiness rests in the God we serve and not the circumstances in which we live. You can find the power to be happy even when things go terribly wrong when you trust that God is in control and that no matter how terrible things get, he will never leave you.

I am convinced that nothing can ever separate us from God's love which Christ Jesus our Lord shows us. We can't be separated by death or life, by angels or rulers, by anything in the present or anything in the future, by forces or powers in the world above or in the world below, or by anything else in creation.

Romans 8:38–39

Is a carefree life a holier life? Not necessarily. It's worth very little to have life just the way you want it, and it's worth a lot to have something in your life you wish wasn't there. Why? Well, because it's through trouble, distress, and danger that you get to know the power of God's love.

God doesn't promise to keep you from all trouble, but he promises to keep you close to him in the midst of it. He never promised the God Girl that her life would be free from suffering or testing. When trials come you can trust the power of God to get you through. Some circumstances will come to you because of your own sinfulness, your own mistakes, and these have to be taken like discipline, with confession and repentance. But when things beyond your power plague you, you can't let them become your undoing. When there's something in your life you wish wasn't there, you can never let that separate you from the fact that God is with you.

Trouble, distress, demons, rulers, mean people, even violent death can't separate you from his love. That means that when you're faced with dangers, you can expect to find more of him. The more trials you overcome and cling to him through, the more your character grows along with your absolute confidence that he is who he says he is. So don't be sorry for the troubles in your life but let them be used for your good, not your destruction. Let them always draw you closer to him.

Who do you think you are to talk back to God like that? Can an object that was made say to its maker, "Why did you make me like this?"

Romans 9:20

s there something that used to be yours but isn't anymore? Has something been taken away, gotten lost, or left you? It helps to remember that whatever you've lost has just been returned to where it came from. **Don't worry about losing what you think you own, because you don't *own* anything in the usual sense of the word.** Everything belongs to God, and he can do with it as he sees fit. Nothing owned by Job belonged to Job, and nothing belongs to you.

So instead of feeling angry or hurt because of what has been taken from you, just tell yourself that it has been returned to God to care for and redistribute or protect. Don't be angry with the one who has taken it from you, either. It's not your job to decide who God uses for what purpose. Instead, be like a traveler who rents a room in a hotel and takes care of it while she stays there but gives it back to the owner when she leaves. When you start to think like this, you don't have to live in fear of loss, and you won't be ruined when you lose something or someone that you love. There is great freedom in knowing and believing that God has it all under control and that he gives and he takes away. Ultimately, the God Girl knows that God's ways are not her ways and that if he decides that something or some-one she loves must go, then she has no need to complain because time will prove that his will is perfect. When you lose what you love, it can be easy to talk back to God, to accuse him of not caring for you. And that's what you do when you let yourself become a wreck because of loss. Certainly losing what you love hurts, but the God Girl isn't destroyed by the loss because of her undying trust in the goodness of the God who decides her destiny.

If you declare that Jesus is Lord, and believe that God brought him back to life, you will be saved.

Romans 10:9

Salvation comes in an instant: at the point when you declare and believe, your life changes, and everything you do and think comes into focus in the light of God's Word. A lot of times you can look at your life and start to question your salvation. Was it real? Did I really mean it? The answer to that question isn't hard to find. When God saves you, he changes you. You are no longer the same, always changing, always getting better. Like a tree producing buckets of fruit, you will start to produce spiritual fruit. Things that were once difficult for you will become easier—not all of them, but a lot of them. And you'll find more and more evidence of God's work in your life.

When a girl makes Jesus Lord, she makes him her master (see Rom. 6:16). That means that she takes

her orders from him and not from anyone else (unless he has given them authority over her here on earth). And this position as slave to Jesus is one that proves your salvation was not a passing fancy, a seed planted in the rocky soil and choked out by the trials of life (see Matt. 13:18–23), but a real, life-saving salvation that can't be lost. The God Girl is certain of her salvation because she wants what God wants. She wants to know him more, to know his Word and to obey it, even though she has the occasional mess-up. Forgiveness is free for those who agree with God that they sinned and who can accept the forgiveness that is there for all who believe. It's this forgiveness and your desire to get it right next time that should prove to you that you are saved. And it's your ever-increasing obedience that proves to the world and to God that you have truly made him Lord of your life (see John 15:14; 1 John 2:3–4; 5:3).

Don't become like the people of this world. Instead, change the way you think. Then you will always be able to determine what God really wants—what is good, pleasing, and perfect.

Romans 12:2

*N*ever say no to a gift from God, even if on the surface it looks like more of a curse than a gift. From your human perspective it might just look a lot different than it does from heaven. Think about the most evil thing that has ever happened in the world: the crucifixion of Jesus. It was horrific. And the people who watched it all happen could see absolutely no good in it as they watched it unfold. But they didn't have the perspective that we have now or that they would soon have when they would see him again. Now we all can look on that horrific event with thanks. For us it's the most important thing that ever happened—still horrific, but so important. God can use anything that has happened to you for good. He promises it (see Rom. 8:28). If you have something in your life that is horrible, something that has happened to you that you can't seem to get over or find any redemption in, don't ask "Why me?" Ask "What glory now?" Trust that God will lift you out of the ashes of destruction to glory. Trust that he'll never fail you and that what he wants is perfect (see Rom. 12:2). Everything that happens in your life can either improve when you trust God with it or destroy you; it's your choice. Let God be God and let your circumstances be the force that turns dirt into pearls. It takes pressure and time to make gems and fire to purify gold and silver, and so it goes with character (see Mal. 3:2–3). Don't resent the hard times, but thank God for purifying you and giving you an opportunity to die to yourself and to live for him (see 2 Cor. 5:14–15).

Bless those who persecute you. Bless them, and don't curse them.

Romans 12:14

When you selfishly fight for your rights, you stab Jesus in the heart. When you demand things go this way or that, you might not hurt anyone else, but you do persecute him and cause him to suffer because of your disbelief. You say you love the Lord and you even teach others about him, but your behavior says something different when you stand for anything other than Jesus Christ himself.

Remember, Jesus' call to you is humility. He says, "learn from me, because I am gentle and humble" (Matt. 11:29). He never demanded respect or stood up for his rights. Instead he "left everything to the one who judges fairly" (1 Peter 2:23). **Don't demand more rights than the Son of God himself would demand.** When you are mistreated, stand up for what's right, but don't take revenge. Let God take care of it (see Rom. 12:19). When someone else gets something better than you do, humbly say, "That's okay, I got much more than I deserve when Christ saved me." Trust God with everything and focus on the needs of other people instead of yourself.

When you live your life as Jesus did, you won't be concerned about being slighted, put upon, or ignored because all your thoughts and hopes will be on him. That is true freedom and true faith. Don't let your thoughts of what you want or "deserve" overpower the life of Christ in you. Instead practice being one with him in meekness and humility.

The person who does what he knows is right shouldn't feel guilty. He is blessed. But if a person has doubts and still eats, he is condemned because he didn't act in faith.

Romans 14:22–23

Are you ever unsure if what you're doing is good with God or not? Whenever you have doubts, you should stop immediately. Doubt signals trouble. It's a red flag in the life of a believer, a sign letting you know you've taken a detour. Don't go any farther on that wobbly bridge.

The best rule of thumb is, **if in doubt, don't do it, because if you doubt and do it anyway, you are in danger of falling into sin.** Take some time to search Scripture so that you can be more informed. Don't jump into things you doubt so quickly that you get used to accepting gray areas as okay areas for you to enter. Find out the truth. Be certain that what you do, how you act, and what you say are in line with what God wants from your life. Doubt is like a car gauge—it warns you when you're about to run into trouble. So read the manual and find out what the sign means and what you need to do next. If you have doubt after reading God's Word, or if someone has given you a reason to believe God is against what you are doing, then slow down and dig deeper.

If you can look at all of Scripture and see no command that would make what you want to do a sin, then doubt has no ground to stand on. So many times we worry about whether God wants us to do this or that when the Bible doesn't address the topic at all. If it's not against his Word, then you can stop worrying about if it's the right thing or not and be confident in what you are doing.

You are partners with Christ Jesus because of God.

1 Corinthians 1:30

*A*t the point when you made Jesus the Lord of your life, everything changed. With that one decision came not only a change in your will but also a change in your makeup. Now you are no longer your own but are filled with Christ himself in the form of the Holy Spirit. Scripture says that "you are partners with Christ" (1 Cor. 1:30). Partners are two people who share in doing something together; they work together toward a common goal. This is a big deal, because it means that even when you feel like you can't do what's right, that's okay, because he can. It means that even though you might not realize it or feel like it right now, you have the wisdom of Jesus on your side—and not only that but his righteousness and holiness as well. That means that he is enough. You may fail, you may mess up royally, but you have been made a partner with Christ, and so he will get you out of your mess if you are willing to let him. You just need to trust him to do it.

As a God Girl you aren't just out there doing life on your own. You have been ransomed or bought away from sin, and that means sin no longer controls you and you are part of a holy team now. You might forget that sometimes and give in to sin's commands, but it's not in charge of you any longer. Now you have the wisdom of Jesus on your side, and that means you can be free from sin and all its punishment. The more you read the Word of God, the more you understand God, but don't underestimate the wisdom that's already yours just because you've become partners with Jesus and accepted his Holy Spirit into your life.

You should not associate with people who call themselves brothers or sisters in the Christian faith but live in sexual sin, are greedy, worship false gods, use abusive language, get drunk, or are dishonest. Don't eat with such people.

1 Corinthians 5:11

*T*ough love can look like anything but love. It's the kind of love that says no to a loved one's requests for kindness and to cries for someone to bail them out when their sin has gotten them into a mess that only their repentance can get them out of. And it takes a stand because it knows that a sin that continues to be adored and protected is a sin that can't be forgiven.

In his first letter to the Corinthians, Paul warned the church in Corinth that they could no longer turn a blind eye to the sins of their brothers and sisters. That's because **the one who accepts another in spite of their desire to continue living in sin commits a sin alongside them.** And that is not love; it's codependency, and it encourages the sinner in their self-deception. This kind of false love is always selfish, because it's afraid to confront someone about their sin out of fear of embarrassment or rejection, and that puts fear before God and before the spiritual well-being of the other person. Being a God Girl means being fearless in the faith, unafraid to confront and reject believers who choose to live in sin without confessing it or attempting to repent.

While we should not be on the offensive, attacking the sin of each and every human being we encounter, you should know that your closest friendships need a lot of honesty, and if you, your friends, or fellow God Girls are rejecting God's law by consciously choosing to live in some kind of sin, then you are called to let them know. You might even have to tell them you can't hang out with them anymore if they choose to keep on sinning instead of to start confessing. A sin accepted is a sin committed. Heed the warning of 1 Corinthians, and don't let the approval of your friends' sinful habits become a conspiracy to sin.

The person who unites himself with the Lord becomes one spirit with him.

1 Corinthians 6:17

*C*an you imagine not wanting anything that Jesus doesn't want? When you surrender your will, you unite it with his, and you don't want things that he doesn't want anymore. A **life spent on Jesus is a life that doesn't want anything that would offend him.** This way of thinking can become as natural as breathing. The more you love him, the more you want of him. And the more you eat up his Word, the more nothing interests you but what he wants. And then devotion becomes effortless. When your heart is one with him and your soul wants nothing more than to please him, devotion takes on a life of its own.

The life of Jesus is your example. He didn't want anything but what the Father himself wanted. And he teaches you to want the same thing: "your will be done" (see Matt. 6:10; 26:42). The really successful believer is the believer who can honestly say that she wants God's will instead of her own. Become one with Jesus, decide you don't want anything that would offend him, and your life will be less about the struggles you face and more about the peace of the Lord.

Don't you realize that everyone who runs in a race runs to win, but only one runner gets the prize? Run like them, so that you can win.

1 Corinthians 9:24

What other people think of you won't determine your success. If it did, you would fail in everything you try to do, because you can't possibly please everyone in the world. So if some people think your way of living or even your calling in life is a big mistake, you can't let that bother you or decide your success or failure in life. You can't let their lack of faith keep you from doing what God has called you to do.

As a God Girl you have to know that if God has given you a passion for something, you should pursue it. You can't always know for sure if the dreams you have are from him or not, so you have to continue to pray that God would guide you, but you can't let people who don't believe in you worry you or stress you out. **If you fail, let it be a failure of ability and not a failure to trust what you believe to be God's call.** If you fail, fail in the direction of faith, not fear.

If God shows you that your dream was of your own making and not his, then be quick to surrender it, but never give up on your dream just because someone else doesn't believe in you. Most often if your dream is from God it will be tested. You will have to work hard and long, but in the end you will see the reward.

Don't you realize that everyone who runs in a race runs to win, but only one runner gets the prize? Run like them, so that you can win. Everyone who enters an athletic contest goes into strict training. They do it to win a temporary crown, but we do it to win one that will be permanent.

1 Corinthians 9:24–25

What does it mean when your life is out of control? Who has moved in and made a mess of everything? When you ask Jesus into your life and make him your Lord, everything comes under his control. So then why do things get so crazy? It must be that someone else has been given the keys and allowed to run the place.

Here's the thing: only you can ever control you or hand the keys of your heart over to someone else. No one can force you to feel or think anything about your life. People can try, and they can work at making your life difficult, but no matter how they hurt you, punish you, slam you, or hate you, they can never control your mind or your soul unless you let them.

So when life seems to be out of control, think about what you've gotta do: remember who you've given your life to and choose to discipline yourself to think only thoughts that are true and right. Think only what God would have you think. Control your mind and your body by obeying God's Word. When an athlete disciplines her body, she tells her body that something else is far more important than how it feels. She has decided her goal is greater than her fear, pain, or even suffering. And as a believer that's what you do when you refuse to let anyone or anything control your mind or your body other than God and his Word.

Every believer can have her body under the absolute control of God. We are, after all, God's holy temple (see 1 Cor. 6:19), so why wouldn't we take great care to let him and him alone be in charge? As a believer you are responsible for your body and its actions. Use your body and your mind for good. Trust God and do all you can to bring him glory. It is well within your power!

I want you to know, brothers and sisters, that all our ancestors who left Egypt . . . ate the same spiritual food, and all of them drank the same spiritual drink. They drank from the spiritual rock that went with them, and that rock was Christ.

1 Corinthians 10:1, 3–4

No matter how lonely you feel or how bad things look, don't ever be deceived into thinking that God isn't there with you, waiting for you to turn to him and be comforted. He is called Provider, and that isn't just a part-time job. He always provides. Even when all seems to be lost, he is trustworthy.

When the Israelites wandered in the desert, they had no hope of finding food or drink, but God provided all they needed in the form of manna from heaven and water from rocks (see Exod. 16:4, 31; 17:6). The same God who gave them exactly what they needed is with you today. As a girl, you can easily let your emotions tell you that all is lost, but once you are saved, you are never again lost, even if you feel that way. **You can't let your circumstances try to dictate the character of God.** He is either God, ruler of all, or he isn't. When the going gets tough, you have to be strong enough to confess that he is still God and you can still trust him, even more now than ever. Because if you can't trust him with the hard times, what can you trust him with?´

He comforts us whenever we suffer. That is why whenever other people suffer, we are able to comfort them by using the same comfort we have received from God.

2 Corinthians 1:4

Your heart's been broken. You feel miserable. Why would God let this happen to you? It seems impossible to fathom from this side of the pain, but the truth is that if you can come to grips with the idea that it doesn't matter what happens to you as long as it is used for his purpose, then heartache won't torture you again. It's through the door of pain that you get into God's presence, but if you collapse in agony before you walk through or tell yourself you just can't go on, then you miss out on God's purposes for your life. If a broken heart is how God's will can be done in your life and the lives of others, then stand up and thank him for breaking your heart.

When you whine and complain or become immobile, you abuse the gifts of God and refuse to do what God calls you to do. So turn off the pain and turn up his voice. What is he trying to do with your life through this pain? Are there others who need comforting like you have needed comforting? Is there a lesson your spirit needs to learn? Get to work and find out God's thoughts instead of focusing on your pain. Heartache can only break you if you let it, and the fastest way to let it is to wallow in it. Refuse to let heartache be your destruction and you'll move out of the pain faster than you would have ever thought you could. You'll be unstoppable if you will just get on with what counts and think about your own pain as nothing to worry about.

Besides, if we suffer, it brings you comfort and salvation. If we are comforted, we can effectively comfort you when you endure the same sufferings that we endure.

2 Corinthians 1:6

*A*re you learning something? Struggling with something? If God is teaching you something about himself or about life, then try your best to understand that truth and figure out how it applies to your life. If you are going through some major remodeling at the hands of God, then get to work and try to share it with someone else. Write about it. Explain it. Figure out how to express it so that it can become a lesson for someone else who will soon be where you are.

When you do this, you will be serving God as well as your own soul. As you labor through a good explanation of his work, your heart will understand it and own it more and more. When you really try to re-say what God is saying to you or showing to you, you get the chance to pay it forward. You can help out another person who will soon need to learn the same thing. But if you refuse to work through what God is teaching you, then your lesson will be of no use to anyone.

You can make a difference and use your grief to change the world; you just have to be able to express God's lessons in your own words. Always make your mind think through what it takes for granted or learns from heartache or trial. Then you will truly own the lessons you have learned. Your mind will hold on to them more tightly, and that knowledge will be there for you and for others in future trials.

Instead, we have refused to use secret and shameful ways. We don't use tricks, and we don't distort God's word. As God watches, we clearly reveal the truth to everyone. This is our letter of recommendation.

2 Corinthians 4:2

*D*o you have any secrets? Secrets that you desperately don't want anyone to know about? When you have things that are hidden in your life, they become a part of your inner life. Even if your values disagree with your secrets, you find a way to get around that conflict by hiding them deep inside of you. If no one sees then no one knows, right? And then you can pretend like nothing is going on at all. But this disagreement with what you truly believe is the very definition of sin (see Rom. 14:23; James 4:17). Secrets need to come out into the open; they need to be fessed up to and shown the way out. If you are afraid of the light being shone on your secret, it's only because the light would cure it. That's what light does: it chases off the vermin and dries up the infection.

It's shameful to know God's ways and his desires for you and then to reject them, even in private. If you want to be free, you have to look at things from God's viewpoint. You have to refuse to hide in the dark any more. If there's a place in your life where you won't invite anyone else, then it's time to reveal your secret to someone you can trust, someone with wisdom and love. Confess your shameful ways and let the truth shine in your life. When you do, the underlying feelings of guilt and shame will be gone.

Our message is not about ourselves. It is about Jesus Christ as the Lord. We are your servants for his sake.

2 Corinthians 4:5

*E*ver said, "I wish I could have gotten that instead of this" or "I wish there was more"? Or how about "This isn't what I expected"? Disappointment with life and what it gives you is pretty normal, but is it godly? How does it relate to Scripture? Does God promise all your wishes will come true? Does he encourage you to spend your energy and resources on getting what you want? Or does he seem more concerned with something completely different?

For the answer on that, all you have to do is look at the life of his Son. Jesus wasn't dissatisfied with the things the Father gave or took away from him. In fact, he was never concerned with himself at all, even when it came to what he would eat or where he would sleep. But nowadays "need" has become the new "want." I "need" new shoes, when I already have five pairs in the closet. I "need" rest, when the lady next door has three kids, two jobs, and no husband. I "need" a bigger room, when the family down the street lives in their car. All your "needs" add up to a whole lot of spiritual arrogance when they go beyond survival. When others around the world suffer, when people don't know the beauty of salvation, when people are starving, cold, alone, and dying, the "need" of the God Girl should be to help, to serve, and to save them.

When your life becomes more about others than about yourself, you'll suddenly be free. You'll be unchained from your childish needs for more and your continual dissatisfaction with what you've already got. How freeing is it to forget yourself, to stop consuming, and to start giving! Become more concerned with what's going on around you than what's within you, and you will find more peace, hope, and love than you ever imagined.

Our suffering is light and temporary and is producing for us an eternal glory that is greater than anything we can imagine.

2 Corinthians 4:17

Your worst fear has come true, and now you are faced with the one thing you thought you could never handle. How do you stand when it seems just too hard to go on? What do you do when your life seems to be on the verge of extinction?

You've got to do the opposite of what your instinct says: don't fight, just surrender. Give up your will to God and stop fighting for your own way, your own survival. Sound illogical? Impossible? Well, it's neither. The place you are now, at the end of your rope, is just the place you are supposed to be. Nothing happens to you unless God allows it to happen. And if God allowed it, then you can be sure it is the very best thing that could have happened to you. But your heart can only get that fact when you completely surrender to God.

You can only win the battle when you submit to it.

Face your trial without fear and refuse to let it lead you to sin. Give your heart, soul, and mind to the one who loves you and will never leave you. Pain can only make you stronger if you don't fear it, so give it to God, and then it will be used for your good instead of your destruction. Stop asking "Why me?" and start saying, "Yes, God, your will be done, not mine. I am content to suffer if that is your will, knowing that all this is just temporary, but life with you is eternal."

Clearly, Christ's love guides us. We are convinced of the fact that one man has died for all people. Therefore, all people have died. He died for all people so that those who live should no longer live for themselves but for the man who died and was brought back to life for them.

2 Corinthians 5:14–15

f people aren't better for having known you, then you aren't loving them like you should. Don't freak—this isn't an accusation but is just something for you to process.

It's an honor and a huge responsibility, but because Christ lives in you, your very presence can and should change lives. Jesus' healing power was so strong that strangers only had to touch his clothes to be healed (see Mark 5:25–34). Even if your faith is as small as a mustard seed (see Matt. 17:20), imagine what you can do with his Spirit inside you. Your very presence can become the hands and feet of Christ in the lives of the people you are around. Live each day and love each person as if the love of Christ in you can completely change their lives, because it will if you will only love them as he loves them.

So care enough to get involved, to say something, to risk embarrassment and even rejection. Put your God above yourself and reach out to a dying world. Be the light on the hill; don't hide yourself so those stumbling around in the dark can't see. Speak God's truth to them. Lift them up when they fall, and assume the position that Christ assumed: the position of humility and meekness. Refuse to be the needy one, because you have all you need in him, but be the one they lean on, the one who loves them and directs their minds upward. Your presence can be a blessing when you make Christ's life and mission your focus. Are people better for having known you? If you aren't sure, study God's Word and find out how he wants you to love a dying world.

Whoever is a believer in Christ is a new creation. The old way of living has disappeared. A new way of living has come into existence.

2 Corinthians 5:17

*D*o you want to identify with Christ? Do you want to be so much like him, so in step with him, that anything that isn't from him makes you sick and makes you run in the opposite direction? It's time for you to make the decision. And that means you've got to tell Jesus either that you don't want sin to die in you or that you want to imitate Christ and die to everything that isn't holy.

When you choose number two, your life will change. The old self will begin to die away and the new self will take its place. When that happens, all the sickness brought on your life by the sin in it will start to lift. Your load will be lighter, and the power of sin in your life will start to be reversed. You can have freedom from the fear and pain in your life if you are only willing to find the sin in your life, admit it, and choose to walk away from it. It's a fairly simple process that requires a very difficult decision: to **confront the truth that sin has become your friend and to choose to make it your enemy.** When you became a God Girl, you became a new creature, one who no longer lives for herself but for him. And this isn't as frightening as it sounds; in fact, it's freeing. When you become a new creature, the effects of your old sin may still remain, but your heart and mind will be set free to thank God for rescuing you from the path you were on. Let Jesus' life and death make a difference to your way of life, and you will find a way out of all your sinful habits and choices.

God was using Christ to restore his relationship with humanity. He didn't hold people's faults against them, and he has given us this message of restored relationships to tell others. Therefore, we are Christ's representatives, and through us God is calling you. We beg you on behalf of Christ to become reunited with God.

2 Corinthians 5:19–20

God's goal for the lives of his children is restoration. He wants them to be reconciled, or restored, to himself and to one another. Restoration means moving away from being enemies and back to becoming friends again. Before you accepted Christ you were an enemy to God, but once you turned to him and confessed your need for him to forgive all the mess-ups of your past, you became his friend.

But reconciliation isn't just about you and God. **If a friend or a family member is on your outs list because of something between you, they need reconciliation** as well. Anything else and you are rejecting God's call to love your neighbor as yourself and even to love your enemies. Something terrible, even sinful, may have come between you, but forgiveness is required in the life of a believer (see Matt. 6:15; Mark 11:25; Luke 17:3).

Reconciliation is like pulling off a bandage: best done quickly. Don't wait to talk to someone who has something against you, but go to them as soon as you realize the problem. Work things out before it's too late. When a sister in the faith is mad at you or hurt by you, there's no time to waste; you've got to do your best, in humility, to talk to her and work things out. As a God Girl you should know that whether you've been hurt, slandered, gossiped about, or judged, you are called to go to your sister or brother and do what you can to make things right. Sometimes that might mean apologizing when it's really the other person who should be apologizing. After all, what's more important, obedience to God's Word or proving that you were right?

The Lord Almighty says, "I will be your Father, and you will be my sons and daughters."

2 Corinthians 6:18

*F*ather is a powerful word to a girl's heart. A father is someone we all either love or wish we could love. A lot of girls have the best dads in the world while others have no father at all. The father is such an important person in the life of a girl because it's the father who protects her, guides her, teaches her, and loves her. This very important and amazing role has its foundation in the Father of the world, God himself. Father God is the perfect father. He protects, guides, teaches, and loves his children. He disciplines as perfectly as he loves. He is the ultimate Father who never messes up, walks away, or forgets his kids. And you became a daughter to God at the moment that you believed and made Jesus the Lord of your life. That means he became your Father. He is the one who knows you inside and out, the one who will always love you and never leave you. He is your Daddy God, and you can trust him. Even when he's disciplining you, he can be trusted.

Whether you have a good earthly father or a bad one, you now have the perfect heavenly Father. All that you want in a dad you now have. He's bigger than you, smarter than you, in love with you, and there to help you whenever you call. Don't let the human father you've had keep you from trusting your heavenly Father. There is a difference between them: one is God and one a man. Obviously every man is weak, fallen, and broken and makes mistakes, but God is none of that. He can be trusted and he will never leave you. You were made in his image, and you can be secure in the fact that once adopted by this Father, you are his forever!

Since we have these promises, dear friends, we need to cleanse ourselves from everything that contaminates body and spirit and live a holy life in the fear of God.

2 Corinthians 7:1

You've prayed to be holy, but you keep sinning. Why? It's not a question of praying but of doing. Don't just ask God to take away your desire to sin and then go on living as normal. Start doing something about it. If there is something that won't seem to let up its choke hold on your life and is making you miserable, then the logical move is to give it up. Let go. Don't just beg God to do it—*you* have to do something too. God gives you the ability to get it done, and he gives you the power of his Word and his protection, but he doesn't do it for you.

God doesn't want you to sin. But he does want you to be holy. So why would you need to convince him of your need for holiness when that's been his goal from the beginning? The only one who's not been willing until now is you. **God doesn't do this holiness stuff for you; he does it with you. The only one not performing here is you.** God has just been waiting for you to agree with him that keeping your sin is harder than giving it up. Until that happens you'll take the easy road and keep the sin alive. So get up and get busy. The sooner you take action, the sooner you'll be free.

> *In fact, to be distressed in a godly way causes people to change the way they think and act and leads them to be saved. No one can regret that. But the distress that the world causes brings only death.*
>
> *2 Corinthians 7:10*

*A*re you as happy with God today as you were when you first met? Is he still your obsession? Or has the passion faded? Have you fallen into a pattern of making demands rather than adoring him? It can be easy to drift away from that first experience of him. It seems like a natural part of the ebb and flow of love, but for the God Girl it can leave you feeling as if you've lost something great.

If your life is off track, if you are unhappy and can't figure out why, know that the joy probably left when you started thinking more about yourself than about God, more about your worries and your dreams than his thoughts and his plans. **When the God Girl isn't continually thinking about ways to make him happy and to please him, she runs the risk of falling into a pattern of "me."**

The answer then is to make him your sole focus, and the happiness will return. If you realize that you don't adore him like you used to, that you've stopped going out of your way for him, and that you are more concerned with yourself and your world, then let that embarrass and shame you. When you are ashamed, you will find godly distress that "causes people to change the way they think and act," and you will get back on track. It is not condemnation that drives you back to his arms but conviction. As a God Girl you can't blame God for the distance between you; your distractions are most often what remove him from the center of your life. You can return to him today—just find out what pleases him and determine to do only that!

We take every thought captive so that it is obedient to Christ.

2 Corinthians 10:5

*A*re you spiritually confused? Is there something in your spiritual life that has you baffled, an area where you can't seem to hear from God or know what to do? Then the answer to your confusion is this: just do it. Just do what God asks you to do in his Word. You will never get life all figured out or "find yourself" through all the soul-searching and crying you could ever do. But when you are confused about life, you've gotta take every confusing thought captive and make it obedient to God's Word by doing what his Word says. In the Bible you will find the answer you need to your dilemma. The answer is for his will to be done, by you, right now. You have to do whatever it is that God is calling you to do right now. It might not make any sense to your mind, but when you start doing what you should be doing, then the confusion will lift.

Is he asking you to get over something or to turn the other cheek? It's gotta be done, and now. Is he telling you to just trust him? Then do it. **The first step of doing what God asks will be the first step toward clearing away any spiritual confusion that you may have.** But don't let anyone tell you all you need to do is "think through things," because when you are feeling any kind of spiritual pressure, the only thing you should do is to immediately do what God is asking, not worry over it. Just doing it brings immediate healing and hope.

We take every thought captive so that it is obedient to Christ.

2 Corinthians 10:5

D o your thoughts ever wander? Do you ever feel depressed, jealous, bitter, or frustrated? When your thoughts turn ugly, when they make you anything but happy, then it's time to take those thoughts captive. Trouble comes when you stop trying to control your thoughts in the light of God's Word. Any thought that you have that is incompatible with Scripture is going to bring you some kind of grief—if not now, then tomorrow or the next day.

The answer is to take every thought captive to make it obedient to Christ. This might sound impossible if you aren't used to doing it, but with practice it gets easier. And when you work at it you will be set free to find the happy in your life. As a God Girl you can't forget that your thoughts define you. They are more than just random ideas; they are either sin or holiness. God is listening. He knows what you think about, dream about, fantasize about. If you would be embarrassed about God watching what you are thinking, or if what you are thinking is making you feel something you don't want to feel, then it's time to take charge of your thoughts so that they are obedient to Jesus, and that means to his Word. Take the lies you are believing and reject them, and replace them with the truth of Scripture. So much of your emotional grief is a result of the sin in your life. Sure, there will be times to mourn, but to spend too much time sad over what you don't have is to deny what you do have: the very Creator of the universe calling out to you to take his hand so that he can see you through. Don't reject him by majoring in your darkness and despair.

Taking your thoughts captive starts with knowing what thoughts need to be chained up and tossed away and what thoughts are beneficial. The way you do that is by becoming intimately aware of God's Word. Know truth, and the truth shall set you free!

We can't do anything against the truth but only to help the truth. We're glad when we are weak and you are strong. We are also praying for your improvement.

2 Corinthians 13:8–9

Control your thoughts. No matter how impossible that sounds, you can do it. Don't let your emotions tell you what to do or not do.

Faith has to do with believing, and belief takes place in the mind, not the emotions. That means faith doesn't change with your emotions. It is strong and determined, relentless in the face of trials or fear. But your faith can only stay strong if you can keep your mind from wandering. Don't let your mind take you to the place of fear or resentment. Don't let your mind wallow in the emotions of grief or rejection. **Your mind has to find its rest in faith.** It needs to seek the higher ground of truth. You need to understand that emotions don't respond to truth any more than a crying baby responds to a talking-to. It's your *mind* that can take in truth and make it an instrument of change, in spite of your emotions.

Thought control is essential to the life of a God Girl. Without it your faith is gonna get weak and tired out, and in the end your emotions will turn your faith into doubt. But you can change all that by not always believing what you feel but instead leaning on what you know to be true about God and his Word. Even when everything screams against that truth, hold on to it as if your very life depended on it, because it just might.

Am I saying this now to win the approval of people or God? Am I try-ing to please people? If I were still trying to please people, I would not be Christ's servant.

Galatians 1:10

Trying to control what others think about you is a waste of time and also the hardest thing to stop doing. Sometimes all your energy seems to be wrapped up in what other people think about you. From what you wear each morning to what you do all day, somewhere in the back of your mind you're always thinking about what other people think and how to control those thoughts so they are in your favor. "Am I kind enough, smart enough, cute enough, faithful enough? Do they think I'm wise, bright, honorable?" You spend all your energy trying to look better to the rest of the world, but all of this is a waste of time because what others think is not your responsibility. You can never really control what other people think. Sure, you can try to. You can dress so they get who you are and act in a way that reveals your values and all that is good about you, but if they think something of you that isn't true, you can't freak out. And you can't decide to fix their thoughts. Changing another person's thoughts is not your job and not something you have the strength to do.

You have to fight the urge to justify yourself. After all, it's Christ who justifies and God who de-fends, and can't they do it a whole lot better than you? What others think or don't think of you should never become your obsession. Listen to what they say, consider its truth, and then if it's false, move on, knowing that God will speak for you if anyone needs to speak.

If we receive God's approval by obeying laws, then Christ's death was pointless.

Galatians 2:21

*N*o one gets right with God because of how good they are. You get right with God by believing in the resurrection of Christ and by making him Lord of your life. When you say, "God can't forgive me; I've done something too awful" or "I'm just not good enough for God," you cheapen the cross. You are saying that you are a particularly difficult case and Christ's death just wasn't enough for you because your sin needs more work, more effort on your part, for you to get right. But that is absurd. If more work needed to be done to save you, then Christ died for nothing, a pointless death.

You can be certain this isn't the case. His death was anything but pointless. It was meant for a supreme purpose, and that was to save sinners by taking on their sins. Not one sin sneaked through uncovered; *all* the sins of his children are forgiven. And you are his child if you believe in him and make him Lord of your life. The God Girl can't allow her feelings to convince her that her salvation requires more effort than was exerted on the cross.

Once you accept the gift of kindness and grace from God out of love instead of obligation, then you start drawing closer to him. And it is love, leading to obedience, that proves to God, yourself, and everyone around you that you are truly a God Girl. But be certain of this: **your love and obedience isn't what saves you. Christ's love and obedience is what saves you!** What you do as a God Girl doesn't save; it only proves that you have allowed the Spirit to work in and through you. Don't count on what you do to save you, but know it will prove you faithful.

Did you receive the Spirit by your own efforts to live according to a set of standards or by believing what you heard?

Galatians 3:2

The law is useless to save you. Before Christ came, people were expected to do exactly what the law said, but since no one could do that perfectly, sacrifices needed to be made. Their sins were too great and happened too often for them to be holy without some kind of sacrifice. And nothing is different now: you were saved not because you were so perfect and holy but because Jesus was your sacrifice. When you accepted that fact, you were immediately saved. Nothing you did, other than accepting him, saved you. Accepting him as Lord of your life is the foundation of all of your faith.

When he became your Lord he also gave you his Spirit, and that Spirit is what changes your life. A lot of times you mess up, you do what you don't want to do, and you feel terrible. You wonder how to fix it, how to make it right. And sometimes you feel powerless to change, and that is true—sometimes you are powerless, but the Spirit is not. Remember, it's through the Spirit that you were saved. And if he has the power to save you, he has the power to change you.

When you fail, don't hate yourself, don't fret, and don't give up. Just remember what you did when you were saved and do it again: turn to him, confess your sin, and accept his forgiveness and cleansing. The ability to know the right thing to do and the strength to do it all come from the Holy Spirit who lives in you. Don't try to do it all by yourself. Call on him, beg him, and trust him to make you more like Christ every day. When you fail, get up, wipe yourself off, and keep moving forward. You can do all things through him (see Phil. 4:13). Trust that and accept his forgiveness.

Those who belong to Christ Jesus have crucified their corrupt nature along with its passions and desires.

Galatians 5:24

Giving up sin isn't just about giving up things in your life; it's about giving up the right to your life. Jesus didn't say it was going to cost you *something* to follow him; he said it was going to cost you *everything*. If you can't give up your right to want what you want, then you aren't following Christ; you're following yourself. You have to be willing to give up your independence and become totally dependent on God and what he wants for you. As long as you rely on yourself to decide what you need, you will be unhappy. You'll be forever looking for the next fix, the next thing to lift you up or pull you through.

You aren't holy by nature; holiness takes sacrifice and practice. If you can't sacrifice your wants, then you haven't truly crucified your corrupt sinful nature. And without crucifixion there is no hope for a new life free from the bondage of sin (see Gal. 2:20). If your sin has gotten the better of you and you are finally ready to ditch it, then you have to learn to say no to yourself. But look out—sin will continue to make you think that you can't live without it, but that's a lie straight from the lips of the devil. Don't buy it one more day. Not only can you live without the sin, but you will thrive without it. Giving up sin turns you toward God and away from the devil. Who are you focusing on? Do you need to say no to yourself and turn around?

We can't allow ourselves to get tired of living the right way. Certainly, each of us will receive everlasting life at the proper time, if we don't give up.

Galatians 6:9

*F*ace it: even God Girls can make bad decisions. We get our advice from the wrong place. We complain about the things God has let into our lives. We work to get free from trials instead of persevering through them, and then we wonder why our faith is so weak and our peace is gone.

Think about these questions and what they mean for your life. Then consider God's thoughts on the matter and ask yourself where your life needs to change:

Why do I exist? To satisfy myself or God?

What is my number one goal—finding comfort or persevering?

What do I ingest more of—TV or the Bible?

When I need help, where do I most often get advice—God's Word or another person?

When life gets hard, do I most often complain or praise?

Am I happy or worried?

Am I content or fearful?

Am I a believer or a doubter?

Through the blood of his Son, we are set free from our sins. God forgives our failures because of his overflowing kindness.

Ephesians 1:7

Beware of taking advantage of God's forgiveness. If you're about to do something wrong and you think, "Well, at least I know that God will forgive me," you've sorely misunderstood the Word of God. Remember, the only reason you are forgiven is because of the horrific death that God's Son died on the cross. To take advantage of that as a free pass to sin is to choose his death for him. I know that's not your intent, but that's the outcome. Never forget that the forgiveness that is so easy for you to take from God cost his Son sheer agony. Never forget the price at which you were bought.

God is good and kind. He loves you. He is there for you, but never, ever think that it is because of this love alone that he is able to forgive you. Your sin required something more: it required that payment, or ransom, be given in return for your transgressions. It's only because of Christ's blood and suffering that he can say, "Your sins are forgiven." This unfathomable gift of God—the persecution, torture, and death of his Son—is what gives you instant access to forgiveness. Never take God's forgiveness for granted, because it comes to you by the blood of his child. Christ hung on the cross so you could have forgiveness. Remember that the next time you are about to take advantage of this amazing gift.

I also pray that love may be the ground into which you sink your roots and on which you have your foundation. This way, with all of God's people you will be able to understand how wide, long, high, and deep his love is.

Ephesians 3:17–18

A tree gets much of what it needs for life from its roots. And its roots grow proportionate to the soil they're in: in shallow ground plants grow low and weak, and in deep soil they grow tall and strong.

Where you sink your roots will determine how much you grow. Sink your roots in the shallow soil of the world, and your growth will be stunted. Because the world doesn't know love, it can't feed your soul or give it life in abundance. But a life buried in the soil of love will blossom and grow into an impressive and strong life, unshakeable in strong winds and able to protect anyone who comes under its impressive branches. Right now you are just a sapling, but one day you will be a mighty oak. Right now you are sinking your roots deeper and deeper, searching for rich soil, digging for water and nourishment from the love of God. The more you drink of this love, the more you ground yourself in it, and the more you offer it as shade to others, the deeper your roots will grow and the more unshakeable you will become.

The girl who has her life's roots sunk into the ground of love is a girl who is determined to react to everyone she encounters with love. She refuses to allow anyone else's sin to become her sin. She doesn't consider bitterness, resentment, revenge, or retaliation to be an option, but instead she digs herself deeper into the meaning of love. She gives while others take. She smiles while others scowl. She forgives while others hate. You, God Girl, will grow strong and become an impressive young woman to those around you when you ground yourself in love and only love. Refuse the world's standards and live only according to God's, and your roots will go deep.

You were taught to change the way you were living. The person you used to be will ruin you through desires that deceive you.

Ephesians 4:22

How much have you changed since you got saved? When you look at who you were before you knew Christ, what do you see? What problems, what sins, what issues did he save you from? And what things in your life have you sacrificed for him?

As a God Girl you are taught to change the way you were living pre-Christ. According to God's Word, one reason is because the person you used to be will ruin you with all its deceitful desires for the things you used to love. When you became a God Girl, you became a new person, completely different from the old you. Some of your bad habits dropped off immediately. But some things you didn't let go of so easily. Some things seemed either too insignificant to worry about or too powerful to overcome. But either way, you can get rid of those things that control you. You can be free from their bondage, and you have to be. You have to change the way you live so that it's consistent with the Word of God. If you find part of your life that's inconsistent, then you have to change that today or it'll be your ruin. **You can't be deceived by the things of this world like you used to be in the past.**

If you're willing to look honestly into your life, then sit before God and ask him if there's anything in you that needs to be kicked out or any allegiance or affection that is lying to you. Then when you see it, get rid of it immediately. Walk away and never look back. If you want to live in the freedom of Christ, then let go of the chains that bind you to this world and become the new person you were taught to be (see Eph. 4:24).

You were taught to have a new attitude. You were also taught to become a new person created to be like God, truly righteous and holy.

Ephesians 4:23–24

*D*on't overanalyze everything. When you do, you stress out. Overanalyzing the things in your life keeps you from trusting God. When you trust God, you don't have to analyze anything other than his Word. You don't have to talk out all your issues or spill all your troubles on someone. You don't have to spend all your time obsessing over your past, trying to figure out how it affects who you are today, because none of that analysis will bring you the peace that God's Word can bring you.

When you trust God and you know that he's got everything under control, then you don't have to spend all your energy trying to figure out how to fix your life. He promises to fix it for you, and it won't take years of analysis to do it. In the blink of an eye he can restore your life and make it new—born again, as the saying goes. That means all that has happened in the past doesn't control you or define you. Even what happened yesterday can be let go of. You don't have to figure it all out. The only thing you need to figure out is how to love God more and to worry less about yourself. The happiest girl isn't the girl who is obsessed with fixing herself but the girl who is obsessed with letting God love her, no matter what she's been or done.

Don't let sexual sin, perversion of any kind, or greed even be mentioned among you. This is not appropriate behavior for God's holy people. It's not right that dirty stories, foolish talk, or obscene jokes should be mentioned among you either. Instead, give thanks to God.

Ephesians 5:3–4

*W*hat comes out of your mouth gives away what's in your heart. When you let yourself talk the way the world talks, you show that your heart prefers the world's ways. In the life of the God Girl it's not only what you do but what you say and even what you think that's gonna be judged. And I don't mean just judged by God, but also judged by the people who hear the thoughts coming out of your mouth and make a judgment about your faith. When you join in with people in joking and talking about ungodly stuff, you aren't just listening to sin but participating in it. Before you knew the truth you joined in because you didn't want to condemn them or to embarrass yourself, and that's understandable. But now that you know the truth you can't keep acting the way you used to. That would be a slap in God's face. Whose judgment are you more afraid of, God's or your friends'?

As a God Girl you are bound to see some changes in your life. The things you used to think were normal will start to disgust you because they disgust God. If you want to be accepted by people more than you want to be accepted by God, then you have to do all you can to say no to your heart's desire to be loved and use your will to act and to think the way God wants you to. Don't let your feelings of embarrassment determine your obedience to God.

Don't let anyone deceive you with meaningless words. It is because of sins like these that God's anger comes to those who refuse to obey him. Don't be partners with them.

Ephesians 5:6–7

The life of faith can't be partners with a life of darkness. When you as a God Girl partner with people who have rejected God by not making his Word the word they live by, you sin. These people aren't obeying God, they are running from him, and so you can't partner with them. When you bind yourself to them, you bind yourself to people who are in opposition to God—in other words, to his enemies. And to make alliance with God's enemy is to become his enemy. You can't let yourself get too close to the enemies of God. And even if they give him lip service by saying they believe in him, if they don't act like it, they're still enemies.

All this doesn't mean you have to remove yourself from the world or even from the presence of these people, but it does mean that they can't be your best friend or partner. They can't have access to your heart or they'll start to deceive it. Certainly you can **serve them, love them, and share with them, but don't think you can rely on them for advice, counsel, or insight.** That would be like going to the enemy for advice about godliness. Their thoughts aren't of any value for your decision making because thoughts that are founded on disobedience will never bring you the salvation of God.

Determine which things please the Lord.

Ephesians 5:10

When your plans are interrupted, when your rest is stopped short, when your comfort is unattainable, how you react proves your faith. When the unexpected happens and the unwelcome comes, what you do reflects your heart and your commitment to love the Lord and to serve him no matter what he asks. Obedience is proven not on your good days or in the things you saw coming but in the dark nights and shocking situations. God's Word is for those moments as well as the planned ones.

You don't get a free pass to sin when life is just too hard. Sure, God offers forgiveness for all the God Girl does, but the beauty of faith is found in your sheer determination to believe no matter what's going on around you and to do what's right no matter how you feel.

Determine what pleases God and do it. When you commit to that kind of trust and obedience, you get perseverance, character, peace, and hope. Each time you reject your dark and sinful nature and do the opposite of what your emotions are yelling at you to do, you get stronger, and doing the right thing the next time gets easier.

But obedience isn't all about duty; it's really about true love. It's something you do for the love of your life. And just as an added bonus, it brings true freedom from those painful emotions and the challenges of life! **God's commandments are designed to make life better, not to make it more miserable.** No matter how crazy or counterintuitive they might sound to the world, they really are for your benefit. When you trust him, you trust what he says—all of it. How much of God's Word do you trust with your life? If the answer is all of it, then you are a true God Girl.

Children, obey your parents because you are Christians. This is the right thing to do. "Honor your father and mother that everything may go well for you, and you may have a long life on earth."

Ephesians 6:1–3

*P*arents. Even if they don't deserve it, honor them. Even if they're crazy, honor them. They might not be right or good, but honor them. Yes, God's Word commands honor, and honor doesn't have to be earned; it has to be given, period. "Honor your father and mother" is the only one of the Ten Commandments that also comes with a promise—that "everything may go well for you, and you may have a long life on earth" (Eph. 6:3). For some reason God found it important to bless honor. Maybe that's because of all the commands, this one is the hardest. Whether it's because of how close you are or because of the permanence of the relationship or some other reason, honoring your parents is probably the commandment that comes the hardest to you. But think about this: **honoring them is not giving them what they deserve but giving God what he deserves, and that is your obedience.**

Soldiers at war have to be willing to obey the commands they are given without any hesitation, because the mission depends on it. Commanding officers know the whole mission and have more information than the soldiers, and because of that they have to be obeyed immediately. In the life of the God Girl your commander is God, and while he might give orders to your parents that are then given to you, he is still your commander. And even if your parents don't have serving God as their mission, you still have to serve them because that's your assignment for the first eighteen years of your life. For some reason God saw fit to choose them as your parents, and that's worth noting. Don't miss that: life isn't luck of the draw. God is actively working in your life. Nothing happens unless he lets it happen, and you can be sure that he let these two people be your parents. So unless they ask you to sin, you have to honor them and obey their rule in your life.

Finally, receive your power from the Lord and from his mighty strength. Put on all the armor that God supplies.

Ephesians 6:10–11

*H*ow many times a week do you feel beaten down, attacked, worn out? How many times do you lose your strength and wanna give up? And how many times a week do you put on the armor of God? If you want peace—if you want self-control, hope, and strength—then you've gotta put on the armor that God has laid out for you (see Eph. 6:10–17).

Every day when you get up, make it your first job to ask God to dress you up in the helmet of salvation, the breastplate of righteousness (God's approval), the belt of truth, and the shoes of the gospel of peace and to put the shield of faith and the sword of the Spirit in your hands. As you imagine actually putting on each thing, remind yourself what each piece does for you. The helmet reminds you of your salvation and assurance of God's hand in your life. The breastplate of righteousness is there to cover you with the righteousness that comes not from your power but from Christ's. The belt of truth is there to remind you of everything God has shown you and will show you. The shoes of the gospel of peace represent the power of the gospel in your life and your ability and call to share it with the people in your life. The shield of faith protects you from all the flaming arrows the evil one shoots at you. And the sword of the Spirit—the Word of God, the Bible—is your most powerful weapon against the attacks of the enemy. With it you can fight off attacks and pierce hearts with God's truth. You need to hold it tightly in your hand every day.

If you want to start experiencing the power and protection of God in your life, then **pray through putting on the armor of God and remind yourself of the protection that is yours!**

My dear friends, you have always obeyed, not only when I was with you but even more now that I'm absent. In the same way continue to work out your salvation with fear and trembling.

Philippians 2:12

*D*on't be jealous of someone else's spiritual strength. They worked hard for it. It's something that doesn't just come overnight but grows over time when you work at doing what God says patiently, hopefully, and confidently. With time and a lot of practice, your spiritual life can be just as amazing as theirs, but it's gonna take some work. You can't give up and whine, "It's just too hard!" Giving up doesn't take you anywhere but backward. But standing firm, refusing to be knocked down, or getting back up if you've lost your footing will take you great places.

Remember, no one climbs Mount Everest in one step. Getting to the summit takes thousands of difficult and trying steps. Don't let the sharp cliffs and rough patches of life scare you; they're all a part of the climb to the top. Understand that you will never achieve what other people you admire have achieved unless you work as hard as they did. Faith isn't simple, it isn't instantaneous, and it takes hard work, but hard work won't kill you—it will only make you stronger.

If you want what someone else has, then find out how they got it. If they are prayer warriors, they had to start somewhere. If they know a ton about the Bible, they didn't learn it overnight but by working and working. Find out how to get from point A to point B—then get moving. God's gifts are amazing; they give you the ability to know more and to be more. But they also require dedication on your part. The cool thing is that once you set your mind to it, God comes right along and helps you. It's as simple as that. So dive in today and work out your salvation. Overcome your weaknesses and enlarge your faith.

Do everything without complaining or arguing.

Philippians 2:14

*D*on't complain—it's a sin. Familiar with it? When it comes to the weather, your clothes, friends, family, grades, work—how many times a day would you say that you sin by complaining? And while we're on the subject and you're getting all real with yourself, how does all this complaining make you feel? Better? Does it make people around you feel better about life? Just something to think about.

But wait, there's more. This little verse in Philippians also says no arguing, making that a sin too. Ugh! Really? So when it comes to your friends, family, politicians, enemies, bosses—how many times a week would you say that you sin by arguing? And how does arguing work for you? Does it usually pan out how you planned it, or does it make things worse? Does it make people happy with you or more angry?

Complaining and arguing both promise to make things better, or at least to make you feel better, but the truth is that both not only make things worse but also lead you away from God, because sin separates you from God. The good news is, Jesus promises to set you free from your sin when you confess it and turn away from it. So here's your chance. If things aren't great in your life and you want more of him in your life, then say no to complaining and arguing. All the time. Every day. Always. Confess those times when you've messed up and done them anyway, and then commit yourself to not doing it again—and I mean really commit yourself, not just say it.

When you start to make God's Word more important than talking, you become more holy and ultimately more happy. Just give it a try and see if it isn't so.

My life is being poured out as a part of the sacrifice and service I offer to God for your faith. Yet, I am filled with joy, and I share that joy with all of you.

Philippians 2:17

When God uses you, he pours you out like wine and he **breaks you like bread.** But what does all that mean? How can you become wine? How are you broken? Well, it's really an amazing analogy. Wine is made from grapes, but before grapes can be drunk they have to be crushed, smooshed, turned to nothing but juice. Their former shape is destroyed, their very being translated from one essence to another. Have you ever felt crushed, squeezed out of all your energy, even your very being? Don't be so quick to complain. It's very normal for the God Girl to be crushed, but it's for a very good purpose: so that she can be poured out as part of the sacrifice of service.

Okay, you can almost handle the idea of being broken by God, but what about when you are crushed by someone else? What then? Can you look at the crushing and still say, "Thank you for pouring me out, dear God"? Or do you buck against the torment and turn away from the strain? When you are being crushed by someone other than God, don't start to wonder what you're doing wrong, but think about how wine gets made. You can't be poured out till you've been squeezed. So if you want to be turned from bitter grapes into beautiful wine, then you've got to accept the fingers that are squeezing you, even when they aren't God's. If God chooses to break you by letting you be squeezed and smooshed by life, then don't start to worry that you've been forgotten or abandoned by God—quite the opposite is true. When the pressure comes, don't sin because of it but stand in the face of it, and then you will be poured out as a part of sacrifice.

In the end they will be destroyed. Their own emotions are their god, and they take pride in the shameful things they do. Their minds are set on worldly things.

Philippians 3:19

Is there something about you that gets you into trouble? Do you have some way of thinking or acting that you don't like but you feel powerless to change? "I can't help myself. It's just part of my personality," you complain.

If that's you, then you just found yourself in possession of a little god. If something or someone controls you, it's not just a habit or a personality trait. If it rules you it has become your idol and has taken the place of the one true God. Sometimes that idol is your own self-ishness or laziness, fear or inability to change. But that's no excuse for bowing to any god other than the great I Am.

You are not alone in your misery, though. We all have to continually find those gods and reject them. When you find a particularly painful or sinful situation happening in your life over and over again, it's time to look for your little god, and when you find it you have to decide to give it up. That means if your god is your stomach and you can't seem to refuse its call for another piece of cake, then you've got to label it as it is, a god, and refuse to serve it any longer. Eat to live; don't live to eat. Or if you think that being negative is just who you are, then you are lying to yourself. As a child of God you are not meant to be a negative person. You've found your little god. Now get rid of it. Don't let your negative "nature" be an excuse for sin.

Whatever is in you that isn't in step with God has to be rejected and turned away from. If God brings you face-to-face with your idol, then you've got to pay attention and vow to destroy it. Don't get comfortable and live with the destructive power of this unwanted guest.

Always be joyful in the Lord! I'll say it again: Be joyful!

Philippians 4:4

ome say that **happiness is based on circumstances while joy is based on focus.** When your focus is your own happiness, most often you end up disappointed, but when your focus is serving and pleasing God, look out, 'cuz the happy train is coming round the bend. In the middle of the most horrible trials you can be happy, or rather *joyful*, when you know that God's hand is on your life. Take the life of the apostle Paul. While locked up in prison for preaching God's Word, Paul wrote the book of Philippians. In it you will find out more about the ability to find joy no matter what the circumstances. The secret to being happy or joyful is not getting what you want but being content with what you have, and Paul has learned that secret.

What you focus on will affect how you feel.

Focus on the negative and you'll feel bad, but focus on the positive and you will feel much better. Your mind is where your faith is or isn't. If you let your mind wander into areas of negativity, fear, and worry, then your faith will suffer, but if you refuse to worry but instead trust God in everything, then your joy will be unstoppable. Your faith, your future, and your feelings all find their foundation in your thoughts. Consider what you think about the most and direct your thoughts upward. Watch how the apostle Paul kept not only his faith but also his joy in the midst of his trials, and you will find an answer for your own.

Then God's peace, which goes beyond anything we can imagine, will guard your thoughts and emotions through Christ Jesus.

Philippians 4:7

*O*ne of the best signs of a life full of faith is peace. A faith-filled life doesn't have room for worry and stress. Peace is a result of faith, so you can judge the distance you have come in your walk of faith by looking at the peace in your life. Do you have more peace now than you used to? More peace should always be your goal. It's much better to be a poor person living in peace and contentment than a millionaire living with worry, grief, and fear.

Learn to master your emotions and set them on the path of faith instead of letting them stay in the rut of circumstance. If you want more peace and less stress, start with something small like not blowing up when you spill juice all over your white shirt or not having a fit when you get stuck behind a slow driver. Tell yourself that being calm in the face of this hassle is the price you are willing to pay for the peace that goes beyond anything you can imagine. Peace isn't something that just happens; it requires some work on your part. But as you work toward peace through faith in the giver of everything good, you will find it coming easier and easier. Peace is the result of your faith and trust in God as the one who not only can handle it all but is involved in it all. Accept the peace that he offers as you work toward resisting any urge to sin that leads away from peace.

No matter what the situation, I've learned the secret of how to live when I'm full or when I'm hungry, when I have too much or when I have too little. I can do everything through Christ who strengthens me.

Philippians 4:12–13

Is there something you are asking God for? A request that you have made with all your heart but haven't heard a peep out of heaven about? When you have passionately asked God to do something but you haven't seen him make a move toward doing it, you might think he's not listening. But that's not the case. Remember, he has a greater purpose in mind than any human.

The thing to remember is that the problem isn't as important as your relationship with God. What you are asking might be getting in the way of your relationship with him, and he wants you to want him more than you want relief from your problem. In fact, he lets a lot of problems come your way so that you will come to him, trust him, and believe him. And when all you want is a way out of the mess, you can miss the very rock in front of you that will protect you from the waves of the storm. **He never promised that the crashing waters would stop—only that you would find peace in the midst of them.** If stopping the stress is more important to you than finding God, chances are the stress will keep up until you get your priorities right.

So instead of begging him to do this or that, try telling him that no matter what the situation, no matter what the problem, you will still trust him, search for him, and rest in him. Stop making the problem bigger than God. When you truly trust him, even the biggest storm won't move you. And the more you trust, the more you will see the storms calm down.

He is the image of the invisible God, the firstborn of all creation. . . . God was pleased to have all of himself live in Christ.

Colossians 1:15, 19

It's super easy to listen when the world talks, to see all the pretty things it has to offer, and to fall in love with them. It's so easy to make the world's way of thinking your own because, well, everyone is doing it. But the world has worked out its own way of living that is completely different from the life of faith. The world makes do with what it can figure out, deduce, and arrange on its own because it puts no hope in the life, death, and resurrection of Jesus. But the truth is, the God Girl needs only one hope and one salvation, and that is found in Jesus Christ, who was the full representation of God on earth.

A lot of people would say that Jesus was just a prophet or a wise teacher, but that is a lie that leads to the destruction of faith. If Jesus was only a prophet, then he was a crazy prophet, because he claimed to be the Son of God and to be one with the Father. The apostle Paul was fighting the same battle against the world that we fight today. He spoke up so that our faith wouldn't get all watered down with the half-truths of this world. As a God Girl you can't allow the world's thoughts on Jesus to be your own. You have to understand his divinity and your need for him. Many other ideas may come at you every day, but just like the early church, you have got to reject these false teachings and hold on to the truth of who Jesus really is.

You are surrounded by the world and inundated by its voices and its visions of beauty. So keep your eyes focused not on the physical but on the spiritual. Look for the truth found in God's Word, and look away from the lies of this world.

Christ is in charge of every ruler and authority.

Colossians 2:10

hen someone has authority over you, they have it for a reason. Whether it's a parent, a teacher, or a cop, no one is put into a position of authority without the approval of Christ himself. While obedience to people in power can seem impossible, when you think about it as obedience to the God who put them in charge, it gets easier. It might seem like a stretch, but by obeying the people in authority in your life, you prove God's authority over your life. And while many authority figures can be harsh and even cruel, that doesn't change the fact that God commands your obedience (see Eph. 6:5). No matter how crazy their demands on you, as long as they don't conflict with God's commands, you need to do what they want.

When being told what to do becomes almost unbearable, the God Girl has a way to freedom. She has to recognize how her actions relate to her faith in God and that her decision to obey authority will result in blessings, even if for a while she's gonna have to endure the hardship of doing what she's told without argument. After a time this kind of response will pay off, if not in this present world, most certainly in the world to come.

Keep your mind on things above, not on worldly things.

Colossians 3:2

Heavenly, by definition, is better than earthly. Who doesn't want heavenly things in their life? But your mind can't want both earthly and heavenly things at the same time. So if you want more heaven and less earth, you've got to quiet your mind and chuck all of your earthly passions and cravings to make room to contemplate more heavenly things.

For example, lust and thoughts of God can't exist in one mind. And earthly pastimes like anger, envy, and greed can't exist in your mind at the same time as thoughts of God's provision, mercy, and love. In order to be truly happy, you have to take out those thoughts that war against the presence of God in your life. Anything that takes your focus off of him and puts it onto you is meant for your destruction. God calls it sin because it stands in direct opposition to what God wants for your life. Why would you want something that God doesn't want for you?

So in order to get the earthly stuff out and let the heavenly stuff into your life, you have to agree with God that what you want is wrong. Call a sin a sin and agree that you won't go there again. When you confess and turn away from the things of this earth, you'll have more room for the things of heaven, and your life will naturally become more heavenly.

You've gotten rid of the person you used to be and the life you used to live, and you've become a new person.

Colossians 3:9–10

When someone points out one of your weaknesses or bad character traits, have you ever said, "Well, that's just the way I am. I can't change it"? If something seems just too hard or even impossible to change, do you just accept it, live with it, and claim it as an inborn tendency? For example, you might say, "I worry, I'm a type A personality, so sue me," or "I'm prone to anger because it runs in my family."

The truth is that sin (or your weaknesses) will always be there nagging at you, pulling at your sleeve, begging for you to listen, but that doesn't mean you have to accept this sinful nature as a part of your very soul. Do you really want to choose the call of sin's voice over God's? Well, that's what you do whenever you say, "That's just the way I am." That kind of giving in to your weaknesses is not only rebellion against God but also setting yourself up for failure. Do you want to be a victim of your weaknesses or a victor over them?

Don't let your sinful nature be an excuse for sin. We all have a sinful nature; that's why we need Jesus. You are not a particularly hard case, but you will have to choose what you're gonna follow: the voice of God or of your sinful nature. And you'll have to choose not just once but daily, even hourly.

Never be comfortable with the part of your nature that causes you to sin. And remember, it's not the boss of you anymore. Maybe it used to be, but Jesus came to set you free from all that, so take him up on his generous gift and say no to your old self.

As holy people whom God has chosen and loved, be sympathetic, kind, humble, gentle, and patient.

Colossians 3:12

*P*atience might not be *your* virtue. In fact, you might have none of it. So how do you get patience? How do you learn to do what God commands when it's something so incredibly hard to do—wait? Waiting might be your least favorite thing in the world, but if you can master it, then you have gained patience, and patience is a good thing. If you lack patience and you wanna get some, then why don't you start where patience has its foundation? Wait on God.

Waiting on God isn't about sitting around doing nothing while you count on him to do it all. Waiting is more about what you are thinking than what you are doing. When you wait on God, you trust God. You know that no matter when his help comes, it's coming. You know that if he wants you to have something, he'll give it to you at the perfect time. Waiting on God means trusting him to do what only he can do and in the meantime doing what you can do.

And patience is learned in these moments. As you learn to wait on God you practice patience, and that same way of thinking can transfer to all areas of your life. Anything in your world that needs patience can be thought of as your waiting on God. And since you know that God never disappoints and that his timing is perfect, waiting isn't such a misery. It becomes more anticipation than drudgery.

Patience can be your virtue; it is something that you can practice. You just have to choose to trust God in all areas of your life and to know that waiting is just an essential part of the process.

Children, always obey your parents. This is pleasing to the Lord. . . . It is Christ, your real master, whom you are serving.

Colossians 3:20, 24

*D*o you think that God speaks to other people besides you? Do you think that God is in control? If you said yes, then why do you argue when people in authority tell you to do something you don't want to do?

Scripture is clear that you are to obey the authority in your life. If you were in a court of law arguing a case and when the opposition stood up to present their side, you stood up and started screaming, "That's not fair! He's wrong! He's wrong!" what do you think the judge would do? He would bang his gavel and say, "Order in the court!" And if you wouldn't shut up and respect the opposition, you would be held in contempt of court. So why would you stand in such contempt in God's court of your life? Why do you argue with your parents when God has put them in authority over you?

Living well under authority is just as much a command on your life as loving God and serving others. You can't cherry-pick his commands, choosing only the ones that suit you. You have to obey God at every turn, and respectfully obeying the authority in your life is part of his commands.

Living under authority is also a chance to trust God. You have to believe that God can fix any situation, that he is always in control, and that he does talk to other people besides you. No matter how much you disagree with your parents, you have to agree with God by respecting the authority he has given them. If you've struggled with this in the past, now's your chance to turn things around. Instead of fighting, pray and obey. Talk to God about the situation, trust him to bring about a good solution, and then move forward with obedience.

Be wise in the way you act toward those who are outside the Christian faith. Make the most of your opportunities. Everything you say should be kind and well thought out so that you know how to answer everyone.

Colossians 4:5–6

*W*isdom is required when dealing with those "outside the Christian faith." You can't act the same with them as you do with believers. They don't understand your faith, they don't love God, and so they have to be treated differently.

Take friendship for example. Best friends share their deepest thoughts and emotions with each other. They look to one another for advice and guidance, and they help each other make their way through life. But nonbelievers can't understand things of the Spirit, their advice isn't godly advice, and their thoughts aren't godly thoughts. And so the God Girl has to get smart about her nonbelieving friends. They'll never be best friends, because she can't share with them the way she shares with sisters in the faith. Because her actions are based on her faith in God, she can't always expect to get good advice from someone who rejects her God. She can't dump her emotions or concerns on them; like it or not, she has to be the stronger one, the one they can turn to for guidance and hope. She represents God in their lives, so she has to represent well.

"Be wise in the way you act toward those who are outside the Christian faith" (Col. 4:5), because how you act may either lead them to salvation or lead them to believe that your God is too weak to care for your emotional, spiritual, and even relational needs. **You, God Girl, may be the only Bible your friends ever read, so be wise in your relationship with them.** Be strong, guide them, comfort them, and give them hope, but save your needs for believers who are stronger than you and can lift you up in truth.

We were gentle when we were with you, like a mother taking care of her children.

1 Thessalonians 2:7

ow gentle are you when it comes to your faith? When you talk to other people about Jesus, are you kind and gentle or frustrated and angry? How you act with people who you think just don't get it says a lot to those same people about who Jesus is. So how you say it is just as important as what you say. And don't kid yourself—if you are judging someone but think you are being kind by telling them about their sin, they know the truth. They can sense your judgment, and it turns them off.

As a God Girl you are to judge right from wrong, to see sin, and to educate people on their wrongdoing, but you are not to judge them as if there is something peculiar about them that isn't the same as you. Remember, you're a sinner too, just in different ways—after all, you know God and still you sin against him! Someone who doesn't know him might not even realize they're doing something wrong. Witnessing to a nonbeliever can be an uncomfortable thing, and it can get even more uncomfortable when you don't show much kindness, compassion, or gentleness. **If you have trouble talking to people about Jesus, then maybe it's because you want them to agree with you so badly that you forget that saving them isn't your job, it's God's.** Your job is to love them and to show them how being a Christian improves you as a person and makes you more compassionate and kind.

Never stop praying.

1 Thessalonians 5:17

*O*nce you stop analyzing and manipulating life and start living it, you can start to live in continual prayer. When you put your entire focus on the gift of God himself instead of on the troubles around you, that's when continual prayer becomes something attainable. When the apostle Paul says, "Never stop praying," you may laugh and say, "That's not possible"—oh, but it is! When your focus is God and God alone, when what you want and need are the farthest thing from your mind but what others need is at the front of your mind, then you start to understand how you can pray continually.

Wanting something so badly that it becomes your obsession is an act of idolatry. Even if your obsession over it leads you to pray nonstop for it, if it's something that you want for you, then it's no longer about God. Then your worry and fear over not getting what you are praying for has become more important than him. If this is you, you have to decide that whatever he wants for you is what you want and decide to pray continually for others and for God's will to be done. Then you will slowly be set free from the obsession that is starting to overtake your life like prayer should be overtaking your life.

Never stop praying. Whatever happens, give thanks, because it is God's will in Christ Jesus that you do this.

1 Thessalonians 5:17–18

*T*here is no such thing as an unanswered prayer. It's easy to believe that God is too busy or just not interested in what you want and need, especially when you pray and pray and never get what you ask for. But the truth is, he isn't ignoring you. He's heard every word and knows every need, and he has answered you—you just haven't heard his voice.

God never lets prayer go unanswered when it comes from the mouth of his children. The only prayer he ignores is the prayer of those who ignore his law and don't truly love him (see Prov. 28:9; John 9:31). For the God Girl that means you can be certain that all your prayers are being answered. It's not always the answer you wanted—sometimes he says no. And he might not show you the answer immediately—sometimes he says to wait—but it will come. And when you are certain of that fact, you can rest in trust and not worry about every little thing.

God always answers in the best way—not occasionally but always. God knows what you need, and he will give you just that. And when he does, it will be the best thing at the best possible time. So don't give up praying for everything in your life. Never stop praying (see 1 Thess. 5:17), knowing that he hears every word and he will respond in just the right way at just the right time.

Brothers and sisters, in the name of our Lord Jesus Christ we order you
not to associate with any believer who doesn't live a disciplined life and
doesn't follow the tradition you received from us.

2 Thessalonians 3:6

Frenemies: those girls who you think are your friends, but some days you really have to wonder. Once they were nice but now they are 50 percent mean. When you have a friend who has changed and now her behavior is ungodly, what do you do?

God's Word has a prescription for you: if your friend is a believer and she has become mean, vengeful, a gossip, or a slanderer, or if she is abusing you or hating you, then it's time to break up. You can't let her sin become contagious. You can't take on her disobedience and make it your own.

The trouble with staying close to believers who desert God's truth is that it can lead you to sin. You sin when you hate her back, retaliate, want revenge, or start thinking negative thoughts or complaining.

The God Girl trusts God's Word and attempts to live it every day. A godly friend might mess up, she might make mistakes, she might even hurt you, but there is always redemption, always confession and reconciliation. But for some girls there is none of that because, truth be told, they are done with God's Word. It is no longer a part of their lives, and instead they live by their own emotions and desires. That kind of girl is not good for you.

So think about your frenemy: will confronting her work? Can there be reconciliation, or is it time to cut the strings that bind you? Don't be afraid to walk away if you have to. It doesn't make you a loser; it makes you a follower of Jesus. You have to obey God's Word no matter what others think or say.

I encourage you to make petitions, prayers, intercessions, and prayers of thanks for all people, for rulers, and for everyone who has authority over us.

1 Timothy 2:1–2

God commands us repeatedly to pray for ourselves and for others. But a lot of times you might think that kind of prayer is something reserved for the mega-spiritual types. So you bow out because of your inability. But prayer isn't just for the super holy; it's required and possible for everyone, and it's how you overcome the world. Prayer moves the hand that moves the world. Why wouldn't you access his power in the challenges of this life? Why wouldn't you want more of him?

Prayer releases the power of God, especially when your prayer is for other people. It's called intercessory prayer, and it's just asking God to help, guide, and save others. If you trust God with your life, then your prayer can be focused on the needs of others instead of your own. That doesn't mean you don't ask for what you need, but the God Girl is never selfish. She doesn't hoard God's blessing for herself but thinks about others every single day.

When your prayer is purposefully focused outside of yourself and you are always thinking of the needs of others, your faith, your hope, and your happiness all increase. Your life begins to mean more as it becomes less about you and more about others. So practice intercessory prayer. It doesn't take any special gift, just a heart that wants to serve God and others.

Don't let anyone look down on you for being young. Instead, make your speech, behavior, love, faith, and purity an example for other believers.

1 Timothy 4:12

*D*o you ever feel like adults are looking down on you? Let it be because they don't know you, not because they do. Your actions, your words, and your love are the ways others know you truly are a God Girl. If they judge that you are bad based on some false idea of who you are, then be thankful that it is false. Would you rather they look down on you because of how you act, talk, or love instead? No, your life should be proof of your faith. People will know you are a believer by how you act, so act like one.

You can't let people look down on you because you act immature. Just being young can't be an excuse to misbehave. Joining the crowd and doing things just because everyone else is doing them makes you a follower, not an example. The God Girl is a leader of people and a follower of God, not the other way around. So follow his lead in everything. A lot of people might think you're not old enough to make a difference in this world, but remember that some of the people who made the most spiritual impact on the world in history were teenagers. Youth isn't an obstacle unless you choose to act your age. Enjoy your youth, but rise above the insanity of defying God just to fit in or have fun. Make sure people look favorably on you because even though you are young, you already act godly and mature. When you think about the fact that others are watching you and making decisions about who God is based on how you act, it's a sobering thought. Don't let them look down on you, but help them to look up to him.

Don't let anyone look down on you for being young. . . . Continue to do what I've told you. If you do this, you will save yourself and those who hear you.

1 Timothy 4:12, 16

*M*any young believers have "spiritual parents"—those who aren't your flesh and blood but who have raised you in your faith and taught you what you need to know in order to lead others into the same kind of faith. These spiritual moms and dads are really important and often can give us as much wisdom and hope as our earthly parents give us, if not more. The spiritual family is a valuable part of the life of a believer, as it has been for centuries. The apostle Paul could be considered the spiritual father of Timothy, whom he loved like a son (see 1 Tim. 1:2). And the books of 1 and 2 Timothy are Paul's final lessons and inspiration meant to encourage and teach Timothy to carry on the torch of Paul's ministry.

Paul knew that Timothy's faith was strong but that he was prone to being sick a lot and was a bit shy. He wanted to encourage Timothy and teach him how to be the pastor of his own church in Ephesus and prepare him to continue his ministry after Paul was dead. Though Timothy was young, he had been very helpful in serving with Paul for years. Paul had learned to trust him and to love him. Now Paul would soon die at the hands of his persecutors, so he wanted to prepare his friend and leave him with the information he would need to keep the faith alive.

As a God Girl you are not alone in this world. Others who are older and wiser have gone before you and are now leaving you direction and guidance as Paul did. You should learn from the wise, seek their counsel, and learn from their experiences in the faith. Like Timothy, you may have a challenge ahead, but keep the faith, knowing others have gone before you who can help. Seek them out, learn from them, and know that you are not alone.

Before the world began, God planned that Christ Jesus would show us God's kindness.

2 Timothy 1:9

*B*efore the world began, God planned to send Jesus Christ to die on the cross to save you from your sin so that you could be his own. Your sin doesn't surprise God. He isn't shocked when you fail; he knew you would, just like he knew all of us would. Knowing all along that his Son would have to die for our mistakes and bad choices, he created the earth and all of humanity in order to show his kindness.

Never underestimate how much God loves you. He loved you enough to bring you into this world even though he knew you would fail. He knew you would sin against him, but he also knew how much he was willing to pay for you. God's kindness ought to be your inspiration, your hope. You are never a lost cause—never! **Your sinfulness is nothing new. Millions before you have sinned just as badly, if not worse, and have been forgiven.** God didn't save you because you were perfectly holy—he saved you because he is holy.

Whoever serves in the military doesn't get mixed up in non-military activities. This pleases his commanding officer.

2 Timothy 2:4

*A*re you caught up in non-military activity? When you're a soldier you work for your commanding officer. You do what he says and you don't argue. But sometimes the non-military people around you have different ideas of what should or shouldn't happen. They might not like what you and your unit are doing. They might want to get you to walk away from your post and come to their side, but that would be desertion. Nope, you have to follow commands, even if the civilians are whining about it.

As a God Girl you follow God's commands, and non-military activity can get all mucked up with your orders. The people around you are involved in some kind of drama, and they want you to take sides or to join in their coup, but **as a God Girl you cannot get involved in civilian affairs.** You can follow the orders of your commanding officer with regards to handling non-military activity, but you cannot let yourself get wrapped up in their petty fights or issues. As a God Girl **you are the voice of reason, the hand of God in the lives of the people around you,** and that's why you can't let those who aren't listening to God drag you into their mess. Like a soldier patrolling a certain region, you have to stay out of the fray, only inserting yourself to preserve the peace or to protect the Father's territory.

If you feel like you've left the base and wandered into civilian territory, you can get back under the command of God by deciding to live with him in mind, under his authority and law, and then you will be free from the chains and the scandals that plague those around you. So stay focused. Get your orders and carry them out, and you will continue to get the direction you need from your commanding officer.

Every Scripture passage is inspired by God. All of them are useful for teaching, pointing out errors, correcting people, and training them for a life that has God's approval.

2 Timothy 3:16

God's Word: good for living or just good for your soul? You trust God and read his Word, but could he really expect you to live that way? To turn the other cheek when someone hits you? To love the people who hate you and hurt you? To die to self and say no to the things you really, really want? Surely God doesn't mean for you to live your life as if all of the Bible applies to your modern world. After all, you aren't a saint. Things are different now. Your situation is unique. The Bible is good to read and meditate on, but you've gotta live and you've gotta protect yourself. Right?

Yeah, some of the stuff he asks seems to go against every ounce of self-protection you have. And that is exactly why it has to be done. If his Word is to be considered true, it has to be considered true at every point. All of it is not only useful but essential for your life as a God Girl. You can't pick and choose which parts of your life you apply it to.

At any point that you are unwilling to make the Word of God a part of your everyday life, you have crossed over into sinville. No matter how risky following his Word sounds, no matter how hard it may be, it's gotta be done. You can't just decide that certain commands don't apply to you; that's just an excuse to disobey. Forgiveness of sin is not for those who refuse to obey God's Word but for those who want to obey but don't succeed at it. Learn what pleases the Lord and do it, and your life will be full of faith, hope, and love. When you mess up and get it wrong, fess up and then thank him for his kindness and his quick forgiveness.

A time will come when people will not listen to accurate teachings. Instead, they will follow their own desires and surround themselves with teachers who tell them what they want to hear.

2 *Timothy* 4:3

*B*eware of wanting to hear only what makes you feel good. God's Word convicts, it rebukes, it calls you on your darkness. But it's easy to want teachers and preachers to say only things that inspire you and to talk only about God's kindness and forgiveness. Although these things are good, a steady diet of them will leave you spiritually sick. Your soul needs to be shaped to be fit, not flabby, and that means doing the hard work of looking in the mirror and seeing where your soul needs some truth, correction, and direction.

When the truth is applied to your dark parts, it hurts. The lights go on and the brightness can hurt your eyes, but that's no reason to flip the switch back off. It's a spiritual illness to want only good news from God and not conviction of sin. When you are being taught, don't turn away from harsh news but embrace it. Though for a while you may feel pain, freedom is the ultimate result. **Those who fear the initial sting of truth don't grow and never overcome the sin that controls them.** But those who courageously accept what God's Word says about the sin in their lives grow more and more into the likeness of Christ every day.

A true friend doesn't just tell you what you want to hear; she tells you the truth. Have too much of just what makes you feel good and you will grow spiritually lazy. But you can never get too much of the truth. When you meet someone who is willing to tell you the hard truth, you have found a friend. Embrace those who love God more than they love you and who aren't afraid to hurt you with the truth in order to help you.

Believers shouldn't curse anyone or be quarrelsome, but they should be gentle and show courtesy to everyone.

Titus 3:2

*H*ow you communicate says a lot about you. Most girls love to talk, no question, but how you talk says a lot. Is your speech kind, compassionate, generous, and loving? Or is it sarcastic, bitter, frustrated, or defiant? No matter who you are interacting with and no matter what they say, do, or command you to do, in your reaction you cannot sin. If what they say is unreasonable, vengeful, angry, or slanderous, your words cannot be. Their actions or sins are no excuse for you to sin in return.

Instead your role is love and kindness. Your role is to speak gently and courteously to everyone.

Your speech proves who you are to those who listen. When they hear you, do you sound like a God Girl or a griping girl? Do you complain about those who have authority over you? Are you quarrelsome, or are you less concerned about being right than about being faithful?

Fighting is not a characteristic of a God Girl. Fighting is an irritating habit that usually just frustrates and angers those around you, and as a result it only gives you less of a bargaining chip in the negotiations of life. If you want to be obedient to God's Word and if you want success in your relationships, then change your speech. Make it kinder, more gentle. When you do, you will prove your love for God and for the people he's put around you.

Maybe Onesimus was gone for a while so that you could have him back forever—no longer as a slave but better than a slave—as a dear brother.

Philemon 15–16

t's pretty easy to knock people who have hurt you or have stepped on your rights. And it can be just as easy to want to get even with them or find justice, but justice can't be looked at from a human perspective. A lot of times God's justice, true justice, looks like unfairness. The mere fact that the girl who has been a believer since she was old enough to understand faith and the girl on her deathbed who's led the most evil life imaginable can both find salvation and full acceptance from the Father is baffling, if not unsettling, to the human mind. In our lives here on earth we have set up our own ideas of justice and what is right and wrong, but God often has a different idea. His ways are far better than your ways, his thoughts far better than your thoughts, so when things seem unfair and justice doesn't seem to be served, just remember that God's plan is not to make you happy but to make you holy. **How you *react to* the situations in life that demand justice, not how you *feel* about those situations, will determine your holiness.**

God's word is living and active. It is sharper than any two-edged sword and cuts as deep as the place where soul and spirit meet, the place where joints and marrow meet. God's word judges a person's thoughts and intentions.

Hebrews 4:12–13

*D*epending on what you need, the Word of God can hurt or heal. The healing is obvious. When you are aching, fearful, or lonely and you read about his faithfulness and love and you are comforted, that's obvious, a no-brainer. But when it's time for a revelation in your life, when the old you is still lurking around and the new you needs to come out, the Word can hurt. Its job is to divide soul and spirit, joints and marrow, and no other pain is so deep. **The beauty of the sting of God's Word is that it makes you desperate for God's help.** Nothing else seems important and you're finally willing to let go of the old you. Through this pain truth sinks into your gut, moves deeper into you, and changes you.

If God's Word isn't "asking too much of you" or breaking your heart, then you're not letting God reveal himself to you fully. Don't run from the pain of revelation; revel in it. Only when you're cut open and uncovered, laid bare before him, will you know without a doubt that you have been touched by the Word of God. So don't be afraid of what he'll ask of you, but look for it with hope and excitement, knowing that out of this painful process will come the glory of your soul.

*We have a chief priest who is able to sympathize with our weaknesses. He
was tempted in every way that we are, but he didn't sin.*

Hebrews 4:15

Sinful feelings don't have to lead to sinful actions. When you
feel angry, bitter, resentful, or any other bad emotion, you
don't have to act on it. When it first comes into your heart,
it's a temptation. It is attempting to get you to do something so that
it can be satisfied. Someone has offended you and so your emotion
wants vengeance—a smart remark, a bitter response, something to
hurt the other person as badly as you've been hurt. But this feeling
of revenge is a part of your sinful nature, not your spirit. No matter
what you're feeling, you can't let it control your spirit.

How many times has someone hurt you and your immediate
response has come from your emotional aches instead of God's
Word? At that point your emotions are your Bible, the word you live
by. And this word is destined to hurt. Not only that, but it sets itself
up as a little god, demanding you do what it wants so that it can be
satisfied. But satisfaction is never the result, is it? When you take what
belongs to God, like vengeance, you're in for heartache.

At **whatever point that your emotions dictate sin in your life,
they need to be shut down.** Just because you feel it doesn't make it
right. And denying your nasty, sinful, and childish decisions isn't bad
for you; it's good and right. As a God Girl you can't let the lie that
you should obey your feelings be a natural part of your life. When
you made Jesus Lord of your life, you were set free from the bondage of emotions, and now you have the ability deep within
you to say no to their sinful wishes and to put them under
the power of your will. The God Girl has been given a
new code, a new wiring that gives her freedom from
negative feelings, and she learns it through the training of
her mind and her will in the classroom of God's Word.

We have been set apart as holy because Jesus Christ did what God wanted him to do by sacrificing his body once and for all.

Hebrews 10:10

The blood of Jesus makes you holy. At the point when you accepted him as your Savior, you were no longer a lost sinner but became a saint because he did the work of being your sacrifice. But what does that mean? Do you feel holy? Are you now sin-free? Doesn't holiness require perfection? It seems like the Bible contradicts itself when it says "not one person has God's approval" (Rom. 3:10) and then in the next breath that you were "set apart as holy" by the sacrifice of Jesus (Heb. 10:10). How can you be both a sinner and a saint?

The answer is this: Jesus' death and resurrection makes you holy in the eyes of God. It gives you access to the Father and justifies you. In this sense, you are innocent before God, because Jesus took your punishment for you. But this doesn't make your character holy. You still have sinful tendencies. You still fall and get back up. Your character will become more holy as you confront the sin in your life and choose, by the strength of your will, not to do what you desperately want to do. **The more strength you show in controlling your will, the more valuable you are to the kingdom,** because it's by accepting the things of God and denying the things of this earth that your actions become holy and therefore useful in bringing God glory.

Don't allow yourself to be comfortable with the thought that Jesus makes you holy so you don't have to work at holiness. Holiness always requires determination of the will, and the practice of it will develop the character of Christ in you. Your battle is not just against sin—Jesus fought and won that battle for you. Your battle is also against your own will, that part of you that argues and cries to be left alone and not be controlled or denied. Take charge of your will and you will reveal the holiness of your character.

Brothers and sisters, because of the blood of Jesus we can now confidently go into the holy place.

Hebrews 10:19

I'm not good enough. I can't do all this Christian stuff. I'm just not perfect. Sometimes it seems like there are so many rules, so much to do in order to be holy—how can you do it all? The answer is that *you* can't, but *God* can. For centuries the Hebrews tried to be good by doing what God commanded them to do, but they just couldn't be perfect. So God did something about it: he sent his Son to be the final sacrifice for all sin. Now, this side of the cross, the commandments still stand, but faith in Jesus is the answer to your failure to be perfect in your attempt to obey God's Word. And so as a believer, when you have a desire to follow and obey all the commands of God but fail, even daily, you can be sure that you are still accepted by God because of the sacrifice of his Son.

Your faith will grow in direct relationship to your access to God, and Christ is your all-access pass to the Father. Before the cross, the only way people could have access to God was through the act of sacrifice. But now, through the forgiveness of sin allowed by the blood of Christ, we all have access to the Father every minute of the day. Take advantage of that access to the one who moves mountains. Don't wait a second longer to talk to him, listen to him, and learn from him. You are now a child of God and can knock on his door and enter in anytime you want to.

If we go on sinning after we have learned the truth, no sacrifice can take away our sins.

Hebrews 10:26

God's forgiveness is generous, but it is not free. The forgiveness that comes with salvation **demands something from you: a confession of sin and a promise to turn away from that sin.** People who "go on sinning" will never find God's forgiveness, according to Hebrews 10:26. But of course we know that we all sin, we have all turned away, so how can the Bible say no sacrifice can take away our sins?

The answer is simple: there are two kinds of sinful actions. One is a sin of the flesh, which Paul talks about in Romans 7. That's when you know God's Word and you want to do God's will, but your flesh is weak and you just can't seem to do what you want to do. This kind of sin makes you "distressed in a godly way" (2 Cor. 7:10), and that leads to repentance. But when a person knows God's Word but decides that it's either not worth it or not necessary to do what God wants, they commit a sin of the will—that is, they willfully disobey. They are rejecting God and removing him as Lord of their life. This kind of deliberate act of the will is what Hebrews 10:26 is talking about when it says there is no sacrifice for our sins if we "go on sinning."

The rejection of God is a terrible thing, and for the God Girl it's an impossibility. Though you might fail over and over again to get it right, your will really wants to get it right; it's just having a hard time. When that's your state of mind, you can be sure that the forgiveness of sins is yours, no matter what the sin or how hefty the mistake.

Faith assures us of things we expect and convinces us of the existence of things we cannot see.

Hebrews 11:1

Your life is filled with so many things that are a given and so many people who have everything planned out for you—your parents, your teachers, your friends. But what happens when you're faced with the unknown? When the future's not a given but a big old question mark? Do you freak?

Living with everything figured out is a piece of cake, but having no clue what's gonna happen next leaves you with nothing but faith. Your future might be unknown, but your God is well known. **Don't let an uncertain tomorrow erase what you know about God, and that is that he is in control of it all.** No matter what you know or don't know and no matter who attempts to intervene, he's still the ultimate authority in the life of the believer. You may be unsure of what's coming next in the journey of life, but big whoop—you are sure of God. And that means you can be sure of his protection and peace.

The evidence of the spiritual life in you is when your heart is okay living with the unknown, because the unknown is where faith lives. Without a few mysteries in life, your faith would be weak and useless, because it wouldn't be "convinced of the existence of things we cannot see." So don't freak when life seems all foggy and iffy, because those moments when you don't know what comes next are when your faith gets stronger and your belief gets a boost of encouragement. Without faith you would be like the nonbeliever, all worried about tomorrow and using all your energy to make sure there were never any unknowns. Be different! Accept the idea of uncertainty in your life, look to the one who is certain, and life will be a great adventure.

Endure your discipline. God corrects you as a father corrects his children. All children are disciplined by their fathers. If you aren't disciplined like the other children, you aren't part of the family.

Hebrews 12:7–8

When you ask God for help with something that just won't go away and you see no change, maybe it's because you're looking in the wrong place. A lot of times the problem is not outside of you but inside of you. A lot of times sin disguises itself as a problem, pretending to be an attack on you or an uncontrollable desire that you have no power over. If you've prayed and prayed and that thing in your life isn't changing, you need to start looking inside.

A lot of times trouble in your life is something sent by God as discipline for your sin. As Hebrews says, God corrects you as a father corrects his children, which means you're part of the family. So be thankful for the trials in your life, especially when they are discipline pointing to a particular sin you were previously oblivious to.

Don't ignore this stuff anymore. If your progress in the faith is as slow as molasses, then you've gotta start to search out your hidden sins and work to get rid of 'em. Ask God to show you the sin that's hiding out, be ready to see things you didn't know were there, and be willing to call a sin a sin. Find out by praying and reading your Bible what sin you have in you that is sticking its tongue out at God saying, "You can't make me!" and decide to stop acting like a naughty little girl. Get your act together by digging deep into God's truth, and you're gonna run this race with the best of them (see Heb. 12:1).

> *Don't forget to show hospitality to believers you don't know. By doing this some believers have shown hospitality to angels without being aware of it.*
>
> *Hebrews 13:2*

*S*trangers are strange. You don't know them, they don't know you, and who knows what they're like or what they'll say if you say hi or, God forbid, start talking to them. Eek! Yep, fear of the unknown can keep you from reaching out to others. You see their need but you fear their presence, so you walk away, and we all end up alone in the crowd. And you fail to do what God says is the greatest thing you could do: love others as yourself.

But guess what? Strangers are around you for a reason. And you'll never know that reason until you get your eyes off the ground and notice them—but don't just notice them; invite them into your life. How can you share the love of God with someone you're afraid to talk to? How can you help when you're afraid to reach out? You can't make friends with everyone, obviously, but you can take a risk and reach out to other girls who cross your path on a regular basis, like that girl who sits next to you on the bus but never looks at you, or that neighbor you see at the mailbox but never talk to.

If you want to be a bridge to God for a dying world, you've gotta open yourself up and offer kindness and compassion to strangers. This isn't just a good idea; it's a command: "Don't forget to show hospitality to believers you don't know" (Heb. 13:2). Be willing to trust God and to step out, even though you totally fear people's response. This life is not about how they're gonna respond but about how you respond to God's call to love. Be brave, God Girl, and you will most definitely be rewarded!

Don't get carried away by all kinds of unfamiliar teachings. Gaining inner strength from God's kindness is good for us. This strength does not come from following rules about food, rules that don't help those who follow them.

Hebrews 13:9

Food can play an important role in the life of the God Girl. It can be abstained from in order to pursue God and wait for an answer. It can be managed so that it doesn't control you. There are vegetarians, vegans, and chronic dieters. There are girls who purge and girls who avoid food as much as possible. For a lot of us food can become our obsession. Through our effort to control it, it ends up controlling us. But God's Word makes it clear: following rules about food doesn't help us, but his kindness (or grace) does.

As a God Girl you have to **be careful about "rules" on eating.** Whether you have created them yourself or followed others who brag about the benefits of eating a certain way, beware—you may be creating an idol out of a way of eating or not eating. Food is not responsible for your ultimate health or holiness. Certainly you should control yourself when it comes to eating, but control that is reasonable and not obsessive is best. If **you feel controlled by your commitment to eat a certain way, then start to ask yourself if you could be in danger of having an obsession, also known as an idol.** If fear is involved in your food routine, then that is a red flag. Any kind of sin, or distrust of God, associated with your diet points to trouble. That means fear, worry, stress, guilt, depression, or self-inflicted pain associated with eating are all signs of dangerous "rules" or routines.

The best thing to do is to turn your life, body and soul, over to God's care. Then eat a normal, balanced diet, trusting that God will not only protect your body but heal you where healing is needed.

Talk and act as people who are going to be judged by laws that bring freedom.

James 2:12

*H*ow can the law set you free? Have you ever wondered that? I mean, "law" sounds like something that holds you back. It's the great "don't touch that" or "I said no" of the spiritual world. If all you do is read the law but don't do what it says, that's exactly what it is: a bunch of dos and don't-dos. But a funny thing happens when you actually do what the Word of God says to do and avoid what he says not to do: you get set free.

See, you have all these things in your life that you have let control you without even realizing it, and all these things are actually sin, because letting them control you contradicts God's Word. Doing whatever you want, giving in to your passions, and just letting loose for a change might feel like freedom, but take a look at your heart. Does this thing that takes your eyes off God really give you the payoff it promises? Or does it eventually lead you to fear, depression, worry, loneliness, or anger?

When you disobey by looking at God's Word and then deciding doing what it says just isn't worth the trouble, you miss out on your chance to be set free from all that hurts you. Everything bad in your life is a result of sin. If you were to refuse to sin and choose to obey God's Word, you would find you have everything you've ever wanted. Freedom would be yours because **God's Word sets you free from the bondage of unmet needs, worry, and fear.** It opens up your heart and your mind and sets you free from what your corrupt nature wants. So whatever you do, remember that you will be set free by the law, should you choose to follow it.

You see that a person receives God's approval because of what he does, not only because of what he believes.

James 2:24

Contrary to popular belief, **Jesus wasn't half human and half divine; he was 100 percent of both.** He was equal to God but "he did not take advantage of this equality" but as a human "he emptied himself by taking on the form of a servant" (Phil. 2:6–7). When you look at the life of Jesus and the commands of God's Word, you can't use your humanity as an excuse for not getting it right. Jesus never used his divinity to get through the hard parts of life. He didn't overcome temptation in the desert or come down from the cross by virtue of his divine nature. When human trials came his way, he survived them as a human so that you would have not only a sympathetic God but also a perfect example of holiness on earth, human style.

The good news for you is this: **the life of Jesus proves that you can do it too.** You can overcome temptation; you can love God no matter what; you can resist the devil—because if Jesus could do it, so can you. Temptation is nothing new, and in resisting it you are not alone. Millions of others have come before you and resisted temptations as hard as if not harder than the ones you have in your life, so use that idea to strengthen yourself. Overcoming temptation can be done; it has been done. You are not powerless; you can say no to temptation. You just have to decide that serving God is your number one priority and that nothing else can trump that. There is no excuse for sin—not your weakness or the power of the tempter— nothing can be used as an excuse for giving in to temptation. So the next time temptation comes along, remind yourself that beating it can be done, that you can resist as you believe you can, and that God is right there with you. But if you do fall, quickly admit defeat, not blaming it on the temptation but accepting full responsibility as the guilty party. Then and only then will your sin be forgiven (see 1 John 1:9).

When you pray for things, you don't get them because you want them for the wrong reason—for your own pleasure. You unfaithful people! Don't you know that love for this evil world is hatred toward God?

James 4:3–4

Be careful what you ask for when you pray, because the things you ask for can actually distract you from God. It's better for you to ask for nothing and just let him decide what you need than for you to become so obsessed with asking him for what you want that your prayer becomes more about your needs than about worshiping him.

Praying with the goal of having some kind of experience or to get something out of God will get you into all kinds of trouble. You start to lose sight of why you live, and that's not for you but for him. The best thing to do is to pray humbly, knowing that whatever God gives you will be the best, and to tell him and yourself that you trust him no matter what the outcome of a particular prayer. When you internalize the fact that what God wants for you is always so much better than anything you could ask, prayer becomes more about saying "your will be done" than "please, God, I really want this." It is good to pray continually and to ask for everything you need, but make sure you always ask with the idea that God's will is ultimately all that you want. **When you pray for God's will to be done, you can be sure that everything you ask will happen, because God's will always comes to pass.**

Humble yourselves in the Lord's presence. Then he will give you a high position.

James 4:10

When you are in the middle of a dark spell, don't rush to get out. Don't clamor for guidance or for someone to help you. Just listen. What is God trying to teach you? If you look somewhere else you'll only cover the voice of God with your complaints. Dark times are your time to listen, not to whine and complain. If you are willing to give up looking for a quick answer and ready to wait for his response and his response alone, then you will find truth and hope. And at the end of your darkness you will find two things: happiness and humility.

Once you have truly heard God, you will feel like saying, "I'm such a dork! He's been talking this whole time and I haven't listened!" You will see your own sinfulness and be embarrassed by it. That's the humility part, and it will soften your heart and leave it ready for the seed of God's truth. Then you are ready to get the peace and hope that was promised you. Then your outlook will change from sadness to expectation, and your focus won't be on yourself anymore but will be on your powerful God, and what a better view that is!

Humility saves you from your emotional slavery. It brings you back to a correct assessment of who you are and who Christ is in your life. It's weird but true: when you truly let go of fighting for yourself and your rights, that's when you get all that you need. What do you think can lift you higher—your own effort or the hand of God? God promises to lift you up!

We consider those who endure to be blessed. You have heard about Job's endurance. You saw that the Lord ended Job's suffering because the Lord is compassionate and merciful.

James 5:11

You have to face some painful trials in life or your perseverance would never be put to the test. If your life was without
pain, then you wouldn't be brought to your knees where
the Father can create something new in you. The prodigal son is a
good example of what it means to return home from a life of pain
to a Father who is waiting with open arms (see Luke 15:11–32). If
you want to return to him, you can't deny the pain, and you can't
choose to wallow in it, medicate it, or ignore it either. What
you need to do is confront it and figure out why God
let it in your life and what he wants to change in you
to take it away.

See, his changing you is the only thing that can
really take the pain away from you. Running from it
by focusing on distractions like TV, people, or love only
pushes it down inside of you so that it can come back
later. Wallowing in it only gives it more strength than it already has by letting it have more impact on your emotions.
But letting it speak to you about how God desires for
your life to change will help make you a new creation,
one who is continually growing closer to the image
of Jesus Christ himself. And this will eventually take
away the pain completely and replace it with the peace
of God that goes beyond anything you can imagine
(see Phil. 4:7).

God the Father knew you long ago and chose you to live holy lives with the Spirit's help so that you are obedient to Jesus Christ and are sprinkled with his blood.

1 Peter 1:2

*G*od chose you. He chose you! Can you believe it? You didn't just show up at his doorstep, all wet and stinky; he chose you and made you his own. But why? What was his purpose for picking you? According to 1 Peter 1:2, it was for you to be holy. A lot of young people want a purpose in life. They want to know why they were created. But you don't have to crave the answer anymore, because it's right here, written in this book: you were chosen "to live holy lives with the Spirit's help so that you are obedient to Jesus Christ" (1 Peter 1:2).

You were created to be holy. Wow, betcha didn't know that. How's it going? Feeling holy today? If you aren't, don't fear. You can achieve your purpose; in fact, you will achieve it. See, when God says you were meant to be holy, he isn't expecting the impossible. That would be cruel. That would be like asking a six-year-old to figure out a problem using the Pythagorean theorem and then punishing her when she can't do it. Crazy! But God isn't crazy. He's got a plan and he's part of it.

First Peter 1:2 tells you how you'll get it done: "with the Spirit's help." **All you have to do is be willing to let his Spirit work with you, teach you, and guide you.** And the way you start to do that is through the process of spiritual discipline—prayer, confession, repentance, study, and more prayer. Holiness can be yours, your life can be changed, and you can be a new creation by trusting God with your life and being willing to do whatever he says, no matter how hard it might sound. If you're ready for that, then ask him for the power to do it, and believe that he will help you. Easy as one, two, three.

God wants you to silence the ignorance of foolish people by doing what is right. Live as free people, but don't hide behind your freedom when you do evil. Instead, use your freedom to serve God.

1 Peter 2:15–16

The freedom the Bible talks about is not the freedom to do whatever you want, whenever you want, with whomever you want. It doesn't give you permission to argue with authority or to disobey orders from those in charge. The freedom spoken of here is **the freedom to be a servant of God.** The world may tell you that freedom is following your heart and giving in to your desires, but that isn't freedom—it's actually bondage to your flesh, which most often has anything but God's will in mind. A life bent on serving yourself is ultimately a life of bondage to the cravings of your sinful nature. And it leads to all kinds of trouble like fear, worry, stress, bitterness, addiction, and fights. When you serve yourself you serve a small and ineffective god, but true freedom comes when you become the servant of the one true God.

Being called a "servant" doesn't much sound like freedom to the untrained ear, but serving the perfect being who wants only what's best for you, knows all things, sees all things, and protects and saves you isn't the normal kind of servitude. **Serving God is serving perfection, it's serving love, and it's the best enslavement there ever was.** And since God is perfect in all he does, serving him equals freedom from all that is imperfect and bad—freedom from the sin that controls you when you live to serve yourself.

God called you to endure suffering because Christ suffered for you. He left you an example so that you could follow in his footsteps.

1 Peter 2:21

When it came to suffering at the hands of mean people, the apostle Peter knew what he was talking about, but he also knew where God was in the whole thing. So he wrote to tell people that suffering at the hands of others, though it hurts to no end, has a far greater purpose. He also wanted them to know that other people's sin was never an excuse for their sin but was their chance to prove themselves to both those watching and to God himself.

Suffering might seem impossible to handle, but in the grand scheme of things it's only temporary. And when you live through it with faith that God will use it all for good, you learn more than you could ever learn in the good times. **You, God Girl, should not fear suffering but should know that it is far better to suffer for doing good than for doing wrong** (see 1 Peter 3:17).

Think about the life of Christ: he suffered beyond belief on the day they hung him on that cross, yet he never fought back or resisted the trial. He never argued his case but did the very thing he now asks us to do: endure hardship in faith, knowing that God can be trusted. You have to remember that suffering lasts only a while and then the reward comes. And what a reward it will be! You have nothing to fear, because no one can harm your soul or take you away from the Father. All you need to do is trust that and obey God's Word no matter what the world throws at you, and you will be sure to overcome.

Christ never verbally abused those who verbally abused him. When he suffered, he didn't make any threats but left everything to the one who judges fairly.

1 Peter 2:23

*F*orget about fighting fair—it's never holy to fight back, period, end of story. It's never godly to argue in anger or resentment. Revenge is not for the God Girl. When it comes to your friends and enemies, you've got to trust God to judge the situation fairly and to work all things out for what he knows to be the best, not what you think is best. No matter how bad the mean, no matter how hard the test, the God Girl who wants to imitate Christ (see Eph. 5:1) doesn't retaliate, get even, or fight back.

The world tries to convince even strong believers that their battle is against flesh and blood people and that they have to fight back, when in fact the opposite is true. The battle isn't ours; it is the Father's. When people attack you, slander you, or cut you down, your natural reaction is to want revenge, but that is never an act of obedience. If Christ, whose very life was being beaten and drained from him, didn't find it necessary to retaliate or to fight back, then why would we who aren't facing anything nearly as gruesome think we have a fight on our hands?

The lesson of God's love is the lesson of dying to self. When your friends, family, or enemies attack, you have to resist the urge to viciously fight back. You have to know and trust the Word of God, choosing to live by it rather than to deny it and instead live by your own strength and reason. Be very happy when others attack, because the testing of your faith develops endurance and maturity (see James 1:2–4). You can trust that these words are true and that God's power is sufficient.

Even if you suffer for doing what God approves, you are blessed. Don't be afraid of those who want to harm you. Don't get upset. But dedicate your lives to Christ as Lord.

1 Peter 3:14–15

*Y*ou probably have mean people in your life, people who hate you and want your destruction. Does that surprise you? Do you believe everyone should adore you? Why? Did you know that the world hated Christ too? It shouldn't shock you when people are mean or spiteful toward you, especially when it's for doing the right thing. It should give you faith in God's Word, because he promised you would have trouble (see John 16:33).

Don't be afraid of those who want to harm you, and don't get upset. Their sin is their sin, and you can't make it yours. But what you can do is pray for them and love them. Obey God's commands, especially with those who hate you, and you will prove yourself faithful. What good is obedience in the easy parts of life? That proves nothing. But obedience in loving your enemies, in doing good to those who hate you, and in not fearing what others fear proves your faith and delivers you from all their evil.

Therè will always be mean people, but the God Girl can't allow their mean to become her mean. Rather, she has to act as Christ acted and refuse to retaliate or hit back. Don't get upset. Trust God and turn away from their sin and disobedience by refusing to join in with them. Obedience to God's Word demands love, and you must fearlessly offer it to others in the name of him who first offered it to save you. Your freedom and your faith are in your hands and no one else's. Suffer for doing good (see 1 Peter 3:17). Prove God's Word is trustworthy by doing what it says, and your faith will get stronger than you ever imagined.

342

The end of everything is near. Therefore, practice self-control, and keep your minds clear so that you can pray.

1 Peter 4:7

F aith takes practice. You can't decide to do the right thing in the middle of the trial without doing the right thing now, before the test hits. Self-control comes through repetition. Start with the small things so that when the big things come, you'll be able to control yourself. When you're in the heat of the moment, obeying can be super hard if obedience isn't already your natural response to life. Letting yourself get away with the small things doesn't do you any good.

Remember, obedience is a noble thing, and noble things are hard, even heroic. Doing what's right might take all your energy, but it gives back as much as it takes by changing your character and strengthening your faith and your resolve.

If you find yourself failing the test of obedience, it might just be because you haven't practiced enough. Be faithful in doing the small things, and then you'll have the strength and ability to be faithful in the big things. Living through a crisis will let you know if you have been practicing or not. Every day you have to do what God has designed you to do and helped you to do by his Spirit. Then when the crisis comes, you'll have both God's grace and your nature on your side. Then you will succeed. You will overcome temptation, rise above, and resist the enemy.

Be happy as you share Christ's sufferings. Then you will also be full of joy when he appears again in his glory.

1 Peter 4:13

The next time you have a problem in your life, don't look at the problem itself but look at God. When trouble hits, your gut instinct is to react to the person inflicting it or to the circumstances surrounding it, but the best thing you can do is to remove yourself from the situation and react to God and what his Word says about it.

The purpose of problems in your life is to see if you are going to look away from God and to the people and things around you. The right answer is always doing what God wants instead of what your sinful nature wants. You might want to fight, you might want to fear, or you might just want to worry, but your spirit has to overrule your sinful nature and decide to look to God and his Word for direction instead of looking to your emotions. Every time a problem pops up, look up—don't look in or down or over, just up. Every time you successfully look up, you get closer and closer to the likeness of Christ, and the more you do, the more you will be able to endure all things and to overcome anything that might set itself up against you.

When you truly trust that God's Word will give you all you need in times of trouble and you fearlessly do whatever God commands, then you will be out of the reach of problems that can damage your life. Troubles might come your way, but they will never again shake you or break you—only make you stronger.

Turn all your anxiety over to God because he cares for you.

1 Peter 5:7

*A*s a believer you have to be aware of the fact that obsessing about the things of this world—success, money, clothes—will suck out of you anything that God put in you. The world is continually on the verge of breaking in on your soul and overwhelming it with worries about "not enough." Not enough money, food, friends, whatever. It never stops. And if you let yourself obsess about those things you lack, you lead yourself into dangerous waters. That's when your mind walks away from truth and dives into the lies of this world. The next step is drowning in them.

But Jesus offers you a lifeline. He says, "Don't worry about it. **Obsess only over one thing, your relationship with me, and then everything else will fall into place.**" The world will say that's ridiculous. You have to worry about the necessities of life, don't you? But Jesus says, "No, you don't. I'll take care of all that stuff. Trust me. Just keep your mind on my abundance, and you will never lack anything."

Are your thoughts faltering? Have you let worry become your obsession? Turn away from it now and put your thoughts onto him who saves. You will not be disappointed.

Because of this, make every effort to add integrity to your faith; and to integrity add knowledge; to knowledge add self-control; to self-control add endurance; to endurance add godliness; to godliness add Christian affection; and to Christian affection add love.

2 Peter 1:5–7

Self-control is good. Even though it can feel like self-torture, it's actually good. Self-control is evidence that you have made God the Lord of your life instead of yourself. The most effective and powerful people in the world of faith are not people who pampered themselves but people who denied themselves every chance they got, like athletes training for a big race. Believers who train their bodies and minds with self-denial become strong and effective in their work.

Self-control demands hard work, but the payoff is thousandfold. With self-control comes peace, hope, and strength. Instead of telling yourself "I just can't," you will be telling yourself "I have to, and he will help me." The believer who chooses self-control never does it alone but with the help of God himself. You have to work at taking back your body and mind for the work of faith instead of the works of this world. **Self-control increases not only your strength but also your faith and your effectiveness.** Your purpose on this planet, whatever it is, starts with self-control. Master that and then you will most assuredly reach your purpose.

In their greed they will use good-sounding arguments to exploit you.

2 Peter 2:3

*P*ersecution from nonbelievers isn't always the only danger to the church. Sometimes the danger is people inside the church who take the truth and change it to fit their own ideals and experiences. That's why knowledge of the truth is so essential for all believers. Without it you can easily be led astray by people pretending to teach about true faith but really teaching a lie. As a God Girl you can't simply accept what you are taught without considering how it aligns with God's Word.

Oftentimes teachers of God's Word allow the ideas of the world to seep into their way of thinking, and then over time they forget what is the world and what is the Word. Their motives may be pure but their words evil. **You are never too young to judge truth for yourself,** and the only excuse you might have is that you don't know enough. But you can't let that stop you. **The Word is available to everyone who is willing to look into it.** Knowledge is a powerful thing and an essential for the life of faith. We can't let people draw us away with enticing arguments that appeal to our desire to be happy and comfortable. We need to bring everything back to God's Word. Ask yourself, "Is what I'm hearing or thinking consistent with God's Word?" If not, then you must reject it.

As a God Girl you can't allow the world to infiltrate your faith, even if it has infiltrated the lives of those who appear to know more than you. It's easy to let lies seep into your mind and become a part of your worldview (your beliefs about faith and living), but as the world starts to make its lies look like God's truth, your faith can become distorted. If you believe something to be true, check it against God's Word. You might be surprised how many "truths" you find out to be complete and total lies. Don't let the world pull the wool over your eyes. Run it all by God and his Word before you believe a word of it. Be smart and be a faithful God Girl!

Grow in the good will and knowledge of our Lord and Savior Jesus Christ.

2 Peter 3:18

*E*veryone God touches changes. If your life isn't changing, then you haven't given it over to him. Once you meet face-to-face with the Creator of the universe, you are no longer the same. Each time you meet him you soften, you learn, you gain wisdom, self-control, and strength. Each day you grow and become more like Jesus Christ himself.

Is your life changing? Do you have encounters with God through his Word that shape you and rub off your rough edges? Staying the same should never be the goal of the God Girl. A lot of girls have no desire to grow and to mature, but the God Girl knows that change is a crucial part of spiritual growth. A plant that stops growing doesn't live, and no girl who has stopped growing is taking her life from the branch (see John 15:4; James 2:26). Growth, including even your daily perseverance in good times and bad, is a public and private reminder of your salvation.

Do you want to conquer life, to conquer your sin and weaknesses, to overcome challenges, and to gain the strength to do more than you've ever done before? When you want that, you have taken the first step to maturity. Accepting the status quo doesn't help anyone, but an irresistible thirst to go deeper proves not only your spiritual maturity but your emotional maturity as well.

Grow like a weed. Cling to the branch, accept its life-giving power, and grow as if your life depends on it, because it does. If God is changing you, then thank him, embrace the future and his hope, and let go of the old girl and welcome the new one—the new and improved you!

If we say, "We have a relationship with God" and yet live in the dark, we're lying. We aren't being truthful.

1 John 1:6

*G*race and forgiveness are two powerful gifts from God. They take away your sins as far as the east is from the west. They give you access to the King of Kings so that you can ask him for whatever you need. But grace and forgiveness aren't cheap. Of course they're free, but that doesn't mean they're cheap. To cheapen grace is to treat it with disrespect by using it as an excuse to sin. Knowing that God will forgive you anything you might ever do can make it easy to decide to just go ahead and disobey since forgiveness is free. But knowing what to do and deliberately choosing not to do it because you know you have God's grace is insanity. God's kindness, or grace, is an amazing gift, not a "get out of jail free" card. Sin happens, you fall down, you get back up, and you get forgiveness. But when you deliberately choose to sin because you're just too tired or lazy, you cheapen grace and treat it with disrespect, and you have to wonder what you really believe about God. Do you serve God or yourself? You can't serve two masters.

The God Girl doesn't want an excuse for sin; she wants to run away from sin. Who decides to sin because God is good and he'll forgive you of anything? The girl who misunderstands or rejects God's law, that's who. Even though sin might feel good or have an instant payoff, ultimately it's destructive. **God declares things off-limits for your own good, and choosing sin is not only breaking the law but damaging yourself.** The God Girl has to know God's law and decide that obeying is the best thing she could ever do. Disobedience comes with discipline and even punishment. So decide not to choose sin and to run away from it instead. But also know that if you should fall into sin, you will be forgiven, but if you choose it, you will be disciplined.

If we say, "We aren't sinful" we are deceiving ourselves, and the truth is not in us. God is faithful and reliable. If we confess our sins, he forgives them and cleanses us from everything we've done wrong. If we say, "We have never sinned," we turn God into a liar and his Word is not in us.

1 John 1:8–10

*J*esus died on the cross so that anything anyone could ever do could be forgiven if they wanted it to be. There are no restrictions on salvation. Jesus said, "So I can guarantee that people will be forgiven for any sin or cursing. However, cursing the Spirit will not be forgiven" (Matt. 12:31). That means that anything other than not believing in the Holy Spirit can and will be forgiven. Look at 1 John 1:8–10. The answer to your sin is confession—in other words, agreeing with God that what you did was wrong—and then determining to never do it again. And you're cleansed, all white and pure as snow. That's how it works.

It is pride talking when you think that your sins cannot be forgiven. "I'm the worst person in the world." "No one is worse than me." "God isn't big enough to pardon my sins." If you think you're special, harder to forgive than others, that speaks of pride.

The apostle Paul, writer of a lot of the New Testament, was a horrible sinner. He chased early Christians and persecuted them; he sent them to jail and to death. And God turned him around, forgave him, and made him into a mighty man of God. The Bible is full of people like that, from prostitutes to King David (who had his lover's husband killed!). Millions of people have been forgiven for things just as bad as if not worse than anything you've done. **Don't be fooled into believing the lie that your sins are more important than others or that God isn't big enough** for your particular situation. He is, and he forgives you as soon as you confess what you have done.

God is faithful and reliable. If we confess our sins, he forgives them and cleanses us from everything we've done wrong. If we say, "We have never sinned," we turn God into a liar and his Word is not in us.

1 John 1:9–10

You cannot and will not be saved if you say, "I've never sinned." Why would you? You don't need salvation if you've done nothing that would condemn you. But as a God Girl you are fully aware of your own sinfulness, and that's why you came to the foot of the cross begging forgiveness. It's tempting to live a life where you make your own rules about what is right and what is wrong, because when you do, you never get it wrong—after all, you made up the rules yourself. But that's not the life of faith. The life of faith is continually taking God up on his offer of forgiveness. Daily, even hourly, the life of faith spots one more sin, one more selfish act that is inconsistent with faith, but because God makes it clear that this happens to everyone, faith doesn't fret.

The book of 1 John makes some very strong statements about sin and obedience. It's a great place to look for inspiration to be obedient. It's a great reminder that what proves your love to God is not your words but your actions, and specifically the action of obedience, that is, doing what he asks. Anything else is rebellion, not love. But thank God that his love is greater than ours and because of that he never deserts us! He never leaves us but is always there waiting for our next confession.

Whoever obeys what Christ says is the kind of person in whom God's love is perfected. That's how we know we are in Christ.

1 John 2:5

Is there some spiritual darkness in your life? Do you wish you could sense God's presence but he seems distant and inattentive to your pleas? Then check yourself. Are you waiting to do something that needs to be done? Is there something you are unwilling to do for fear that it isn't his will or you aren't strong enough? Doing what God wants you to do is the way you live in the presence of God (see John 15:10), and if you lack that presence, it may just be because of your unwillingness to do something you know you should be doing or to stop doing something you know you shouldn't be doing.

In the life of faith you are going to have good days and bad days, mountain peak days and dry old desert days. You can't let either one of them become your obsession. Don't worry and fret over how you feel; just do what's gotta be done. When you are a God Girl, your best example of how to live is how Jesus lived. Of course that doesn't mean walking on water and healing the blind, but it does mean having compassion, showing mercy, being kind, loving others, being humble, and caring. You could add a lot of things you see in the life of Jesus to your life today. But do you know right now what they are? **If you want more of God, then learn more about Jesus.** Learn how he walked, what he did, and how he loved, and you'll find yourself closer to God than you could have ever imagined.

Those who say that they live in him must live the same way he lived.

1 John 2:6

Face it: everyone sins. No exceptions. But Jesus came to set you free from sin, and that's exactly what he's done. The Bible says that no one goes on sinning if they know Jesus. "What?" you scream. "How is that possible? Does that mean I don't know Jesus if I still sin?" No, it doesn't mean that, but it means once you turn your heart and will over to Jesus, something changes inside you.

Look at it like this: you are on a freeway, the freeway of faith, and you see an exit. It looks like it has all kinds of exciting attractions and services, so you get off. You weren't planning on exiting; you just lost control and before you knew it you were stopped at the light waiting to pull onto the city streets. But suddenly you realize this isn't a good place and you shouldn't be here—that God told you not to exit here but you did it anyway—so you immediately get back onto the freeway. Phew! Sin noted and quickly confessed!

But let's suppose one day you take an exit again, and this time you not only get off but also meander around the neighborhoods till finally you end up moving in. You don't get back on the freeway; you just stay where you don't belong. In this scenario you are continuing to sin, rather than sinning and then getting right back on the road to redemption.

Everyone sins. We all mess up—daily, in fact. That's why we need confession and repentance, or turning to God. But there is a difference between falling into temptation but confessing it when you realize it, and deciding that this sin is acceptable and you're going to keep living in it. So look for the signs and don't get off into dangerous territory, but stay on the route God wants you on.

Those who have been born from God don't live sinful lives. What God has said lives in them, and they can't live sinful lives. They have been born from God.

1 John 3:9

*D*o you feel the need to sin? Are there areas in your life where you can't do without some delightful or refreshing sin in your life? Sin isn't always dark and ominous; sometimes it seems bright and wonderful. It's a date with a gorgeous guy who doesn't believe in God. It's a chance to go somewhere everyone is going but you are forbidden to go. Sin offers a big payoff, and that's why resisting it can be so hard. But when you want only what God wants, suddenly sin doesn't look so appealing. Its offer isn't as enticing as before, and saying no starts to come easy.

When you want what God wants and nothing more, then living a sinful life disgusts you. You certainly don't feel a need to sin, because you have all you need in God and God alone. If you feel a need you think only sin can fulfill, then it's time to find out why that's a lie and to realize that only God can meet your needs. Sin talks a good talk; it offers a lot, but in the end it delivers more pain than you bargained for. Look at what you think are your "needs," and then look in God's Word to find out what he has to say about them. Don't accept the need to sin as a reality—it's a lie. You've been born from God, and you therefore are no longer controlled by the power of sin.

To love God means that we obey his commandments.

1 John 5:3

f you love God, you will want to do what he says. But if you not only don't want to do what he says but *refuse* to do what he says and are okay with that, then according to his Word there is no sacrifice left for you (see Heb. 10:26). As a God Girl you **prove your love to him by doing what he says.** It sounds like a tall order. Obedience isn't normally presented as a part of the salvation story. Kindness, forgiveness, and restoration, yes, but obedience? How hard is that? But God's Word is clear: you must make him Lord of your life, and that means more than a verbal agreement that he is God; it's a willful choice to obey his Word (see Rom. 10:9; James 2:14–26; 1 John 2:3–4).

This doesn't mean you won't mess up or that God doesn't forgive you when you do—oh yes, he does (see 1 John 1:9)! But it does mean that as a God Girl you will want to love him, and love obeys. Love doesn't want what God doesn't give; it doesn't turn away from truth; it doesn't make its own way; it stays faithful. It may fall down, it may get tempted or even distracted, but it never willfully disobeys. When love makes a mistake it corrects it; it doesn't hide from it.

As a God Girl, if you want the blessing of God's Spirit, then you will want to do what he says. And in order to do that, you have to know his Word. Study it, memorize it, teach it. Make it part of the very fiber of your being. When you do you will find that blessings abound.

We are confident that God listens to us if we ask for anything that has his approval.

1 John 5:14

What's more important, getting what you want or getting what you need? It can be really easy to spend all your thoughts and energy on what you want and completely ignore what you need. But God is like a good parent who doesn't allow their toddler to eat all the candy they want but makes sure they eat good stuff too. He wants to give you what you want, but not to the extent that it will hurt you or your relationship with him.

If you aren't getting what you want, maybe it's time to look at your wants and needs. Why do you want what you want? And how might that not be what you need right now? **When God says no, it's because no is the best answer for you in this situation.** Discover why. Ask yourself what getting what you want would do to your faith, your emotions, and your self-control. Then ask yourself what not getting it can do for all of those things. For the God Girl, getting God's best is always best. If there is something you wish you had but can't seem to get, don't be fooled: God isn't to blame; he's to thank. Maybe you aren't spiritually prepared for what you are asking for, or maybe what you are asking for wouldn't be the best for you. Whatever God's reason, you can trust that what you have right now is all that you need to survive and even to thrive. Trust God with your life. Put it into his hands and rest assured that when you do, he will take perfect care of it.

*From the beginning we were commanded to love each other. Love means
that we live by doing what he commands. We were commanded to live in
love, and you have heard this from the beginning.*

2 John 5–6

The early commentary writer Jerome tells a story about the
apostle John in his old age speaking to a crowd and only repeating these five words: "Little children, love one another."
When the people got tired of hearing the same thing over and over
again, they said to him, "Master, why do you always say this?" The
old apostle said, "Because it is the Lord's command, and if only this is
done, it is enough." John, the apostle of love, knew what was needed.
But love is a big word, and how do you know if you have it?

Love isn't a gushy feeling that you get from your feelings or your
hormones. It's not the feeling of contentment you get when you are
with someone who loves you back. According to God's Word, it's
something totally different: it's doing what God tells you to do. Not
what you thought love was? I know, it seems like something totally
different, but did you read 2 John 6? "Love means that we live by
doing what he commands." Love calls you out of yourself and into
a life of caring and concern for others. You have to get this idea.
You can't love the way the world loves and call it good. You have to
look at God's Word for the whole truth about love and know what
it means for how you treat others.

How do you know if you are loving someone? **You are loving if
you are doing what God tells you to do in relationship to them.**
Then and only then can you be sure that you are truly loving the way
you were meant to love. That means that if you want to love well,
then you've got to dig into God's Word and learn what he's asking
of you. Study his thoughts on relationships and loving. Learn what
true love is and then offer it to the world, regardless of whether or
not they ever offer it back.

Dear friend, never imitate evil, but imitate good.

3 John 11

f she jumped off a cliff, would you?" Following the crowd can sometimes seem like the safest route. No one notices you, no one calls you out, no one judges you. But when the crowd is jumping off a cliff, how smart is diving to your destruction just to fit in?

The world doesn't know Jesus, so they think he's crazy. They create their own rules and values. They focus on what the eye can see and avoid what can't be seen. But as a God Girl you know there is more than the physical world. You are aware of the spiritual, that unseen world that surrounds you and fills you. Temporary happiness might be found denying the existence of God and the commands of his law, but permanent happiness comes when you drop what the world believes and trust only what God says.

It's human nature to want to fit in, but when you act, look, and think like the rest of the world, you prove not your faith but your distrust. True God Girls follow not the world but the Savior. Going against the grain and doing what God wants you to do not only proves you believe but also increases your faith. Each time you risk disobeying the world by doing what is right, your faith grows.

Some people have slipped in among you unnoticed. Not long ago they were condemned in writing for the following reason: They are people to whom God means nothing. They use God's kindness as an excuse for sexual freedom and deny our only Master and Lord, Jesus Christ.

Jude 4

God's kindness can never be an excuse for sin. His grace shouldn't be a loophole to disobedience. Knowing that he forgives everything you've ever done or ever will do isn't a reason to turn your back on him and to sin. If you tell yourself it's okay to disregard his law because of grace, you lie to yourself and prove that you love yourself more than you love him. God means nothing to the person who uses his kindness to do whatever she wants.

You can't be a slave to two masters. You can serve two people, like having two jobs, but you can't be a slave to more than one master. When you're a slave you don't have the freedom to work a second job. And when you are a slave to God, you don't abuse his kindness but obey him and him only, in spite of his ability to offer grace for your disobedience or crime.

A lot of times disobedient and self-serving people slip into your life without you noticing. They talk a good talk, they preach, they teach, and they lead you to believe that grace is the most important and useful thing in the life of the believer. And while God's kindness is essential because without it you wouldn't know God, it can't become a replacement for doing what is right. You are saved by God's kindness or grace, but you prove your love by your faithfulness. Don't let deceivers say otherwise. Enjoy the grace of God, accept it when you fall, and when you discover areas of your life that were in the dark, know that he can and will forgive as soon as you repent and confess. But don't use that knowledge as an excuse for premeditated sin, as a free pass to selfishness, or you will prove that God means nothing to you.

Show mercy to those who have doubts. Save others by snatching them from the fire of hell.

Jude 22–23

*J*ust because someone claims to be a believer doesn't make it so. The best way to tell is from the fruit of their lives. Do they act like a believer? Do they teach things that are consistent with God's Word? It's easy to say you are a Christian but harder to prove it by how you act and what you say. When you find believers who fail to live out their faith, you have to find the desire and the mercy to help them understand that they have been living a lie so they do not continue to live in darkness.

As a God Girl you don't have to save the world, but you should look out for believers who might be mistakenly believing and even preaching a falsehood. You can't allow a fellow believer to be deceived because you think that they aren't your responsibility. Your job as a God Girl is to remind them of the truth they may have forgotten or never known, but your job is not to save them. God himself will do that. You don't need to worry or become anxious over the sins of others; just share the truth and then trust God to work in their hearts and lives.

Show mercy to others, even though you are afraid that you might be stained by their sinful lives. God can guard you so that you don't fall.

Jude 23–24

Mercy can't be afraid of getting dirty. When you reach out to help those who are hurting and have turned their backs on God, you can't be afraid of getting a little messy. Sure, you have to guard your heart against friendship with the world. You can't go around giving away your heart willy-nilly to those who hate God and haven't made him Lord, but you can give them your hand. You can offer to help.

Mercy demonstrates a desire to show others the God who saves. How will they know if they haven't heard? How will they hear if you don't speak up? Mercy requires your fearlessness. Mercy's target is misery—the misery of those who suffer because they don't know God or understand his love. Because of this darkness of their soul, they don't understand what they are doing; they don't know the depths of their sin. Forgive them, for they do not know what they are doing (see Luke 23:34). Show them mercy because they are in misery.

When people insult you, gossip about you, or otherwise prove their distance from the Father, as a God Girl you should have mercy on them, for their soul is in distress. **You should find ways to serve, rather than to criticize.** Your trademark reaction should always be showing mercy and compassion to those who are weaker than you. "God can guard you so that you don't fall and so that you can be full of joy" (Jude 24), but you must put all your hope in him and turn all your thoughts onto him. Never focus so much on other people's misery that you take your eyes off of God. Obey him, love them, show them mercy and compassion, and pray for them, but never fear them and never turn your back in indifference or hate.

I am John, your brother. I share your suffering, ruling, and endurance because of Jesus. I was exiled on the island of Patmos because of God's word and the testimony about Jesus.

Revelation 1:9

A ccording to this verse, **believers have three things in common: suffering, ruling, and endurance.** As a God Girl you shouldn't be surprised when you suffer and have to endure it. It's what we all do. It's such a joke to think that your life was meant to be perfect, to be all comfortable and happy. Happiness isn't the goal of faith. It may be a symptom but it's not the goal—not that faith is meant to be miserable either, but you shouldn't be so shocked when bad things happen. It's been that way for centuries. Suffering is a constant, so it is a continual duty of the God Girl to suffer. But you are to suffer not as a nonbeliever but as a believer, with the confidence that suffering produces something holy within you. That suffering should never be in vain but should be used for good, for character building, for strength, for perseverance, and for the development of trust.

Don't let the presence of suffering in your life convince you that something is wrong. That

isn't always the case. Sometimes you suffer because of your own sin, and rather than hate the suffering, you must address the cause. Use the symptom of suffering as a signal that you must change what you are doing, and thank God for the redirecting power of suffering. Sometimes suffering comes at the hands of another. But this is just an opportunity to trust that God will do what he says and work it all out for your good (see Rom. 8:28). Don't allow the rough parts of life to convince you that God is absent when they ought to convince you that he is present—shaping you, guiding you, purifying you. Never let the opportunity of suffering go unused. Instead let it do its work within you so that you will be mature and complete, not lacking anything (see James 1:2–4).

You only have a little strength, but you have paid attention to my word and have not denied my name.

*I*f you only have a little strength, use it for God's glory. When you are too weak to move and too tired to go on, all you have to do is obey. Not sure what God wants you to do? Then just do what he tells you to do in his Word. Don't worry about hearing his voice right now. Don't fret over finding his will for your life today. All you need to know for today is found in the pages of the Bible. Truth is written for the taking. With the little strength that you have, reach for truth.

It takes much less energy to take orders than to struggle and wrestle with indecision. A smart girl takes the resources she has and applies them to her life. As you move into adulthood, you will be met with all kinds of different choices that only you can make. When you were a child your parents made choices for you, but now it's up to you. And because of that you will be held responsible. You can't go blamin' your life on anyone else but yourself now. Are you willing to take God at his Word and do what he commands, or will you complain, disagree, and do it your own way? If you only have a little strength, pay attention to God's Word and don't deny his name.

They could harm only the people who do not have the seal of God on their foreheads.

Revelation 9:4

Worry might be your first response when things get tough. When everyone around you sees disaster coming and fears the worst, it's easy to jump on the worry train. But worry isn't meant to be a part of the life of a God Girl. Sure, things might look bleak. Trouble might be all around you, the earth may look like it's about to stop spinning, but no matter how bad things look, you can be sure of one thing: God has it all under control. Fear isn't useful unless you're talking about the fear of God. He's the only one you need to fear. No one and nothing can take you away from him. So don't fear and don't worry when things seem tragic. Your life is in his hands, and even if the sky falls and the oceans all dry up, he won't let go.

When things get rough, don't let worry prove your lack of faith. Instead prove how much you trust God by refusing to believe that he's not in control. Worry calls God a liar, but trust proves your faith in him. So don't fear the future, don't fear what God has ordained, don't fear what others fear. Your life is in his hands from beginning to end. He knows your destiny, he knows how the world will end, and he knows how to protect and care for you.

It [the beast] was allowed to wage war against God's holy people and to conquer them. It was also given authority over every tribe, people, language, and nation.

Revelation 13:7

arth. **Who's in charge? Satan. But he only has control insofar as God allows it.** That's one of the reasons we have nothing to fear. The enemy might plot against you, he might plan attacks, he might even succeed, but he doesn't win. The thing to remember is that **no one has control or authority unless God allows them to have it.** So when Satan "wages war against God's holy people" (see Rev. 13:7), it's because God allowed it. Why God allows the enemy to do such things is a mystery, but one that we have to trust.

If God allows something to come to pass, he must have a good reason. The God Girl is fear-free and full of peace because of this. She knows who is in charge and who wins. She knows whose side she is on and the protection he offers. Even if God allows an apparently terrible thing to come into your life, don't fear, but trust that it is for your good. All you need to do is choose to seek him, and you will find in God's Word the answer to how you are to react to trials and suffering. When you willingly obey and refuse to accuse God of not living up to his promises, you will over time find yourself exactly where you need to be. And peace will be your constant companion.

I warn everyone who hears the words of the prophecy in this book: If anyone adds anything to this, God will strike him with the plagues that are written in this book.

*H*ave you heard the voice of God? Has he told you to do something? To go somewhere? What will you do? These are the times when knowing God's Word is crucial, because if you are unfamiliar with his ways, with his voice, and with his truth, you can easily fall prey to imposters and to adding things to Scripture that aren't really there. God's Word says to test every spirit that you hear, because not every spirit that claims to be *the* Spirit with a capital *S* really is (see 1 John 4:1). **Satan pretends to be God by dressing up as an "angel of light"** (2 Cor. 11:14), **so you can't be too quick to say "God told me" when there's a chance that the one who told you was only pretending to be someone he's not.**

So how do you know who's talking? If what "God told you" contradicts God's Word, you can be sure that what you heard wasn't God's voice. How many times have you been sure God wanted you to do something or to have something, only to find out it wasn't gonna happen? Do you blame God? Or do you stop and think that you might have been too quick to call the voice in your head the voice of God? Just because you hear something that sounds amazing and wonderful doesn't mean that it is God speaking to you. So resist the temptation to say "God told me," because the only thing you can be sure God told you is what he has told the world in his Word.

godgirl.com

Quick Relief

godgirl.com

*H*ayley **DiMarco** is founder of Hungry Planet, where she writes and creates cutting-edge books that connect with the multitasking mind-set. She has written and co-written numerous bestselling books for both teens and adults, including *Dateable, Mean Girls, Sexy Girls, Technical Virgin*, and *B4UD8*. She lives in Nashville, Tennessee, with her husband and their daughter.

The *Ultimate Bible* just for the *God Girl!*

With special features like Ask Yourself, Prayers, God Girl Stories, and Know This Devotions, all written by bestselling author Hayley DiMarco, the *God Girl Bible* is a must-have for girls thirteen and up! If you're ready to grow closer to God, grow in your faith, and join an online group of girls from around the globe growing together, the *God Girl Bible* is for you!

Available Wherever Books Are Sold
Also Available in Ebook Format

Revell
a division of Baker Publishing Group
www.RevellBooks.com

Hungry Planet
www.hungryplanet.net

God Girl.com

Hungry Planet Helps Girls Become the Women They Are Meant to Be

When you become a God Girl, your life will never be the same.

Available Wherever Books Are Sold
Also Available in Ebook Format

Revell
a division of Baker Publishing Group
www.RevellBooks.com

www.hungryplanet.net

GodGirl.com

At GodGirl.com, you can be mentored by bestselling author Hayley DiMarco in what it means to be a God Girl and get help with the challenges of life in the process.

Here are just some of the features of GodGirl.com:

- Free books, resources, and an online Bible to grow in your relationship with God.

- God Girl Academy is a four-part spiritual mentoring course you can go through on your own or as part of a group.

- Quick Relief section gives you Bible verses organized by the topics you need at the moment.

- Exclusive live online events with Hayley and her friends.

- Design Your Own GG Bible cover hints and templates for the one and only all-white blank canvas God Girl Bible.

- And much, much more!

And if you're a leader of a small group, you can use GodGirl.com as a meeting hub and resource library full of tools for discipleship and mentoring young women.